# Names, Titles, and Characters by Literary Writers–Shakespeare, 19th and 20th Century Authors

# NAMES, TITLES, AND CHARACTERS BY LITERARY WRITERS– SHAKESPEARE, 19TH AND 20TH CENTURY AUTHORS

Robert F. Fleissner

Studies in Onomastics
Volume 2

The Edwin Mellen Press
Lewiston•Queenston•Lampeter

032104

**Library of Congress Cataloging-in-Publication Data**

Fleissner, Robert F.
  Names, titles, and characters by literary writers--Shakespeare, 19th and 20th century authors / Robert F. Fleissner.
      p. cm. -- (Studies in onomastics ; v. 2)
  Includes bibliographical references and index.
  ISBN 0-7734-7524-9
  1. English literature--History and criticism. 2. Shakespeare, William, 1564-1616--Characters. 3. Characters and characteristics in literature. 4. American literature--History and criticism. 5. Names in literature. 6. Titles of books. I. Title. II. Series.

PR401 .F58  2001
820.9--dc21

                                                                00-050059

This is volume 2 in the continuing series
Studies in Onomastics
Volume 2 ISBN  0-7734-7524-9
SO Series ISBN  0-7734-7725-X

A CIP catalog record for this book is available from the British Library.

The Edwin Mellen Press                    The Edwin Mellen Press
Box 450                                              Box 67
Lewiston, New York                           Queenston, Ontario
USA  14092-0450                              CANADA  L0S 1L0

The Edwin Mellen Press, Ltd.
Lampeter, Ceredigion, Wales
UNITED KINGDOM SA48 8LT

Printed in the United States of America

# TABLE OF CONTENTS

## Part III: NINETEENTH AND TWENTIETH-CENTURY AMERICA (AND SOME EUROPEAN INFLUENCE)

# FOREWORD

Because the literary name-game, as it is sometimes called, can lead to so many variations and reactions (comical, abstruse, even serious), it is useful to start off by at least warning the reader of what to expect (and what he or she may want to dwell on and what possibly to dismiss). First, I had thought of naming the compendium of my work here after probably the most famous phrase on the subject known, but one also used differentially by many critics: "What *IS* in a Name?" The most famous usage of the rhetorical question is no doubt Umberto Eco's *Il Nome della Rosa* (The Name of the Rose), because he makes use of Juliet's response to her own question ("A rose by any other name would smell as sweet"). Incidentally, I followed suit then with a booklet, in a nice roseate binding, entitled *A Rose by Another Name* (Locust Hill P, 1989). I had tried to be more subtle in my symbolism. Now by stressing the verb *is* in my proposed title I was repudiating the rhetorical quality of Juliet's question by pointing to the validity. But the general editor of the series, Dr. Leonard Ashley, frowned on my suggestion as perhaps too derivative or informal, and so I had to come up with something else.

In any event, owing to quite an accumulation of papers (delivered orally as well as in print at times) on literary onomastics (the technical term for all this), I have had to make some notable decisions regarding organization. First, a certain chronological order seemed desirable, and because my main interest has always been in Shakespeare, I decided to provide revisions of essays on his plays. Not all appearing in journals are here reproduced, in somewhat revised form, because there were too many.

Possibly owing to my old-time interest in relating two great geniuses (the subject already of my published doctoral diss.), I chose to follow the Shakespeare section up by one on Dickens. My main nomenclatural interest has been on the unfinished novel *The Mystery of Edwin Drood*. By no means all of my printed essays on this subject are now duplicated because I did not feel required to plunge into the whole volcano of ideas once again, thus avoiding any new, unforeseen eruption. For example, there is the question of what the so-called "survivalists" believe. Did Drood *not* die, in spite of all the well-known hints for this in advance? Or did he indeed perish, most probably owing to Jasper's machinations, and then was resurrected in a Christ-like manner (or so it may be interpreted)? I see nothing wrong with the "death-urge" approach myself (owing especially to the protagonist's racist behavior toward a Ceylonese) but have to admit that one of the great characteristics of nineteenth-century writing has been termed "organic form," meaning that a fragmentary work has its own Romantic resonance. Yet, then again, Dickens was more Victorian than Romantic.

Because I start out the book with Shylock, I bring in, in passing only, the plausibility of the name *Rosencrantz* having been Jewish too, even back then, and deal with other ethnic etymology with regard to the name of the Noble Moor. Cordelia's name, on the other hand, sometimes suggests a religiously Christian, not an ethnic,factor to some, especially if it is thought of as an anagram for "ideal *cor*" (or heart). But that raises further controversy. As for the anagrammatic quality of Oliver Martext's name in *As You Like It*, as reflecting back, let us consider, on that of Marlowe (whereby *Ol.* as the abbreviation for *Oliver* is correlated with the first syllable of the dramatist's surname—in reverse fashion), I have dealt with that in my book on Shakespearean cruxes published in 1991 by the Mellen Press and so would rather not rehearse that again.

The Caliban problem is another source of delight for me, and I have to admit I do mention it more than once throughout, though the paper I delivered which was then printed in conference proceedings, "Caliban Converted; or *The Tempest* as the Tempering of the Pest," has not been reworked here, so that the reader at least may not be taken aback at such paronomasia on the title of the play. Yet some lightheartedness cannot be avoided from time to time, and I only hope to be forgiven for a bit of informality (not beyond my subject-matter in any case).

I deleted one essay on Shakespeare's rival contemporary, Marlowe, again, as being perhaps a bit too technical for the general reader, namely that on *Dr. Faustus* regarding the discrepancy between whether the name *Wittenberg* or *Wertenberg* represents the true label of the locale involved. Because I deal with titles of works as well as names of characters, I do consider the exact naming of the most famous of the so-called Apocryphal plays, usually called *Arden of Feversham*. This then led to other titular resonances in general. Regarding Dickens, the title of his religious work written for his children is readily debated too. Although the label usually given it, *The Life of Our Lord*, sounds more orthodoxly Christian than anything else, we have to remember that this novelist had his Unitarian sympathies as well.

Originally I had meant to include a section on the Victorian poet Tennyson because I have been involved in a dispute in print in Europe regarding the title of his famous poem "Crossing the Bar," which he wanted at the end of any collection of his verse. Yet again the matter of orthodoxy enters the picture. *Can* the "Cross" connotation validly work here in a Christian way when the Poet Laureate was not a very bona-fide Christian? I believe it does (and the poem is actually included in my hymnal too), but the matter is somewhat disputatious. The same can be said of the very first article on onomastics which I managed to get into print, "The Name Jude." —Is there a hint nominally of St. Jude? Or rather even of the word as being German for *Jew*?

My long-time concern with Conan Doyle then brought me to include a Sherlockian section, one based on articles here and abroad which have led to debate, even when Dame Jean Conan Doyle entered the fray and wrote me about it. My general feeling is that she disputed Sherlock's original first name being *Ignatius*, as suggested in print before I got into this, possibly because of the Jesuitical connotations—when he was a lapsed Catholic. But then *Innes* would work just as well for personal reasons, as we shall see.

Regarding Eliot, another old-time favorite of mine (my having been a dutiful member of the T. S. Eliot Society for many a year), I dwell again on "Prufrock," the subject of another collection of articles of mine, but decided finally to eliminate some of the overly controversial issues, such as whether there was a hint of the name of J. Verdenal, his one-time friend, even in that isolated first initial of his own name. After all, brotherly love has its place.

Finally it seemed desirable to deal with American twentieth-century literature in general, especially with regard to my locale, so I dwell on Frost as well as Sinclair Lewis, not to forget such a leading African American as James Baldwin. Many readers no doubt associate Frost mainly with Middlebury, Vermont, near his cottage in Ripton, and indeed my essay on him was delivered at the Frost conference there in '99. Yet he had good connections with Ohio too, even my area, as my *Frost's Road Taken* indicates. He delivered a sermon, for instance, for his good friend Rabbi Victor Reichert in his temple in Cincinnati.

In summary, what better can be done than to end with a concluding chapter of sorts. I deal with Kafka for various reasons. First, it concerns my overall focus on this country for the past century with his very book title. Second, it happens to represent the very latest publication of mine on onomastics, here slightly reformatted. And, third, it somehow relates or combines the literary writers on whom I have been dwelling in the second half of the book, notably Dickens and Lewis. Here the matter of race as well as ethnicity enters the picture one more time: my contention is that it was Lewis, not Twain, who represented the true American Dickens for this reason. See also Part IV concerning the conclusion.

RFF

# ACKNOWLEDGMENTS

Chapters in this book represent revisions of articles often in journals, the titles remaining practically the same except for Chs. XII and XXVI which represent a combination of two notes. Chapters IV, VI, XVII, XXII, and XXIV are brand new, their having been only read at conferences as indicated, except for Ch. IV. The chapters appearing in earlier draft form in journals are indicated below (and then are not given in the "Works Cited" at the end of the book).

| | |
|---|---|
| Ch. I | *American Notes and Queries* 5.4 (1966): 52-4. |
| II | *Names* (Journal of the American Name Society) 41 (1993): 282-87. |
| III | *Names* 39 (1991): 95-102. |
| V | *Notes and Queries* 223 (1978): 72-3. |
| VII | *Names* 22 (1974): 254-6. |
| VIII | *Names* 39 (1991): 42-6. |
| IX | *Names* 40 (1992): 295-8. |
| X | *Susquehanna University Studies* 10 (1977): 169-72. |
| XI | *Analytical & Enumerative Bibliography* NS 6 (1992): 208-15. |
| XII | *Pucred* 2.4 (1974): 1-2; *Word Ways* 23 (1990): 171. |
| XIII | *The Armchair Detective* 13 (1980): 12-6. |
| XIV | *Names* 40 (1992): 117-22. |
| XV | *Research Studies* (Washington SU) 49 (March, 1981): 35-5. |
| XVI | *Names* 37 (1989): 65-8. |
| XVIII | *The Mystery Fancier* 8 (May/June, 1984): 21-4. |
| XIX | *The Baker Street Journal* NS 4 (1991): 226-9. |
| XX | *Clues: A Journal of Detection* 16 (1995): 67-76. |
| XXI | *Thalia* 15 (1995): 77-79. |
| XXIII | *Sinclair Lewis Newsletter* 2.1 (1970): 10-11. |
| XXV | *Word Ways* 27 (1994): 125. |
| XXVI | *Notes on Contemporary Literature* 3 (May, 1973) 5-7; *Word Ways* 27 (1994): 249-50. |
| XXVII | *Studies in Black Literature* 8.1 (1977): 4-5. |
| XXVIII | *Germanic Notes and Reviews* 31.1 (2000): 8-13. |

# PREFACE

This book is Professor Robert F. Fleissner's latest stop in a long onomastic journey through the years in his study of the sources of naming in works of literature. Some of the essays here are new, while others are revisions of previously published work.

Fleissner delves into biographical, historical, literary, and philosophical aspects of an author's choice of names for his characters. His discussions are always informed by broad knowledge of the subjects he pursues. He reports on the work of other scholars, discusses areas of agreement and disagreement and, generally, offers an exhaustive background of the subject. This makes the book useful for further study.

This book is part of an honorable tradition in the examination of influences on an author in naming his characters, setting his locale, and choosing the title for his work. The extent of his work in this discipline is indicated in the Bibliography, which cites twenty-four new titles on onomastic research under his name.

The influences he suggests are often ingenious and provocative. The book's coverage is broad; literary names are examined for the Early Modern Period in England, for the nineteenth century in America and England, and for the twentieth century in England, America, and Austria.

His suggestions are always recognized by Fleissner to be no more than that, given that certain proof is unavailable. His style is leisured, a bit informal at times, and detailed, geared to the undergraduate. He tells, for instance, of discussions with scholars at conferences he attended, when he has a particularly knotty problem to grapple with.

There are eight essays on naming in Shakespeare's plays; these are placed at the beginning of the book because, as he tells us, "my main interest has always been in Shakespeare" (see the Foreword). These essays explore the name of Shylock in *The Merchant of Venice* (Chs. I and II), the name of Malvolio in *Twelfth Night* (Ch. III), Rosencrantz's name in *Hamlet* (Ch. IV), Othello's name (Ch. V), and the problem of Othello's self-referential "base Judean" or "base Indian," the key textual crux in the play (Ch. VI).

*King Lear* is examined for the origin of the king's own name and that of his daughter, Cordelia (Ch. VII). Caliban's name, like Othello's, is allotted two chapters (IX and X). Fleissner goes on to examine the title of *Arden of Feversham*, a play once attributed to Shakespeare, although it is now universally accepted as apocryphal. Fleissner tries to establish a Shakespearean link in the play's title, *Arden*, which is the maiden name of Shakespeare's mother. We are also offered other examples in the play which might sound a Shakespearean note. At the same time, Fleissner recognizes that we "might all too easily get bogged down in some kind of biographical fallacy here admittedly, and, in any case, the Ardenic association does appear rather speculative to some readers" (68-69): this is part of the author's modest, self-effacing style; he leaves his evidence open for the reader to ponder himself (Ch. XI).

In Chapter XII he examines the titles and subtitles of Shakespeare's plays for puns and bawdy implications not previously noticed. By placing the apocryphal *Arden of Feversham* before the chapter on Shakespeare's titles, it would appear that Fleissner intended to focus the reader's attention on the apocryphal play's possible role within the Shakespeare canon.

The book then moves toward the nineteenth century. Charles Dickens' naming in *Edwin Drood* is discussed in two chapters (XIII and XIV). In Chapter XV, naming is set aside for an examination of religious elements in Dickens' work, supported by other scholars' contributions.

We return to naming patterns in Thomas Hardy's *Tess of the d'Urbervilles* (Ch. XVI); to Robert Louis Stevenson's in *Doctor Jekyll and Mister Hyde* (Ch. XVII).

The name of Sherlock Holmes is then engaged for three chapters. His name is discussed in regard to a cryptogrammatical allusion, to etymology, and a possible link to the name Shylock (Ch. XVIII). The next chapter deals with Sherlock's initial, and a link with Edgar Allan Poe's detective C. Auguste Dupin (Ch. XIX). Finally, the pedigree of the name Holmes, as that of a detective, is explored (Ch. XX).

The reader is then led to American literature, in a study of the title of Walt Whitman's *Leaves of Grass* (Ch. XXI), to the name of the eponymous hero in T. S. Eliot's "The Love Song of J. Alfred Prufrock" (Ch. XXII), and to the place-name Zenith in the work of Sinclair Lewis (Ch. XXIII).

The chapter on Robert Frost and Robert Burns is directed toward naming (Ch. XXIV). It is particularly interesting for its gathering together of gossip, as well as more serious evidence, in an enlightening discussion.

Teenagers and those who have not long ago left their teenage years will find the next three chapters particularly interesting, for they deal with books that they have surely read and enjoyed, Thus the name of Nancy Drew is discussed with regard to the influence of Charles Dickens (Ch. XXV); the name of Holden Caulfield is also suggestively linked with Dickens' influence on J. D. Salinger (Ch. XXVI).

Again, Richard Wright's *Native Son* is probably included on every high schooler's reading list. Fleissner, in a particularly provocative essay, discusses the historical, psychological, and linguistic evidence for his argument, in which he links Bigger Thomas with Shakespeare's Othello onomastically and finds as a parallel Iago, equated with white society. In order to establish the fact that Bigger's naming goes beyond what is known of authorial intent, Fleissner cites the essay which Wright wrote, "How Bigger Was Born," which doesn't support any link between Bigger and Othello, or with *Uncle Tom's Cabin* which Wright also suggests. Fleissner follows the birth metaphor with a philosophical and practical discussion of the time when the soul is believed to enter a fetus, or when it brings to life a work of art. He goes on to argue for unconscious influences which may supplement authorial intent. The discussion is graceful and illuminating. Typically, the works of other scholars are conscientiously cited and discussed.

The last essay deals with Franz Kafka's *Amerika* and the influence on that author by the work of Sinclair Lewis and Charles Dickens.

The student, and whomever this engaging book is introduced to, will find a compendium, a rich store of information and scholarship in every work of literature examined here. It is indeed a state of the art of the names therein discussed.

Dorothy E. Litt, author,
*Names in English Renaissance Literature*

PART I:

SHAKESPEARE

# CHAPTER I

# A KEY TO THE NAME SHYLOCK

Lionel Bart's musical adaptation *Oliver!* introduces the conversion of Dickens's Fagin, if not to Christianity (to which Shylock, his familiar literary predecessor, is obliged to turn) certainly to a life based upon the law of love, one fundamental to Christianity and Judaism alike. Thereby the accommodation of the novel *Oliver Twist* is seen as anticipating the characterization of Riah in *Our Mutual Friend*. This is by no means an unwarranted shift inasmuch as Fagin already makes up for us in aesthetic interest (his characterization being superb) for what he lacks in the moral sphere. Very possibly Bart's Fagin was influenced by the treatment accorded Shylock, for "the Jew that Shakespeare drew" (as Alexander Pope called the Macklin Shylock) was by no means wronged according to the true standards of Christianity, the Inquisition notwithstanding. For obviously, if Christianity is right, to be converted to it can be only a reward, though such a verdict may seem bigoted to some.

Since considerable evidence exists that Dickens was creatively influenced by Shakespeare, for which I have recourse to my doctoral dissertation, then put in book form,[1] as well as other studies by such scholars as Alfred Harbage and Valerie Gager, *Oliver!* represents an elaboration on a fundamentally Dickensian theme: namely the re-creation of a certain Shakespearean theatricality.

This leads to the distinct possibility that the derivation of each figure is likewise similar. If Fagin gets his name from the real-life prototype of Robert Fagin, as is often believed, so might Shylock get his name from an Elizabethan. For example, Shylock's name may derive from the contemporary recusant writer Richard Shacklock, whose well-known defense of Roman Catholicism is comparable to Shylock's defense of Judaism. Indeed, A. C. Southern has drawn attention to the similarity between Shylock's defense and that of the leading Catholic apologist, Thomas Harding; in his book on Elizabethan recusant prose, he writes, "Surely the trenchant irony of this passage [one he cites] is of the very same nature as that later magnificent outburst in which Shylock vindicates the essential quality of Jew and Christian" (75-76). So a valid parallel with Shacklock may also be quite in order.

Moreover, earlier conjectures that Shylock's name may relate to that of Richard Shylok, who held land in Hoo in 1435 (for which see M. A. Lower), or to one Shurlock, vaguely related to Sir John Parrott, who in turn was supposed to have been ridiculed in Kemp's impersonation of Falconbridge in *King John* (on which see Hitchin-Kemp), support the view that Shakespeare's creative afflatus may have been under the influence of an English surname or two. For Cecil Roth has produced clear evidence that "in any case, as far as the Ghetto was concerned, the name Shylock was absolutely unknown; and nothing approaching it is to be found in Venetian sources, printed or manuscript" (149).

There is no doubt that the name had some kind of Semitic analog, but Roth finds no specific Jewish source: "Even the name Shylock is obscure in its Jewish connection. It is conceivable that Shakespeare derived it from 'Shiloch the Babylonian' . . . . On the other hand, it has been pointed out that all the Jewish names which occur in *The Merchant of Venice*—Shylock (Shelah), Jessica (Jesca), Chus (Cush), and Tubal—are closely paralleled in two successive chapters of the Book of Genesis" (149). But if Shylock *may* relate to the Hebrew Shelah, it may also relate to the Hebrew Shiloh and Shallach, as John Russell Brown points out, or to the English word *shullock* (for which see the Arden Shakespeare ed. 3).

All these possibilities can be valid, but one so-called possibility surely is not, and it is high time that the theory supporting it is exploded. Consider the Semite Caleb Shilocke mentioned in the 1606 edition of *News from Rome*: a number of scholars have speculated that Shakespeare was acquainted with an earlier version of this work and utilized the surname for his own purposes. The theory has misled the Arden editor and is in great need of being expunged. For there really can be no doubt that *The Merchant of Venice* influenced *News from Rome* and not vice versa.

Here is the proof. M. A. Shaaber states the case for the reverse influence most succinctly, finding that Halliwell's 1853 edition of Shakespeare's plays contains an allusion to an earlier version of *News from Rome*: "a passage from a pamphlet of 1607 entitled *Miracle upon Miracle* which explicitly stigmatizes the story as a hoary fraud: 'witnes the Jewes Prophesie, being an idle vaine pamphlet, as grosse and grosser then John of Calabria, and was printed many years agoe, and this last yeare onely renewed with the addition of 1607'" (236, the passage from Halliwell being in the fifth volume 278). Shaaber mistakenly concludes that "'printed many years agoe' means early enough to have been seen by Shakespeare" from a similar allusion to *News from Rome* in Thomas Nashe's *Have With You to Saffron-Walden* in 1596. Brown observes that "Halliwell showed that it was probably printed 'many years' before 1606 and then re-issued, and M. A. Shaaber . . . quoted a reference . . . which may well allude to an earlier version" (3). That this deduction is ill-advised is evident from the title-page, where there is a clear statement that the section involving Caleb Shilocke was *adjoined* to the pamphlet only in 1606: "*Also certaine prophecies of a Jew serving to that Armie, called Caleb Shilocke, prognosticating many strange accidents, which shall happen the following yeere, 1607.*" Halliwell's passage refers to the "Jewes Pophesie" being a pamphlet "*and* was printed many years agoe, *and* this last yeare onely renewed" (italics added); the earlier form could not have contained the Shilocke prognostications for "*the following yeere, 1607*" and therefore must have been a slightly different pamphlet. The use of the word *and* rather than *that* prompts such a reading; it is surely more than a mere loose grammatical construction. To corroborate the point, the careful reader will note that the allusion in Nashe contains no reference to Caleb and his predictions at all.

W. Jaggard provides a final point proving that the name Shylock (like Fagin) was immediately derived from English surnames, regardless of remote Jewish connections:

> As Dr. Bardsley remarks: "Both Shakespeare and Dickens often took surnames from real life." A Shylock (or Sylock) family existed in Somerset in 1327. The name of Shakespeare's extortionate usurer may be a corruption of Sherlock, Shillock, or Shilcock. It certainly looks, and sounds, essentially British, rather than Eastern, or Italian. (467)

How much better this is than relating Shylock to "an idle vaine pamphlet"! When Dickens decided to call Oliver's master "Fagin," very likely he remembered that his

6

favorite dramatist called a Jew by an English name as well. This is by no means improbable. For instance, P. D. A. Harvey, in "Charles Dickens as Playwright," writes of how "the names he gave his characters were of great significance to Dickens" (25n). Worth comparing is J. Lindsay 125-26.[2]

NOTES

[1] "Shakespeare and Dickens: Some Characteristic Uses of the Playwright by the Novelist," my diss., was then published as *Dickens and Shakespeare* (with a subtitle provided by the publisher). Granted, with two such geniuses there are still bound to be more creative differences on the whole than similarities.

[2] Because of John K. Hale's note "The Name 'Shylock'" in the Winter 1998-99 issue of the *Shakespeare Newsletter*, I resorted in a later issue to citing my original form of this chapter as it appeared in *American Notes and Queries* with the same title. That essay, incidentally, was cited by Joan Ozark Holmer 303, as exhibiting a derivation from a British surname (see also 84). My letter to the editors of *SNL* provided the rationale: "The reason given is that a British Catholic then had a similar name, and the Catholics considered their plight in largely Protestant England as akin to that of the Jews over the centuries" (Summer 1999): 30.

# CHAPTER II

## SIZING UP SHYLOCK'S NAME AGAIN

John Gross's comprehensive book on the moneylender of *The Merchant of Venice*[1] fails to come to terms with the name as such, even when an entire chapter is entitled "Shylock is My Name." Provided are the usually suggested etymologies, including an analogy in the Old Testament and the Hebrew meaning of *cormorant*, but these connections are not very close or helpful in reference to the plot; nor is there any real likelihood that Shakespeare would have had familiarity with such relatively obscure words. Because of the general lack of documentation throughout the book, no consideration of other possible, published etymologies appears. One passing hint, however, happens to point aslant to a previous consideration on which I happen to have worked, one which might now be glanced at again.

First, let me confess to a little titular paronomasia in my initial article on the subject (included here in revised form as Ch. I), yet Shakespeare's own flair for punning provides at least a wholesome precedent. Richard Coates, in his annotated bibliography for the special Shakespeare issue of *Names: A Journal of Onomastics*, was definitely not captivated by my suggestion when he composed his annotation for it (211), but his gloss ("Possible references to historical personages; most implausible") may be also misleading and thus in need of a gloss now itself. Presumably what he *meant* is that I provide such "possible references" in summary form, but specifically reveal then that *most of them* are actually implausible. Certainly I refrain from promoting on my own a variety of references as plausible (a rather

8

implausible thesis in itself to entertain) but instead single out one aspect as worth dealing with among the candidates: my original suggestion then is that an *English* name is the most likely progenitor, whether *Shillock*, *Shilcock*, or *Sherlock*, as W. Jaggard suggests.

For this final listing involves a passing anticipation of the name of the Master Detective: "In the extent of his fame Shylock belongs with . . . Sherlock Holmes" (187). Although a few other forenames are mentioned, the Shylock / Sherlock correlation, however qualified, deserves at least passing reinvestigation under the critical lens. Let us see how.

Let us hasten to affirm from the start that no pre-Shylockian Sherlock is now in the record. On the other hand, it is of curious enough fascination that both Shylock and Sherlock have had their nomenclature traced back to the name of Shacklock, though in the first case it is that of a Catholic recusant and in the second of a cricket player. Still, two things related to the same sort of thing may, in some quasi-mathematical guise, also correlate. Gross's hint therefore offers a re-examination procedure which, even if coincidentally, may be of some assistance to the alert reader open to plausible new resonances.

The most important point is that a certain Richard Shacklock belonged to a well-known group of British recusants who compared their alienated plight to that of the Jewish people historically, one such recusant even being on record for linking up the story of Laban in the Bible that way, even as Shylock himself happens to later, though in a rather different context (*The Merchant of Venice*, 1.3.71).[2] Shylock's being legally required to convert to orthodox Roman Christianity at the end (the play taking place in Catholic Italy) means that his name lends a properly ironic touch to his conversion-to-be; that is if a Catholic-sounding name already prompts what is readily in store for him. It might be added then that this latent irony is evident also in the familiar "pound of flesh" motif: the fact that his demand for this, which cannot be literally obtained without the drawing of blood (and hence murder of his victim), can be met on the preternatural level through his having to accept perforce and thereby consume the Real Presence in the Holy Eucharist. Although, to some, such a reading can enlist a "cannibalistic" interpretation of what was clearly meant to supersede such a primitivistic view, it need not be taken on any such pagan-like level, but can instead be relegated to what anthropologists and psychologists have allowed for as acceptable omophagia. The extent to which Elizabethan

9

playgoers may have been *consciously* aware of this anomaly is open to question, but then the same happens to be true of Caliban at the tail end of *The Tempest*: he, too, is obliged to "seek for grace," as he admits, and thereby live up to a sublimated form of the obvious anagram which his name calls forth (one variant spelling of *cannibal* then having a single "n"). Again, theatergoers may be pardoned for ignoring this submerged meaning, but the basic kinship of Shylock and Caliban in such a symbolic respect augurs for at least a certain subliminal significance. (Caliban, too, has his Italian cohorts, it so happens.)

Demurrers may tentatively arise now owing to the possibility of other plausibly relevant onomastic associations. For example, because Shylock cites Frankfurt (3.1.84), could not his name also have some sort of Teutonic resonance? A modernized production I witnessed at Stratford-upon-Avon (1993) even had him uttering certain German-Jewish or Yiddish expressions. It might be proposed that the German word for *shy* is *scheu* and that a hesitancy to indulge in battle (except when valid self-interest is obviously at stake) has been ethnically linked with German-Jewish people all too often; to express it more decorously, the penchant might better be phrased as their "horror of war." Indeed, Jesus Himself emphasized such passivity, at least in terms of the standard pacifist interpretations of the New Testament. Hence Shylock would exhibit even a certain "shyness" in disdaining to keep company, on the whole, with his gentile brethren (1.3.30-38). Whether such a broad reading would be acceptable as objective enough may perhaps be questioned, at least nowadays in the wake of World War II; in any case, a similar argument could be made for his name as having Scottish rather than Hebrew characteristics, and these ought to be judged on a similar level. *Shy* here can stand on its own without any recourse to German.

For instance, even *if* the first syllable of Shylock's name also might suggest a kind of Germanic origin, so the last may hint at the familiar waterway in Scotland known as the *loch*, the *OED* providing sufficient evidence of early usages of this word this way. So Shylock's concentrated concern with funds even for their own sake, as it were, might then be compared with the age-old English penchant at times for finding the Scots stingy and thereby (informally) money-minded. Their so-called opportunism has even been summoned as providing a basis for the tragedy of *Macbeth*, though admittedly too much might be made of such an analogy.

Yet the trouble is that one such connotation (that of the German Jew) would

10

effectively cancel out the other (that of a possible Scottish innuendo), thereby hinting at both views as being ultimately too subjective for truly serious consideration. The charge of bias could also now be leveled, but the further question then would be whether such prejudice need be wholly on the part of the critic or whether it might not be also (or rather) imputed to the writer himself or perhaps his age, which could well have prompted his critical reactions or attempt at verisimilitude. So, why, we might ask, get involved with all this? But an answer is forthcoming.

In contrast, the "recusant" solution here proposed again would tie in with Gross's own evidence that the playwright's father John Shakespeare, often himself a Catholic recusant at least in part, was a prototype for Shylock. In particular, the father was himself a money-lender (47); the son, as Gross shows, citing the noted authority E. A. J. Honigmann, may even have charged interest on loans. The most curious evidence to this effect, as he points out, is the "one surviving letter addressed to him by his 'loving good friend' Richard Quiney in 1598," for Quiney, originally a fellow Stratfordian but then abiding in London, had "requested a loan of £30" (47). As Denis Kay has also lately shown,[3] "recent research in the Public Records has unearthed some further evidence that John Shakespeare was a business man on a substantial scale and that, as well as trading in large quantities of wool, he was also involved in lending money" (13). The most recent confirmatory evidence for this thesis is that Sir John Falstaff's original prototype, Sir John Oldcastle, though often taken as strongly Protestant, was at times admired by Catholics.

In a note on a Catholic Oldcastle, R. W. F. Martin[4] finds a positive reference to him in Jane Owen's *An Antidote Against Purgatory*, a Catholic work which then alludes to Falstaff as well in this connection. In the same issue of the journal in which Martin's research appears, Eric Sams, writing on Oldcastle and the new *Oxford Shakespeare* edition,[5] claims that although "Shakespeare was said to have 'died a Papist,'" there is "abundant evidence he was held to have lived and thought as one too" (184).[6] Sams's conclusions are at odds with Martin's, in a sense, in that he disputes the entire Oldcastle / Falstaff connection, but, to sum things up, any connection between Oldcastle and either John Falstaff or Catholicism works hand-in-glove with Garry O'Connor's recently stated belief that Falstaff was ultimately based on Shakespeare's father, two of whose "associates who hid from the law and from creditors" being "William Fluellen and George Bardolphe, names which Shakespeare later revived in *Henry IV* and *Henry V*" (19). Ironically, both Falstaff and Shylock may have a similar biographical origin.

O'Connor's authority comes from his practical work on the stage. He was formerly Director of the Royal Shakespeare Company in England. We might compare the similar interplay of syllables and meanings in the names *Fal(l)-staff* and *Shake-speare*. (See Harry Levin's article on "Shakespeare's Nomenclature.") Kay provides evidence that the latter name was sometimes taken as having an unfortunate punning effect and that at least one person is on record for having thereby changed it: "Hugh Shakespeare, a Fellow of Mertin College, Oxford, changed his name to read 'Hugh Sawnders' because it was then said 'Shake-speare' has such a bad repute" (5).

As a final touch, it might be added that Leonard Ashley contends that "Florio (if Rowse is right in thinking he had *marrano* origins) may have something to do with Shylock" so that Shakespeare would have "obtained much" from this friend instead of from any "supposed visits to Italy" (49). This is also plausible, though the Sherlock affinity intrigues me more, for which see Chs. XVIII-XX.[7]

## NOTES

[1]Gross's very title, *Shylock: Four Hundred Years in the Life of a Legend*, reflects the notion that the play appeared as early as 1592, whereas it is generally thought to have been composed in 1596-7. See Halliday 311.

[2]Shakespearean references here and elsewhere are to the revised Pelican ed.

[3]His is the most recent and liveliest of recent Shakespeare biographies, though he does also, to my mind, indulge in some unwarranted speculation, e.g., assuming that Cardenio is the name of a long lost play by the man from Stratford, the evidence for which is extremely sketchy, for which see my paper "The Likely Misascription of *Cardenio* (and thereby *Double Falsehood*) in Part to Shakespeare."

[4]The title of Martin's article can be misleading, for Oldcastle was the leading recognized prototype for Sir John Falstaff, whose only affinity with some behavior of certain Catholics may have been in his indulgence in alcoholic beverage.

[5]Sams is perhaps the most controversial Shakespearean of note operative today. He rejects, for instance, new theories of the *Oxford Shakespeare* ed., in this case notably Gary Taylor's substitution of the name of *Oldcastle* for *Falstaff* in *1 Henry IV*. Taylor's purpose was to try to revert to the dramatist's original intent, but that can at times be considered multivalent.

[6]Yet most Shakespeareans, even some Catholic ones, would still contend that the Stratford Bard was at least later a conformist and thus followed the Church of England, as seen in his prominently echoing *The Book of Common Prayer*, as is widely recognized, in *Hamlet*. See Christopher Devlin's *Hamlet's Divinity*. Admittedly the so-called Lancastrians nowadays disagree,

[7]After composing this chapter I came across Paula Brody's article "Shylock's Omophagia." She posits that Shylock's demand for his "pound of flesh" represents a ritualistic yearning to accept "communion with the spirit of the group," to become initiated into Venetian society. His "hatred" thus represents an unconscious "love-wish." I then suggested to her the idea that has once been put forward that Shylock should have thought of using a white-hot knife which would not have drawn blood. In a review of J. Shatzmiller's *Shylock Reconsidered* in the *New York Review of Books*, Gary Wills provides further evidence that Shylock is somehow of British vintage, at least nominally: "Some who discuss this play assume that only Shylock and his coreligionists are usurers in Venice. There would be no reason for Elizabethans, so familiar with their own Christian usurers, to assume that. In fact, the usurer, a common figure in the drama of Shakespeare's age, is normally a Christian" (24). It might finally be mentioned that Shylock's getting his "Body *and* Blood" (in terms of omophagia in the Eucharist, regularly taken, as amounting finally to a "pound of flesh"), when he is legally not allowed to have one drop of blood, represents one of the great ironies of the play.

# CHAPTER III

## MALVOLIO'S MANIPULATED NAME

The title means rather more than that the steward Malvolio in *Twelfth Night* has a transformed or malformed name. Instead it indicates that he has one which, as we shall see, was manipulated by Shakespeare presumably from Spenser's *Faerie Queene* and Montaigne, although, granted, that is meant only as a calculated, circumstantial deduction. The reader must decide for himself on the basis of the evidence.

In any event, whereas Malvolio's *nose* has received prominent enough attention,[1] his nomenclature has presented more of a muddle. The dramatist's calling attention to the latter is, however, clear enough as in the analogous, familiar name-play on "M. O. A. I." (2.5.107, 110, 120, 139). Various proposed decodings of this abbreviation have included "*My Own Adored Idol*" and (in a more learned manner of course) "*Mare Orbis Aer Ignis*" (Water, Earth, Air, Fire); even John Marston's abbreviated initials transposed, with *J* then signified by an *I* (*IO: MA*); somewhat more pertinently apropos of the plot, "*I AM Olivia*";[2] and of course the suggestion that the letters are "simply the first, second, and second from last letters" and the last in the name *Malvolio* itself.[3] Because no clear-cut consensus exists as to the best etymology, something additional may now profitably be added as a follow-up.

First, let us recognize that obscure lettering is also in the name *Olivia*, which is in itself a partial anagram (if one likes) of *Viola*, the name of the very person to whom she is attached. Insofar as the encoded lettering comes by way of *Maria* (whose letters are also partly in Malvolio's label), these three women are, in effect, symbolizing his nemesis. It has likewise aptly been noted that "[i]ronically, M O A I has all the ingredients of egocentricity: English 'I,' Italian 'MIO,' 'MIA,' 'IO,' and French 'MOI'" (see Petronella 143). Whereas these findings are fairly recent and somewhat helpful, new ones can again be added which are more to the point. Let us see.

Whereas Malvolio is correct that the jumbled letters happen to be ones also in his own name, they are there by virtue of what has been called anamorphosis, but can also be dubbed metathesis, a switching that Shakespeare invested in otherwise. Hence "garmombles" represents, in effect, a well-recognized metathetic variation of *Mömpelgart* in *The Merry Wives of Windsor*; the name *Falstaff* is a variant form (aside from echoing the meaning of *Shake-speare*, as noted earlier) of *Fastolfe*;[4] *Othello* is derivative of *Othoman* but also an anagrammatic version of *Otho* and *Leo* (see Ch. V); *Caliban* is a somewhat jumbled version of *cannibal* with a single "n" (amusingly also symbolizing his drunken nature). But the point can be made that metathesis in itself is meaningless, that the entire purport of the jest played on Malvolio is to make him vainly try to discern intrinsic nominal meaning when there may be none present; this point would then be underscored through Sir Toby's use of similar "learned" language which appears also relatively meaningless in itself: *Pigrogromitus*, *Vapians*, and *Queubus*, names which appear in 2.3.23. The first suggests pig Latin and may be a pun on the word *grammaticus*, but no completely cogent etymology has been put forth. The second possibly had the connotation of "vapid" as derivative of Latin *vapidus* ("flat-tasting"). Although *Queubus* relates to "queer," the best overall explanation for all these terms is that the dramatist was parodying the learned style of Robert Greene or, in the light of the final conclusion of this essay, Spenser's own archaisms. If the meaninglessness of such "learned" effects is present, the so-called M. O. A. I. conundrum would thereby be incapable of genuine solution because none would verifiably exist.

Yet in spite of or even because of such mumbo-jumbo concerning Malvolio and his presumed acronym, his formal nomenclature itself may ironically have had notable significance for his creator which has not yet been satisfactorily explained. Upon first reading, we may notice that the prefix *Mal-* conjures up such an analogous name as that of *Malevole* in another drama, *The Malcontent* (both the name and title being germane here); however, this figure is not comic, and if any debt is indeed present, it would most probably be that of Marston to Shakespeare, not vice versa. In this respect, consult my essay "Shakespeare's *Carte Blanche*," its proposal being that Marston imitated the subtitle of *Twelfth Night* in composing his own play with the title *What You Will*.

Probing a bit further, we can observe that Malvolio has something in common with Shylock, both of them being strongly "puritanical" loners, ones looked down upon by society, and at least initially composed as comic or satirical characters. It is of at least passing interest again that Shylock's own name has occasioned some of the oldest name-hunting recorded in the annals of scholarship, reverting back to the mid-nineteenth century. Moreover, Malvolio's puritanism emerges in his torturing the text of Maria's letter "to make it yield a suitable meaning, much in the style of Puritan theologizing" (Bevington 395, cited by Petronella 139).

Let us observe that evidently Malvolio's name was meant to be taken as a sort of variant of the meaning of the play's subtitle, *What You Will*. (This was transposed and became a main title in the famous German translation, *Was Ihr Wollt*.) In short, if an "ill will" (*Mal* mixed with *volio*) be generated because of the steward, the members of the audience are free to take for themselves "what [they] will" from this. His attitude is clearly in contrast to the presumed merriment associated with the twelve nights of Christmas. What is more, Sir Henry Herbert underscored this import by renaming the comedy *Malvolio* in his Office Book (2 February 1623): "At Candlemas Malvolio was acted at court, by the kings and servants" (Halliday 300), he being the most interesting character, if not the protagonist.

Further, because Shakespeare indulged in such well-known name-play on *Will* in several sonnets, his subtitle here evidently was not merely a throw-away one but meant that the spectator or reader is to take "what [he] will" from Will—hence thereby also from Malvolio as a kind of Will. Such a deduction should not, of course, give playgoers and readers license to do wholly as they please, but only as Shakespeare himself wanted. For consider the last line of the play, "And we'll strive to please you every day" (5.1.397), which relates to the allowance in the Epilogue of the related play *As You Like It*, "as please you" (5.4.12-13). To underscore this, let us consider a plausible source he used, one which bears on the meaning.

Because the name of Malvolio is that of a steward, it would follow that the playwright could easily enough have derived it, however obliquely, from that of another notably named menial servant in the annals of Renaissance literature. One that comes immediately to mind is the porter dubbed appositely *Malvenù* in Spenser's epic, *The Faerie Queene*. The onomastic correlation with the drama is in that Malvenù—playing nominally on the French *bienvenu*, meaning "welcome"—is depicted at the very entrance to the House of Pride in the *Faerie Queene* (1.4.6), and, for what it is worth (which is rather notable here), the first of the Deadly Sins represents clearly Malvolio's own outstanding problem—unless it be instead that he takes himself simply too seriously, though that can be discerned as a side-effect of pride too. Indeed, it is a commonplace that Shakespeare appropriated Spenser extensively elsewhere; for instance, the story of Claudio and Hero in another such comedy, *Much Ado About Nothing*, derives from the epic (Halliday 327), as does part of the plot of *King Lear*. Why not then also *Twelfth Night*?

As a final neatly intriguing bit of evidence here, the initials E. K., which adorn Spenser's *Shepherd's Calendar*, have prompted likewise much debate—and thus could have been also somewhat behind the sport made of the letters M. O. A. I., as related, however tangentially, as we may now notice, to Malvolio's cognomen. Thus Malvolio's name was manipulated, let us say, by way of Malvenù's and not merely malformed in the process. Moreover, if Spenser took over Malvenù's name, he did so much more on the level of half-conscious than fully conscious echolalia. In support, another hint of Malvolio's egocentric behavior is discernible enough in the actions of Braggadochio in the *Faerie Queene*—again on a more general than specific level. The import of this character and his influence is evident enough from mention made of him in the play *Edmund Ironside* (indeed an issue important with regard to the dating of that play with its controversial authorship), but I would not contend that this allusion supports Shakespeare's use of Spenser here, for the overall style of the anonymous play is rather inferior (though it was apparently verbally somewhat indebted to *Richard II*).

Such a Spenserian correlation is closer at hand than the Italian entertainment *Il Sacrificio*, which, as the New Arden editors of *Twelfth Night* point out, included the character with a name similar to that of Malvolio, Malevolti.[5] In any case, as the name of a Puritan, Malvolio conjures up a form of self-denigration which is then ironically turned in upon itself when he falsely believes Olivia has given her humorless steward a warrant to expose his ego on her behalf. His self-importance obviously is responsible for his believing he has license for such self-indulgence. When he finally leaves the stage, claiming he will be avenged on the whole "pack," the import of his name takes on its most literal significance. Whereas Malvenù's name invokes a bad welcome, Malvolio's finally stands for a bad goodbye.

Then some comments are in order regarding recent and not so recent scholarship on this self-indulgent steward. Vincent Petronella's essay has a number of helpful remarks such as the following pertaining to the New Historicism: "[Malvolio's] fashioning of self is in relation to something alien, an illusion, but it is a mock of self-fashioning, a distortion of self-fashioning itself" (144). Stephen Greenblatt's *Renaissance Self-Fashioning* also comes to mind. Leslie Hotson's ingenious but doubtful etymology of *M. O. A. I.* as wordplay on the name of Mall Fitton (108) might also be mentioned, if only in passing, for Fitton was light-haired, not dark as the Dark Lady of the *Sonnets* must have been, and she was sixteen in 1592, when most scholars think the poems were first being written, and so hardly married then. J. J. M. Tobin's finding an allusion in this code to Gabriel Harvey's fascination with capital letters is cogent enough but does not come to terms with the names themselves. Shakespeare could well have derived the *character* of Malvolio from Harvey, not to mention the play on letters, but have taken the Puritan's *name* from a different source.

With this in mind, it seems plausible enough that the abbreviated lettering was intended as a cipher for *Montaigne*, the counsel given regarding Malvolio's behavior being derivative of the *Essais* (3.3 and 3.7), with the name itself relating to the essay "Des Noms," where the phrase "*mal volontiers*" is soon to be found (Guttman 92). This erudite position was set forth by Allen Percy in a letter to the *TLS* (18 Sept. 1937) but overlooked in the extensive bibliographies in the Shakespeare issue of *Names*. In brief, Percy claims that the "fustian riddle" which is in "*M. O. A. I.* doth sway my life" could also imply that "Montaigne influences Shakespeare strongly." The argument, sounding somewhat better than the proposed play on the abbreviation for Marston's full name in reverse cited earlier, runs as follows:

> Malvolio, attempting to link the letters "Moai" with his own name, perceives that "there is no constancy in the sequel . . . *A* should follow but *O* does." Substitute the name "Montaigne" for "Malvolio," and there *is* consonancy; because the letters *Mo-ai* are the first letters of the two syllables of *Mont-aigne*. (675)

Although such a reading may sound at first like a private joke arising, let us say, from wit-combats in the Mermaid Tavern, Percy notes well that the French essayist was himself concerned in "Des Noms" with such cryptograms, as with the names of *Nicolas Denisot* and *Alsinois*, e.g.: "Conte d'Alcinois (cf. Count Malvolio) is an anagram for 'Nicolas Denisot'" (675).

Whereas members of the general audience would not have been expected to detect such codification, it holds up remarkably well, given Percy's supportive argumentation:

> Further, the short essay on Greatness, which follows immediately in that scene, and the rules for Malvolio's future self-conduct, are taken from the third vol. of the *Essays*, first published in 1588; the two drawn upon being III.3, "De Trois Commerces," and III.7, "De l'Incommodité de la Grandeur."

The novice reader, however, may well be nonplussed at Percy's further contention that "Shakespeare must have read the French edition of Montaigne because Florio translates names beginning with *M* into 'those that begin with *P* . . . .'" For, to be sure, *Montaigne* also begins with the requisite *M*. In following this up, I discerned a misprint (Percy's "begin" should be "began" [312]), but also discovered a wealth of helpful data. The point is that, in the very first paragraph of his rendition of "Des Noms," Florio singled out common names beginning with the letter *P* (actually alimentary terms) whereas Montaigne had done the same thing with *M* (1: 292). Shortly after that, the French essayist tells how important it is to have a smooth-sounding name, for that way it will be forgotten by others only "mal volontiers" (unwillingly). Hence Shakespeare presumably was attracted to the singling out of this solitary letter in the original version and so could easily have associated it not only with the fuss made over *M* in "M. O. A. I." but with a sort of French etymology of *Malvolio* itself following shortly.

The notion that Shakespeare could have read Montaigne in the original as well as in Florio's version has been settled affirmatively by Robert Ellrodt in his well-received paper at Stratford-upon-Avon (later published in *Shakespeare Survey*) with its careful research. Could he have even seen Florio's translation when it was published only several years after *Twelfth Night*? If he did, it would have been in manuscript. Yet too much has been made of the supposed Shakespearean autograph in the British Library copy of Florio's *Essays*. Consult, for example, Charles Hamilton, whose main title to fame was in discerning that the supposed Hitler *Dia-*

*ries* were forgeries. Referring to the distinguished paleographer Edward Maunde Thompson as having already published on the signature as a fake, Hamilton went into more detail on its alleged spurious nature, observing that "the forgery is based upon the signature on the bottom of page 2 of the will," for "the *W* is much too large for the rest of the signature," his conclusion then being that evidently "the forger was not familiar with the secretary script and did not know precisely how the letters should be written" (Hamilton 243, 245).

One animadversion to claiming a personal debt to Montaigne here might be that Shakespeare would hardly have wanted to identify himself in any way with such a character as Malvolio. Yet "*M. O. A. I.* doth sway my life" is said by the steward only in quoting the riddling missive he has received, one which he egotistically misinterprets; hence the inherent meaning could still be that Montaigne is the principal swayer of Shakespeare's creativity in producing the comic figure, if not the sole influence. (Greater influence of the Frenchman can then be detected in *Hamlet* and *The Tempest*, as is well recognized.) It can be added that Montaigne's skepticism concerning conventional faith ("Que sais-je?") is then reflected, if not also refracted, in the dramatist's fun in handling the Puritan element in Malvolio's character. With this Francophile allusiveness now at hand, it is further tempting to suspect that he was indebted *both* to "Des Noms" and to Malvenù, whereby the French connection would be reinforced.

NOTES

[1]See Wood 38-39. Feste's allusion (2.3.25-27) may be based on Erasmus.

[2]Lee Cox (360) offered this anagrammatic suggestion to the prior list of possibilities, cited in the *Variorum*. The vowels in Malvolio's name as well as in the abbreviation do point to his being a grossly exaggerated reflection of both Olivia and Orsino.

[3]Chris Hassel (356), finding Cox's riddle hard to decipher, offered this simplified version.

[4]See the two articles by Willson, also Davis and G. Williams. Samuel Crowl has suggested to me additional name-play with Falstaff's name and the form *Fats-laff*, but that was a mere friendly gesture.

[5]See Lothian and Craik xxix; also Levith 3.

# CHAPTER IV

## DECODING THE "ROSE-" AFFILIATION IN *ROSENCRANTZ*

The problem of the correct form of the family name of Hamlet's academically affiliated companions, courtiers Rosencrantz and Guildenstern, who are commonly thought to have been linked as well with the university at Wittenberg, Germany, probably having been undergraduate classmates of the Prince's there, can raise some eyebrows nowadays.[1] This effect is especially true inasmuch as the spelling of the Rosencrantz name, as we presently have it, was initially promulgated by the most famous of Shakespearean emendators, Theobald, in the eighteenth century.

The query which can validly arise is whether the dramatist would have been wont to employ a spelling or linguistic construct such as the *Rosencrantz* variant, that is if he simply had felt obligated to prefer a certain standardized form. What is more, it is clearly known that even though Theobald became a specialist in emendations in a major way, *The Oxford English Dictionary* later indicated well enough that many of his proffered changes were historically supererogatory, if not unworthy, additions. Still, the present-day formulation can possibly have certain merits, so let us re-examine it with care. For there even may be semantic undertones therein favorable to the religious sacrifice of Jewish people historically, evidence of martyrdom, ones lending themselves to the modern-day scapegoat image, for the name could well have been Semitic. As to whether such a reading would appear at all stereotyped, the suitable answer would be that finding intimations of prejudice even then may initially appear trumped up, but still should not be suppressed if valid. We are apt all too easily to recall Shylock.

Thus far the main documentation on this nomenclatural question, duly sum-marized in the standard *Variorum* edition, cites a Danish nobleman with the same name (though the "c" effect here takes then the shape of a "k" spelling) who hap-pened to accompany a Danish politician to England on the ascension of James I; an editorial comment then pointedly adds that "Steevens says it was an ambassador."[2] The main citation is to a brief remark by Walter Thornbury, who posits Shakespeare's plausible awareness of the new King's queen as being Danish herself. Hence we have here what might be termed even a viable, political, "Danish connection," let us say.

Now because of the well-known argument that another tragedy roughly at that time, *Macbeth*, was composed specifically for the same king, James I, thereby becoming the so-designated "Royal Play," it is surely plausible enough to detect some kind of link with the Danish tragedy even in this regal manner. Still (granted) such a tacit association may also be critiqued as but another accommodation of the critical stance commonly now rather demoted as occasionalism, hence amounting to a sort of random deduction, one having to be reconstructed verily "after the fact," as it were. Clearly because Shakespeare started working on the tragedy of Denmark actually prior to the ascension of the Scottish king, any presumed creative link with the royal inauguration and its aftermath is rather open to question, however.

Another piece of research, moreover, should likewise be taken into due ac-count: Raven I. McDavid's argument, about two decades ago, which made some-thing of yet another Danish diplomat, a certain Jørgen Rosenkrantz, who (intrigu-ingly enough) happened indeed to have also attended the university at Wittenberg. In point of historical fact, McDavid then goes so far as to contend that "many men of both families" (namely that of Guildenstern included) were somehow affiliated with academic life there; he claims that this was but "another detail Shakespeare probably included in the interest of verisimilitude" (401). Again, though, no spe-cific proof is provided for the dramatist's having been cognizant of any such corre-lation. Yet, in short, the nomenclature can be reasonably thought of as being itself, let us posit, even diplomatically "in the air" enough at that time in history. The actual proof, nonetheless, is fairly sketchy, to say the least.

So it is time to re-examine the name *Rosencrantz*, as it duly is registered in the early printings of the play, to try finally to discern what indeed happened to such a distinguished surname. The *Variorum* edition first cites the spelling as being *Rosencraus* in the Quartos,[3] that being the characteristic orthography then, though in fact the variant *Rossencraft* also happens to appear in Q1 (plausibly, it may well be then asked, as the result of, say, histrionic mishearing?). Thus Alan C. Dessen remarks, "I, for one, have no trouble seeing (or hearing) how F's *Laertes* could become Q1's *Leartes* . . . Rosencrantz—*Rossencraft*"(66-67).

His parenthetic qualifier suggests that the Q1 version was after the fact, conceivably the result of what has been commonly termed nowadays a veritable "memorial reconstruction." (This popular designation has in recent years been called into question, to be sure, by various revisionist critics but has by no means been ousted in its entirety even now.)

True, it might appear that the presently unacceptable form of *Rosencraus* turned out to be no more than the result of common enough *u:n* orthographic confusion, whether in terms of a disarray by the compositor in setting up type (not merely thereby an inversion of the same letter, but an example of "foul case") or, before that, a result of simple minim-confusion as occurring even in reading the playwright's manuscript. If a reporter's copy happens to be involved with the *Rosencraus* variant, as well as with the *Rossencraft* spelling, then the minim problem could have taken place even there, owing no doubt to a certain haste involved in reporting. Perhaps the best known example of this kind of mishap elsewhere in Shakespeare is in terms of the curious *Indian / Iudean* (*Judean*) reading in *Othello*, 5.2.347 (see Ch. V). In short, *Rosencrans* was originally misprinted, or more likely misread, as *Rosencraus*, the latter hypothesis appearing the more acceptable, at least in terms of modern textual scholarship.

The point is that because this odd misspelling obviously did not make any sense to anyone acquainted with Danish history, an apparent readjustment had then to be introduced in the First Folio, namely a reversion back to the "n" reading, but still not entirely to the better-known Q reading. The result turned out to be the odd spelling of *Rosincrane*.[4] Because in subsequent Folios the new orthography then turned either into *Rosincrosse* or *Rosincros*, the evident suspicion arises that the final vowel in the original Folio variant was here in the same way that it was in the Second and Third Folios, the added "e" being merely appended for effect. It is hard not to be reminded, at least in passing, of a notable analogy with the familiar Spenserian Red Cross knight (sometimes dubbed merely *Redcrosse*) in *The Faerie*

*Queene*, where again the final "e" for effect, actually here a pseudo-Chaucerian imitation, is so often rampant as well. The same "e" ending happens to be in all of the spellings of the first mention of Guildenstern's name as found in Quartos and Folios as cited in the *Variorum*.[5] Although the spellings singled out in this edition as "characteristic" of those in these early texts are not entirely comprehensive, they can be sufficiently trusted, at any rate, given the status of unstandardized spelling evident in those early times. In other words, they constituted sufficiently "representative" orthography for that age.

But then what made later editors confidently revert to the accepted spelling that we presently use? The most cogent or simple answer is that they discerned so much inconsistency in the earlier versions that they quite naturally determined that they were thus compelled to standardize the name for themselves, yet still keep it in effect properly Anglicized in the process—the *-crantz* suffix being, in short, less Germanic-sounding, let alone even Danish-sounding, than the *-krantz*.[6] Another plausible answer is that Theobald, and editors following him, had felt, whether deliberately or not, that Shakespeare's very own orthography was somehow discernible in a sort of nomenclatural conflation of the Qq and F1 versions. In a word, the "s" ending in the Quartos was evidently transferred to become the "cran[e]" effect in the Folio, with the consequence that the sound effect forthcoming from such a link-up would appear close enough to the original Danish family name.

Whether the unusual spellings would be sufficient, even as conflated, to promote thereby a *symbolic* interpretation of the Rosencrantz name as suggestive of something explicitly or implicitly *theological*, let us say, is rather more questionable. In any event, *Krantz* could simply mean *wreath* (or *garland*), whereby any Catholic "rosarian" suggestiveness need hardly be germane here, especially in the name of a male student and in terms then of the Lutheran Wittenberg connection. Clearly it is just as conjectural to assert that the early spellings of the surname needed to reflect, in some form, Shakespeare's own version(s). The point is that numerous reasons can be offered for this mix-up; no particular early variant needs to have priority over another, compositors being capable enough of contributing to the problem with their own individualized reconstructions.

Analogously, Guildenstern's name also underwent some metamorphosis, if less radically, the "i" taking the early variant form of "y" in both Qq and F readings,[7] and the final "e" being adduced for its mannered effect once again. (The Q1 reading was *Guilderstone*, again a likely mishearing by an incompetent or perhaps simply näive reporter.) Curiously, one variant in later Folios became *Guildenstare*, which indicates an Anglicizing of the German substantive *Stern* as *star* (plus the appended vowel). In this instance, actual translation would have been involved. Such an example would indicate that the British were well enough acquainted with the Teutonic language in order to uncover root meanings in both names of the schoolmates. True enough, *Rosen-* then may rather be linked with the sycophant's kowtowing to Claudius' wishes, and in terms of his presumed precious language and behavior, than with any implicit allusion to, say, a *rosary* effect (whether meant literally or perhaps ironically), the abundance of supposed Christological imagery otherwise in this play from time to time notwithstanding. Although the drama embodies references to a university at Wittenberg, as then Lutheran in Shakespeare's time, the dramatist may have had his initial Catholic proclivities, largely through his mother, as evident for example obviously in the so-called "purgatorial" aspects of the Ghost. Wittenberg thus need not encroach upon *Rosencrantz* happening to mean *rosary* in certain strictly religious contexts.

In short, it appears safe enough at this time to pursue Theobald in his variation on the *Rosenkrantz* spelling, even though he is notorious for having made so many emendations and adaptations that his dictum by no means represents always the final word nowadays as being that of a textual editor. (This is hardly to criticize him as being personally disingenuous. The authority of *OED* simply arose later and thus had to supersede him.) This spelling then is most probably what Shakespeare originally desired, even though he spelled the name rather differently in various places (unstandardized spelling being rampant enough then). Indeed, as Giles E. Dawson points out, this so-called Stratford "upstart" turned out to be inconsistent even in the orthography *of his own* name; Dawson mentions, for example, that he had come across no other playwright of the period, or writer at all for that matter, who would abbreviate his surname in the apparently casual way that Shakespeare did. This could suggest modesty no doubt.

Lastly, this textual concern has a bearing on yet another, which has recently come to the fore again, namely the issue of whether Hamlet deliberately planned his escape from the confines of Rosencrantz and Guildenstern to get away on a pirate ship. That interpretation depends on the textual question of whether the word *crafts* could have had the meaning of "ships" then, a matter argued for by David Farley-

Hills in a recent essay. For, if Hamlet did plot his escape, then the likelihood of his making his supposed friends aboard deliberately into scapegoat images becomes more prominent.

NOTES

[1]For an opposing view of their academic affiliation, see Linda Kay Hoff 270-75; owing to Hamlet's friends' spying techniques, she rather considers a Jesuit school a more distinct possibility. Whether such a verdict raises the hint of a bias toward the Society of Jesus is another matter. In any case, the name *Rosencrantz* can be literally translated as *rosary*. Thus cf. the Danish rosary text *Om Jomfru Marie Rosenkrands* (About Mary's Rosary), as cited in Winston-Allen's *Stories of the Rose*, which also includes numerous Germanic connections, e.g. *Von dem psalter und Rosenkrancz unser lieben frauen* (the dates of the two works are roughly 1483 and 1502) (25).

[2]Furness, I, 129.

[3]This is cited, apropos of the first entry on the character, in the *Variorum*. In examining the Folio text, we can discern only two instances of this spelling (29, 72), whereas the name *Rosincrance* appears some five times (30 [twice], 80, 95, 103). Cf. also readings in *Hamlet: The Text of the First Folio*, 1623, passim.

[4]Reference again is to the first entry only; this spelling appears only four times in F (29-30, with two instances on each page), whereas the *e*-less ending occurs six times (71, 72 [twice] , 80, 95, 103). Less authoritative, earlier quarto readings are not considered, especially because of the plausibility of their representing what are called reporters' copies.

[5] Whereas the F editors claimed that they were dispensing with earlier Q readings and following the author's manuscript, they actually carried over many readings in Q, as Malone has already suggested, as is well known. For a full account and critical appraisal thereof, see Margareta de Grazia 43, 61.

[6] This is so claimed with regard to the first entry (*Variorum* I, 129). According to the Scolar Press edition of F (see n4 above), however, this variant is not evident there. Still, spellings then could simply have differed somewhat from one copy to another.

[7] The leading senior member of my Department happened to be Semitic recently, with a heritage stemming from the part of northern Europe where the play took place. This colleague, Dr. Emil Dansker, has assured me that Rosencrantz's name could well have been Jewish at Hamlet's time historically. Another Jewish Shakespearean I know has submitted that it was simply Germanic, but she did not provide any evidence for that distinction here. The fact that Rosencrantz and Guildenstern

were classmates of Hamlet's at a university associated with Luther in Shakespeare's time intimates their not being religiously Jewish; still they could be considered Jewish converts to Christianity, as were Jesus's disciples. So the idea of their being Jewish scapegoats is at least plausible.

# CHAPTER V

## THE MOOR'S NOMENCLATURE

May I add a footnote to the notes of Professors F. N. Lees and Sipahigil on the origin of Othello's name? I concur with both of them that there is evidence that the name somehow derived from that of Othoman and was also Italian in a manufactured sort of way. Since, according to the authority of Geoffrey Bullough, one of the possible sources of the play is Fenton's *Certaine Tragicall Discourses*, which was translated from Belleforest, who in turn adapted his tales from Bandello, the *-ello* suffix to the Moor's name is clearly associated with a common ending for an Italian proper noun (thereby is not a diminutive).

Previously I had noted that the Othello name was a blend of *Oth-* and *ello* (considered as a metathetic variant of the letters in *Leo*—namely John Leo, whose career, as presented in the introduction to Pory's translation of his work in 1600, and whose description of Africa influenced Shakespeare's description of the Moor, for which see Lois Whitney's article in *PMLA* and Jones 21-25). I should like to point out in addition that although the transposition of L-e-o into e-l-l-o (the extra *l* having been added then for the Italian effect) may seem a bit sought after, it is not implausible in terms of the half-conscious level, especially given Shakespeare's penchant for such metathetic and anagrammatic shifts as with *Fastolfe / Falstaff, canibal / Caliban, Thom[as] Nashe* and *Moth, Mömpelgart /* "garmombles," *Florio* and *Holofernes*—all of which are fairly common knowledge.

But did Shakespeare have a precedent for taking over the first part or syllable of *Othoman*? Was he thinking of his character only as a lesser sort of Othoman the Great? He had such a precedent inasmuch as he was also partly basing himself on *Otho*, the Roman emperor who died in A. D. 69. Both Otho and Othello were leaders and from Italy who died in exactly the same manner: they stabbed themselves. Otho also had a problem with his wife, which involved the question of divorce. It is probable that Shakespeare knew about Otho at least insofar as Francis Bacon cited Otho specifically in one of his best known essays, "Of Death," and though the essay was published after the play, Bacon surely would not have used such a reference if he did not think the readership of the times would recognize it. (This is not to suggest in any way, of course, that Bacon really wrote the plays.)

When this essay was published in its initial form in the Oxford *Notes and Queries*, an essay immediately following it was entitled "The Naming of the Protagonists in Shakespeare's *Othello*." I dispute its main thesis here that "Othello is an Italian name (of Teutonic origin) meaning 'rich'" (143). For the *Oth* syllable is definitely not Italian (except in a dialectal way perhaps), and the association with a Germanic name probably confuses it with the name *Odo*, which the *Oxford Dictionary of English Christian Names* relates to *Otto*, and claims is from Old Germanic *Audo*, derivative of *auda*, the equivalent of Old English *ead*, meaning *rich*. Many other variants are given. Now the Germanic connection would appear to relate to the Roman emperor *Otho*, whereas it actually does not, for that name is Latin, derivative from the Greek. The Teutonic association is rather with *Otto der Grosse*, who came much later than Otho, the Roman Stoic.

Since working on this matter initially I decided to have an addendum published in *Names*, which can here be presented in revised form. I observed that G. L. Kittredge, in his introduction to his edition of the tragedy, referred to A. H. Krappe's "A Byzantine Source of Shakespeare's *Othello*" as particularly "interesting" (viii). Krappe noted that "neither the Italian original not the French translation mention the names *Othello* and *Iago*" and then stated that "it has been pointed out that the poet took those from a contemporary work entitled *God's revenge against Adultery*"(156). Careful research then convinced me, however, that this work probably was a ghost, did not exist. For it is not mentioned in the *Short-Title Catalogue* or in any of the standard bibliographies of the period, nor is there an entry for it in The Folger Library Catalog. Watt's *Bibliotheca Britannica* mentions only one work under the subject of "God" that might possibly be related, namely *A Wonderful Judg-*

*ment of God upon Two Adulterers* . . . (1583) but this book is by a minister with whose work Shakespeare would scarcely have been acquainted. Nonetheless, though none of the standard editions of *Othello* (the New Arden, New Cambridge, London, Riverside) cite the work mentioned by Krappe, it apparently achieved a certain recognition. Francis Griffin Stokes in his *Dictionary of the Characters and Proper Names in the Works of Shakespeare* (1949) states, under *Othello*: "With regard to the origin of the name nothing definite is known. Its occurrence in nearly contemporary writings may be due to the play"(240-1). Was Stokes thinking of *God's Revenge*? F. N. Lees, in his note on "Othello's Name," written twelve years later, affirms, however, that the noted authority E. K. Chambers claimed in 1930 that "it is not known where [the name] Othello came from." Since "Ottoman" (or "Othoman") is mentioned in the play, moreover (the third scene of the first act), Lees's view that Othello's name somehow derives from that of Othoman has a factual, comparative basis. It occurred to me that *God's revenge* might have a bearing on John Reynolds' *Triumphs of God's Revenge* . . . (1622), but the dates simply did not fit. Finally, I discovered a reference which linked the work cited by Krappe to Reynolds and suggested that the scholar who first referred to the work was the noted editor of Shakespeare, George Steevens, who stated: "It is highly probable that our author met with the name of Othello in some tale that has escaped our researches; as I likewise find it in *God's Revenge against Adultery*, standing in one of his Arguments as follows: She marries Othello, an old German soldier. This History, the eighth, is professed to be an Italian one. Here also occurs the name of Iago." (No reference was provided. See my "Addendum: Chasing a Ghost.")

But Othello as the name of an old German soldier! Although the connotation of "-hell-" sounds better in German than it does in English (*hell* being German for *bright*), Steevens's contribution is suspect. In examining an early edition of Reynolds's work, I found no reference either to Othello or Iago in any part of the book (certainly not the eighth history). What is more, my industry has been preëmpted by a former student of Brandl's who claimed to examine all the editions of Reynolds's work up to 1708 and found no such references. Her industriousness is cited in Eduard Engle's note "Zur Urgeschichte des Othello" (cited then in S. A. Tannenbaum's bibliography on the Moorish tragedy). Engel concludes that Steevens's allusion is simply fraudulent: "Diese Angabe von Steevens ist seitdem von allen Herausgebern und Erklären des Othello nachgeschrieben worden. Sie ist zweifellos

32

ein Schwindel, eine der nicht seltenen bewussten Irreführungen, die Steevens sich zu schulden kommen lässt" (272).

The odd thing is that such a fraud, documented as such in a Shakespeare yearbook, was overlooked by Kittredge, Krappe, and Stokes. Even more fraudulent is the notable fact that Krappe insists that Shakespeare "took" the names of Othello and Iago from *God's Revenge*, whereas Steevens's statement does not imply that at all: it simply claims that the work may be roughly contemporary with *Othello*, not that it was published previously, as Reynolds's work certainly was not.

Perhaps the best solution is a diverting one. When I confronted a Shakespearean at Cornell University with the problem of locating a work called *God's Revenge against Adultery*, which was surely not a play since it was not mentioned by W. W. Greg, he responded to my query of whether I was chasing a ghost here, with "it certainly sounds ghostly!"

CHAPTER VI

THE MOOR'S INDIAN OR JUDEAN IDENTIFICATION:
THE MAJOR TEXTUAL CRUX

Most Shakespeareans are clearly in agreement that the most famous, powerful speech of the Moor of Venice is his very last long one, wherein he laments his
gross misdeed in executing his wife after he felt that she was guilty of adultery and
so soon after their marriage. In terms of even modern, creative influence, it has led
to Richard Wright's prominent novel *Native Son*, in which Bigger Thomas smothers
a woman in bed, his very first name abbreviated normally *Tho.*, thus slightly alter-
ing the key order of the letters in the first syllable of Othello's, the *-ello* ending there
in effect giving the impression first of a diminutive (at least for contemporary American readers). (For more on this, see Chs. V and XXVII.) The overall pathetic nature
of what the tragic hero says here has led a leading twentieth-century critic, T. S.
Eliot, to dub it, in his prominent essay "Shakespeare and the Stoicism of Seneca,"[1]
a veritable "*bovarysme*" (111), in other words paralleling what Charles Bovary states
apologetically at the finale of Flaubert's *Madame Bovary*.

Yet the most familiar problem of all in this speech is often taken in separate,
textual terms: Othello's comparison of his action to that of either "the base *Indian*"
(whether Asian, or plausibly, but then taken out of context, American), which is the
First Quarto and later Folios reading, or rather what is now so commonly tran-
scribed as "the base Judean" (5.2 347).[2] The point is which textual reading represents the correct one? And could the second variant simply amount to an authorial

revision? True, the *Variorum* edition of the play devotes a number of full pages to this issue, opting at the end for "Judean," whereas presently the bulk of editors still favor "Indian." This is essentially the case with E. A. J. Honigmann, who graciously informed me at the Congress of the International Shakespeare Association, in Los Angeles in 1996, that he is again favoring "Indian" in his New Arden edition of the play, thus happening there to cite my defense in the process. Still, agreed, some readers now feel differently, especially if their own heritage happens to be non-Caucasian (including incidentally many of my students).

Owing to several fairly recent attempts to restore the "Judean" reading—which we still ought to be obliged to remember was found only after Shakespeare's demise, and based only on the *First* Folio reading—further commentary on the textual crux is still worthy of some debate. As a starter, let us revert to one ardent *Judean*-enthusiast here, Rev. Peter Milward, S. J., if only to have to dispute his thesis in the end. (See his "More on 'the base Judean.'")

In spite of his fervent, printed disagreement with my defense of the Moor's comparing himself to "the base Indian," some of his negative, speculative arguments remain seriously suspect and so deserve, in turn, pointed refutation. First of all, he neglects coming to terms with the uncomfortable fact that the original, then altered, phrase in the initial Folio, "the base Iudean," commonly glossed as alluding to a native of Judea (whether Judas or another Jew, even a high priest like Caiphas), simply will not *scan* metrically. In support of such a critical rationale, in some previous documentation of mine on this subject in *Notes and Queries* I then deliberately chose to place an accent on the first syllable of the word in print, at least titularly ("Júdean"), thence following some precedents for this pronunciation already in the eighteenth century; my purpose was to imply that, in its historical context, it simply would need to be enunciated that way to ensure proper metrical sense. Yet fairly recent textual criticism has shown that instances of this tribal designation (even though spelled a bit differently) existing before the 1623 Folio were pronounced precisely as the noun or adjective *Judean* is today. Still, the complete phrase in the initial Folio would metrically make for an awkward anapest at best, the effect seeming rather unaesthetic in context.

In corroboration, George Walton Williams specified in *Shakespeare Survey* that "we must read 'Indian,' the word that scans smoothly in the line" (194). The complete line evidently constitutes a "reversed foot" with four regular iambs; it contains ten syllables reading, with proper phonetic emphasis, this way: "Like the base *Injun*, threw a pearl *away* . . . ." This phonetic collapsing (or "crushing") of *Indian* into *Injun* (as has been commonly done so much in reference to American Indians) happens to be evident again in the very same context here, whereby the term *Medicinable* turns phonetically into *Med'cinable* (5.2.351). Elsewhere (*The Upstart Crow*) I have broached the issue of whether (1) foul case or (2) misread stroke lettering was probably the culprit responsible for the awkward, anomalous reading in the Folio, opting for the latter explanation, as have most others I should think.

Milward would broadly infer that my defense of "Indian" simply does not provide the thematic Christian support offered by "Judean." After all, the whole phrase, "the base Judean," would conjure up most probably, at least first of all for him, vile Judas Iscariot. Although the "Indian" reading does not offer any such biblical affinity, clearly the Moor's allying himself, in such a fraternal way, with a "base" (meaning here, I venture to add, *dark-complexioned* more than just *lowly*, and certainly not *wicked*) person of the historically then accepted social system in India is perfectly in keeping with what might be dubbed the overall religious context which is truly operative in this tragedy.

Conversely, in his defense of the Folio reading, Milward, by then also deigning to dub the play's villain a non-believer, even a veritable "Florentine Jew," is unhappily indulging in a highly questionable religious and ethnic insinuation. As it turns out in this drama, Cassio's remark concerning a friend's frankness ("I never knew a Florentine more kind and honest"—3.1.40) is now generally glossed as alluding in passing to *his own* affiliation, to *his* being from Florence, Iago himself being instead a Venetian, hardly some commercially minded representative of Florence. In a word, then, "a Florentine" in context simply means "*even* a Florentine," which implies being "like Cassio," for "Iago was a Venetian" (for which consult the gloss in the revised Pelican edition 1036). In thereby referring to his "tribe" (3.3.175), Iago is using this collective noun in the common, generalized sense, not thereby harking back to some particular Semitic clan, as would be the case, let us posit, with Shylock's familiar tribal allusions in *The Merchant of Venice* (1.3.47, 53, 106).

So Othello's use of "tribe" rather more naturally ties in with the earlier, Quarto, "Indian" reading than with the superimposed, later "Judean" one. Indeed, the variant spelling in the earlier version, "like the base Indean," reflects *Indian* in effect spelled in terms of the country then known as *Inde*, an example of which has been classified in *OED* (see *tribe*, sub. 3). What is more, no evidence is extant that Shakespeare would have known then that *American* Indians themselves happened to live in tribes. Comparable enough is the phrase "Indian Moors" in Marlowe's *Doctor Faustus* (2.119), for what would such Moorish people then be doing in the New Continent? So, especially because the Moor in this very context in his talk cites Arabia (5.2.350) as bordering on the Indian Ocean, let us reasonably opt for the *Asiatic* Indian connection.

A major critical point is that if Iago happens to be taken in acceptable terms here as even nominally or symbolically Semitic, what then would preclude certain other recalcitrant critics from expending their fantasy in a similar fashion and finding this ensign even, let us say, an intolerant sort of Roman Catholic instead? (Jacobeans, after all, did have their own biases.) Because his name is of obvious Spanish vintage, it might then be taken as reverting back to a certain kind of *Saint* Iago type (whereupon one might analogously revert to comparing the familiar Hispanic city name of Santiago), thus recalling that key figure who rid the Spanish peninsula of Moorish invaders during the so-called *Reconquista*, namely St. Iago (or James). In point of fact, an American specialist, Murray J. Levith, in commenting on the Italianate element in the play (and, incidentally, once again finding Iago a Venetian, hardly a Florentine), is prompted to assert that Shakespeare seems to compound the negative in the villain this way: "he combines the hostile suggestion of England's Catholic enemy with the suggestion of the seamy Italian" (35). To follow up Milward's relating the *Indian / Judean* crux to the drama in thematic, religious terms, one might now even think of this play as embodying in brief an aspect of "the tragedy of Spain." But then such a reading could perchance be thought of as being anti-Catholic in a manner just as perverse as "the base Judean" reading appearing to be anti-Semitic, in spite of Milward's incidental side-remark to me that he did not have ethnicity as such in the back of his mind. Yet, in an analogous manner, because of such a claim of Iago's as "I am not what I am" (1.1.65), this villain *could* be taken stereotypically even as an "equivocating" Jesuitic type then— that is, if one wishes to pursue any such subtle prejudicial matter. It does at least suggest that he is a "Machiavel," believing in the end justifying the means.

Granted, though Milward says he would ignore ethnic implications here, ordinary Renaissance spectators and readers of his view might all too easily have related the Folio reading to the Bible (John 1.11, 19.11),[3] with its purported condemnation (according, at least to some) of the whole recalcitrant Jewish nation. Such a generic reading can turn out to be all too perilously plausible. True enough, Milward would gain support, in deigning to find Iago Jewish, in some passing comments by E. L. Dachslager, who also would discern "some perception of the image of the Jew in the role of Iago" (14), thereby stereotypically stressing, in this connection, the Villain's noted, reiterated admonition "Put money in thy purse" (1.2.229-40), as if almost repudiating the commonplace that a certain prudential conservation of money should amount to a universal human obligation. He further points out then Iago's miscellaneous "blasphemies and heresies." What is more, he would thus loosely accommodate Iago's name even with the translation of the names *Isaac* and *Jacob* in Italian (e.g., Já-cōbi). This is farfetched. When he would credit America's Norman Mailer with finding "Iago, not Shylock, as 'the despised image' of the Jew," he should also then have boldly confronted A. L. Rowse as comparing Iago instead (somewhat portentously) with the leader of the Third Reich (III, 269)—quite a contrast. On all this, compare also Sidney Homan's argument (110). Nonetheless, Dachslager, too, would find Iago a true "Venetian," not a Florentine (15). Incidentally, worth adding is a recent note called "'Most Lovely Jew'" by L. Holford Stevens indicating that the designation "Jew" in Shakespeare's time was in point of fact "a word of endearment" (213).

So, even though Milward's well-recognized conservatism in relating biblical themes to Shakespeare can often enough be applauded, he here engages in special pleading. True enough, he does not go so far as to claim, as some (like Paul N. Siegel) have had to, that Othello is automatically destined for perdition because of such hasty vindictive action. But the point is that just such an implication is still present with the *Judas* association, especially if a general debt to the ninth circle of Dante's *Inferno* is also invoked in this context, as has often enough been done.

Such a dogmatic judgment does not appeal to most readers and audiences accustomed to more multicultural, open-minded approaches. For instance, should it be contended that the letters h-e-l-l are already part and parcel of the Moor's name, thus in effect presumably forecasting where he now has to go (as I indeed have heard seriously suggested in a conference paper), it can be likewise urged that the same four letters also happen to mean *bright* or *fair* in German, presuming here that Shakespeare might have known just enough, thereby in effect annotating in a positive manner the Duke's parting shot to Brabantio: "Your son-in-law is far more fair than black" (1.3.290). What is more, what then about the d-e-m-o-n in Desdemona's name, that is if h-e-l-l in Othello's is supposed to be made something of? Let us re-examine her name again shortly.

Does not a curious inconsistency arise in Milward's attempt to claim that the phrase "the base Judean" would *not* apply generically to the Jewish people—the familiarity of such a phrase as "Judas-Jew" then (say as used by George Herbert, as is well enough known) notwithstanding—and his immediately afterwards still contending that Iago himself must amount to no less than a Semite? Further, what then about the well-known Schlegel translation of the crux as relating to *dem niedern Juden*, meaning (in modern parlance) "the 'low-down' Jew"? Would that not lamentably argue for a disengaging "Judas-Jew" appellation here, especially when applied on stage in our own century? As the critic Schlegel then had it, Jewish people were not customarily on record for discarding their pearls with much ease. But that effect has become a stereotyped one nowadays of course.

Milward would then resuscitate the familiar "pearl of great price" biblical allusion in reference to Othello's describing Desdemona as being like a "pearl" in the context of the textual crux. But such religious analogies can be easily accommodated in so many diverse ways. In this instance, the allusion could just as well rather be to Proverbs (31. 10), wherein a good woman is described as having a price far above—not the standardized *rubies* (that is, in terms of the Geneva Bible, which Shakespeare evidently used) but, in fact, pearls. Also the Old Testament reading fits this context well enough.

In any case, such a passing reference to Proverbs does not have to be taken to mean that Desdemona need be thought of as, in general, a truly wise wife herself—let alone any Christ figure (not to forget in passing, let us say, a Mary figure, not to be chauvinist about all this); for her well-recognized indiscretion in pleading so strikingly for another man's honor, Cassio's, so soon after her marriage, would give any normal husband understandably second thoughts. Her name just happens then to relate to the Italian *desde* followed by *mona*, which literally would mean *from the monkey*, hinting at what would in our time be designated "monkey business," as historically connoted even in the Moor's sudden exclamation in a moment of crisis, "Goats and monkeys!" (4.1.263). In this context let us also recall that Spenser's *Faerie Queene*, Book I, with its well-known pageant of the Seven

Deadly Sins, has lechery characteristically symbolized as riding a goat (1.2.24.2), a faithful historical analogy.

One obvious rationale of Desdemona's hardly representing a bona-fide Christ figure is that, in her indiscretions, so soon after marriage, she fails to follow Christ's terse precept "Be wise as serpents" (Matt. 10. 16), but, at least psychologically, looks upon the Moor more as a sort of father type than as a true husband. Then, in insisting that the rich pearl which Othello has thrown away is "hardly that of an ignorant Indian diver," Milward ignores all the historically strong evidence rejecting "base" as meaning *ignorant* here, proof extant in that essay of my own in *Notes and Queries* on the subject, cited previously. For Othello is much more apt to be alluding to a poor Asiatic fisherman than to any ethnically more diverse Judean. Comparable enough in this context is the analogous phrase "orient pearl" in *Antony and Cleopatra* (1.5.41). True, American Pelican and Everyman editions still opt for "Judean," and William Marshall in his *Othello* film has him using this epithet too; even James Earl Jones, in his well-known production, conveniently varied the phrase to read "the base Jud*as*." (But if that is what Shakespeare meant, why did he not use it himself?) Harold Bloom, moreover, defends "Judean" in his *Shakespeare: The Invention of the Human*; he thinks that Othello compares himself to Herod the Great in his relation to Mariamne. Yet Herod was not a native Judean, it so happens, but an Idumean. More memorably, the leading actor Paul Robeson is on record for using the old "Indian" reference (as I have heard on the recording), as did Fishburne in his own, fairly recent, cinematic version.

It might finally be urged that, as a leading, prolific, initially British, Shakespearean Jesuit based in Japan, Milward might truly be expected to have taken into account as well major documented *Asiatic* research on the crux; yet no evidence of his recounting such fellow scholarship emerges in what he says. Thus, in responding in print to my thesis in *Notes and Queries*, he did not care to observe previous studies of mine which do cite such Asian commentaries, including ones relatively recently even printed in China. Because not too long ago an International Shakespeare Association Congress was held in Tokyo, it might appear almost mandatory for a textual critic there to come to terms with key Asian research as well. As for the translations of the Bible (other than the Genevan text) to which he refers, it is rather debatable how much Shakespeare would have been acquainted with any of these.

So let us stand up for the poor, dark Indian of the old social system of India, not the far-fetched evil Judean, admitting in the process that some imposed religious renderings can become all too precious. No evidence of *Judean*, even of Jud-*a*-ean (its happening to be spelled that way then), was actually on printed record when *Othello* was composed—a point for which Honigmann gives me kind credit in his new Arden edition. So why should the playwright have interpolated such a neologism like *Judean* when he already had a perfectly germane *Indian* operating for him?

Granted, one purported source for part of the play, Knolles's *The General Historie of the Turkes*, does happen to contain the phrase "Judas like" (as I document it in my book dealing in part with *textual* cruxes in Shakespeare),[4] yet the *immediate source* of the crux, as I have indicated more recently, is most likely to be found in the writings of Shakespeare himself, namely the previous vibrant passage about the "man of Inde" in *Love's Labour's Lost*.[5] Comparable enough is the expression in *All's Well that Ends Well*: "Indian-like, / Religious in mine error, I adore / The sun" (1.3.183-85), which seems to allude to bowing to the East (to the setting sun, hence to Buddhism). And if Shakespeare had had Judas specifically in mind, why would he not at least logically rather have specified "like *a* base Judean"? As for whether the veritable "base Judean" in the tragedy is plausibly Iago, let us say, our final verdict may just as well be that certainly Jewish people over the years (incidentally including Harold Bloom once again) have had a hard enough time accepting Shylock. Also worth comparing is Othello's other use of *base*: "Yet 'tis the plague of great ones; / Prerogatived are they less than the base" (3.3.273-74). Here "base" would mean *lowly* (or *humble*), a term never to be confused in context with the modernized expression *low-down*.

What can be discerned symbiotically about the two readings? Can any conclusions of note now be drawn? The important thing is to avoid subjectivity at all costs and to strive for objective, historical understanding. Thus the claim that a man from India could not be meant because he would have known the true value of a pearl (discussed by Othello, as in his talk) overlooks the simple fact that a *poor* Indian fisherman would have been meant here, and that is all. The word *base* simply need not have any truly negative implications in this context; Shakespeare referred elsewhere to "base clouds" (see his sonnets 33 and 34), a perfectly natural description for ones dark and low in the sky. So let us accept that position which is still definitely more standard nowadays anyway, that "Indian" and not "Judean" works best after all. [6]

NOTES

[1]See his *Selected Essays* 107-20.

[2]The Shakespearean text used here is not the Pelican, but the Riverside, edition with its "Indian" reading. Otherwise I cite the Pelican ed., as I do elsewhere in the book, or at times the First Folio of the 1623 text.

[3]"Jesus answered, 'Thou wouldst have no power at all over me were it not given thee from above'"; "He came unto his own, and his own received him not." (The King James version is used.)

[4]See my *Shakespeare and the Matter of the Crux* 7-8.

[5]See my "Love's Lost in *Othello*: What 'the base Indian' is Founded On." This might appear to pay short shrift to Nashe's *Pierce Penilesse*, which contains a well-known analogy about artists being "base minded and like the Indians, that have store of gold & precious stones at command, yet are ignorant of their value" (a passage often cited). See the Wilson and McKerrow ed. of Nashe's *Works*. Still, Shakespeare himself never used *base* in the sense of *ignorant*. The term is applied to Indians elsewhere in a different context, and in point of indisputable fact the key parallel in *Love's Labour's Lost* also relates "base" to "man of Inde" (4.3.217, 220). Admittedly the allusion in Nashe is to an Indian from America, but contextually any connection in *Othello* with, say, the Caribbean would appear to be a bit forced, especially because of the close contextual reference there to Arabia. Cf. also Park Honan 282.

[6]This essay, in early draft form, was delivered at the Ohio Shakespeare Conference at Ohio State University in Columbus in 1997, the theme of which was "Textual Practice and Theatrical Labor: Shakespeare and His Contemporaries." A revised version was then presented in Bristol, England, for the second "Symbiosis" conference in July 1999. The particular forum was entitled "Anglo-American Textual Relations," so I dealt with American and British views on the crux, Peter Milward being originally British but stationed then in Japan.

Worth considering finally is Naseeb Shaheen's position on the textual crux, first appearing in a short article and then in his *Biblical References in Shakespeare's Plays*. Being of Indian background, he is understandably opposed to the "base *Indian*" reading in Q as somehow biased; yet the problem that arises is whether he can follow completely through with the Folio reading of "base Judean" in its place. For example, he observes that "'Indian' was the more familiar word in Shakespeare's day," that "'Iudean' (Judean) was far less common" (600). But he argues from this that "the Q1 typesetter, unacquainted with Fenton [author of the English translator of Bandello's version of the story], and confronted with the unfamiliar and puzzling word 'Iudean,' may well have mistaken it for the familiar word 'Indian'" (601).

This is an unsubstantiated hypothesis. First of all, the records indicate that *Judean*, however spelt, was not in evidence when Shakespeare was alive; the closest approximation was *Iudaean*, in print only after his death. Moreover, the Q printer put the word "Indian" here in italic; that may also suggest more than a chance misreading.

Second, even if Shakespeare intended a possible allusion to Judas in this context, it could have still come about with the "Indian" reading. The point is that the Moor, in killing his wife, whom he presumably had wed in a Christian ceremony (the drama taking place in Catholic Italy), was acting vituperously, in a thoughtless, vindictive manner, suggesting a Judas figure killing Christ (both Judas and Othello having kissed their victim at one point before killing him). This would be true regardless of the killer's ethnic background.

Third, because of the connotations of "the base Judean" suggesting Jewish ethnic heritage, not just one for a "Judas" figure, it would be best to steer clear of the "base Judean" reading—as has been done by most editors and scholars (as well as actors like Paul Robeson).

So why press the point that the original reading must also have been "base Iudean"? First, the adjective *base* did not have to apply *negatively* to racial or ethnic background, even as Shakespeare alluded to "base clouds" in his sonnets, meaning ones naturally dark in the sky. The context suggests an India Indian because of the allusion to Arabia (and thus to the Indian Ocean, in which poor fishermen doubtless found plenty of pearls, as the well-known rumor about the cheap price of pearls in India indicated).

Shaheen notes that "Fenton twice compares the murder to Judas's betrayal of Christ" (601), but in his final moments Othello was also reverting to his original, pre-Christian background, thereby could allude easily to himself as being like a poor, dark-complexioned Indian, yet this need not detract from the overall Christian meaning in the play's larger context.

# CHAPTER VII

# LEAR'S LEARNED NAME

Even as the key word in the first scene of the last of Shakespeare's great tragedies, *King Lear*, namely "love," may derive from the Old English "lofian," meaning "to praise" (see Hawkes 178-81), so the King's name may also have some basis in the language of the Anglo-Saxons. Although *Lear* is usually thought of as a Celtic term (see Schücking 176-90), with a likely analog in the legend of the Irish *Lir* (consult Barton in his *Links Between Ireland and Shakespeare*), there may well be resonances of OE lære ("empty"), which then evolved in ME *lere* (which had the variant form of *lear*, for which see *OED*). The same word in Renaissance times was spelled *lear(e)*, as in Turberville's translation of the Epistles of Ovid: "Some lustfull lasse will not permit Achylles coutch be leare" (in 1567). The origin is approximately the same as the Modern German *leer*.

If Camden was one of the sources of the play, which appears likely, it is noteworthy that several other names which are in the tragedy, and which he also mentions, are of Saxon origin. For further comment on Old English origins of names in this work as derived from Camden's *Remaines* (e.g., Edgar, Edmund, Oswald), see S. Musgrove's article "The Nomenclature of *King Lear*."

Consequently, a resonance of OE "empty" in the name of Lear is a distinct possibility too. The affinity has some bearing on the Buddhist origin of the story of *Barlaam and Josaphat* (Loomis 35-36, citing Geoffrey of Monmouth on this)—an important analog to the Lear story—for it suggests that the "empty" condition of the

King is a state awaiting spiritual fulfillment. The linkage points, moreover, to a "nirvana theme" in the Shakespearean version of the story, implications of which are subtly present already in the name of the protagonist. On this see R. B. Kulshreshtha's "Shakespeare's Feeling for Words."

Is it only an interesting coincidence that the personal name *Lear* and the Early Modern English adjective *lear(e)* ("empty") (<ME lere <OE laere) are homonyms? It is relevant that T. S. Eliot apparently had some understanding of these resonances in his poetry, if only perhaps on the half-conscious level. The concept of hollowness awaiting fulfillment has been noticed in "The Hollow Men" and also in *The Waste Land*, where there are decided echoes of the first scene in *King Lear* (e.g., see D. E. S. Maxwell 107). I should like to add that Eliot's own awareness of the affinity between the name *Lear* and the German adjective *leer* arises in that famous quotation in his major poem *"Oed' und leer das Meer"* (l. 42).

That characters' names in the plays may relate to their function ultimately derives from the Morality Play tradition. Though this correlation certainly need not be thought of as central for most of Shakespeare's figures, a number of etymological connections that have been discovered are worth serious attention. For example, it is clearly more than coincidental that Romeo's name is contrasted with that of his rival for the hand of Juliet, namely Paris (the two capital cities, Rome and Paris, aesthetically balancing each other off). Further, it is remarkable enough that the name of Iago relates to Sant'Iago Matamoros (meaning "Moor-slayer St. Iago"), though given England's enmity with Spain it is understandable. On the other hand, it is difficult to believe that the combination of h-e-l-l in the tragic hero's name would adumbrate his being damned at the end of *Othello*, for, if so, what about the d-e-m-o-n in innocent Desdemona? Her name is scarcely demonic, in spite of the Moor's nicknaming her once *Desdemon* (1. 1651), inasmuch as it derives from the words *desde* and *mona* ("from" the "monkey"), suggesting that her behavior is considered by several characters to be a bit ape-like (or that she behaves as has been thought monkeys operate) (for which see Ch. VI).

Could Shakespeare have been aware of the resonances of OE and ME "empty" in the name of perhaps his most tragic hero? If they work in the play, it is not required to assume that it was directly on his mind, for plausibly the author of the old English source-play of *King Leir* could have been better aware of such etymology, and Shakespeare could then have taken over earlier research inadvertently. For already in Geoffrey of Monmouth's version of the Lear legend, the name *Cordelia* was spelled *Cordeilla*, suggesting *cor de illa* ("with, or from, the heart"). Thus J. S. P. Tatlock writes, "As to Leir's daughters, whatever any earlier form of Cordeilla's name, the good Latinist author must have meant Cor-de-illa to fit her loyal love" (382). Hence it is helpful to think of Cordelia's heartfelt nature as balanced off against Lear's more or less sterile emptiness, with his "darker purpose" ironically already hinted at in a name reflecting his need to be filled with grace. On this issue, Dove and Gamble's article "'Our Darker Purpose': The Division Scene in *Lear*" makes the interesting point that the King's "darker purpose" is his decision to give Cordelia the richest third of the kingdom as a bait for her to remain with him. But it does not work out.

One further etymological hint that *may* work out thematically is that Lear's name reflects the appearance / reality effects in the tragedy inasmuch as it is a true anagram for *real*. The shifting of the lettering in this sense indicates that he is confused as to this interrelationship, as in the opening scene with Cordelia and the ensuing "nothing" interplay.

# CHAPTER VIII

## THE CODIFICATION OF CORDELIA'S NAME

To what extent is literary onomastics concerned with name-play which goes beyond etymology as such? This has always been a question, one not readily answerable. Clearly any responsible scholar or author would take into account etymological suggestions, not deny their historical validity if evident, but might he or she not then add to them as well? In the case of *King Lear*, this problem becomes especially acute, as I have pointed out in the preceding chapter. Although the historical origin of Lear's name may be taken as Celtic, as numerous scholars have also believed, depending thereby on the name *Lyr*, the name as Shakespeare used it could connote those other things, such as *lear(e)*, used by Shakespeare's friend and fellow playwright Ben Jonson, at least, in the sense of "empty." The point is that such an origin may well reflect on the King's needing finally to be filled with grace. Various readers responded to my original article on the subject in *Names* (see Ch. VII), some of them being convinced (in particular the religiously minded), others finding the effect more transient. A similar issue arises now with regard to the name of the King's youngest daughter.

Exactly what does Cordelia's name imply? Etymologically, there can be no doubt that its earlier spelling (Cordeilla) would cancel any suggestion of original codification, as has been offered, for example, by Joseph Satin, who found "*Cor*, which is Italian and Latin for 'heart'" correlated with *Delia* as a "witty anagram for 'ideal'" (15-17). Thus, in the opening scene of the tragedy, she indeed speaks from her heart in an ideal way in responding to her king and father. Or so it is inferred. Such name-play is based on "Drayton's semi-parody of Daniel's sequence" of sonnets dealing with Lady Delia, since Daniel calls his love *ideal*. The anagram of *Delia* being *ideal* was, it seems fair to say, a virtual Renaissance commonplace. Yet the name in the earlier play of *King Leir* is *Cordella*, and there no anagram is involved. Still, Geoffrey of Monmouth's *Cordeilla* version (see Ch. VII) has suggested *cor de illa*, meaning "with, or from, the heart" (for which, see Tatlock 382).

Although many scholars have gone along with the anagrammatic *Cor-delia / ideal* heart conjunction for some time, something new can now be added. For example, the late F. N. Lees, a good name-hunter in terms of Shakespeare's nomenclature, at least with regard to Othello's name (even though I happen to disagree with his finding there, as indicated in the last chapter), has written in response to my note in *Names* on the Learean name, of an Elizabethan play entitled *Richard Cordelion* (*Coeur de Lion*), which he felt might relate to Cordelia's cognomen. He felt that it connected with "'Cordella' and 'Cordell,' the name of the 'good' daughter of Sir Brian Annesley, who opposed her 'wicked' sisters in 1603, and later married Southampton's godfather" (private correspondence). That would provide more etymological suggestiveness or evidence of historical indebtedness. Yet a more onomastic meaning as such arises if we consider the syllabic split in her name as *Cordelia*, rather than *Cor-delia*. The result is that we arrive at a new codification, one in counterpoint with the earlier one.

The hint for this new distinction arises already with the time-honored problem of whether Shakespeare's own name breaks down into *Shake-speare* or *Shakespeare* or both. The first division appears more natural at least in terms of his coat of arms with its crossed spears and then the refraction of such name-play in Falstaff's name (*fall staff*, since he does not fight), a commonplace noted by Harry Levin (87) among others, but the breakdown into the second possibility may be more natural in terms of everyday speech. This raises the question of whether onomastics is based mainly on *parole* (speech patterning as outlined by de Saussure) or supersedes it. A case could be made for *Shakes-peare* as relating just as well to the connotation of a *peer* who *shakes*, in other words an earth-shaking genius of the first rank.

As for *Cord-elia*, the hint for the first syllable as connotatively meaningful has been provided in a useful article by Robert F. Willson, who writes of her as a "figure whose name underscores the image of cords that hold together bodies, families, and societies, as well as suggesting the musical chord whose power can restore order out of chaos, or discord" (82). All of this is missing, adds Willson, in Nahum Tate's 1681 version of the play (which does not end tragically) because "paradoxically, the bond of reuniting with Lear must be broken before the storm within and without men can subside" (86). With all this in mind, what then about the *-elia* ending? Although Wilson does not comment on this, even as *-delia* may be considered an anagram for *ideal* so *-elia* can be taken as another for *a lie*. In other words, Cordelia breaks her *cord* or bond with her father and king when she responds negatively to him in the first scene; in answer to the question of what love she holds for him, she responds, "Nothing," which, in effect, amounts to a prevarication.

The value of this additional anagrammatic reading is that it would help to enrichen Cordelia's character by working in counterpoint with the reading first offered. The point would be that whereas the daughter most loved *means well* in her utterance, she still starts off the tragedy because of her lack of effective communication. In a word, she *cruelly* severs her bond, or *cord*, with the King in answering the way she does, one that is not fully restored till the end, so that eventually out of her "Nothing" ironically comes everything—a commonplace actually in criticism of the play (though not a thematic one).

Whether this response is owing to some stubbornness on her part (as Heinrich Heine among others has felt, i.e.. "Cordela inclines to be self-willed, and this small spot is a birth-mark from the father" [qtd. in trans. in Ralli 1: 247]), to her lack of maturity, or to her undue forthrightness in dealing with a man at least on the edge of senility, is a moot point. (Compare essays by Wilbern and Tayler as well as my tentative offering, "The 'Nothing' Element in *King Lear*.") It can even be argued that she breaks the biblical commandment about honoring one's father. (Lest too much be made of this, it is wise always to qualify such a connection by adding how her older sisters act much worse.)

Further, does she act somehow like a kind of *fool* in her response, so that Lear's reference to his "poore Foole" (5.3.306) being hanged at the end could allude to her? Or rather to doubling in the theater whereby the same actor played her and the court jester? A case could be made for Lear, in his wandering mind, conflating these two characters, but, in any event, it is unnecessary to assume, as has sometimes been done, that they do not appear together on the stage; for the jester may well be part of the King's entourage in the initial scene, can be thought of as a witness to Cordelia's strange behavior, and thus is in a position to refer back to it in his own "echoing" of her "Nothing" later in the play with the King, again a minor commonplace in studies of the tragedy's imagery. To my mind, the bulk of the evidence, including the orthographic (the capitalization of the final "Foole" allusion), suggests that Lear had only his jester in mind during the last scene (the two characters being so totally different in terms of their voice and characterization). Hence Cordelia's initial action may best be thought of as not foolishness, but rather an effect of deliberate tragic happenstance.

One other effect of saying that her name embraces both an "ideal heart" and a "cord" that has become, at least for the time, "a lie" is that it might detract from her being considered a true Christ figure. Granted, this may be an obstacle, mythically speaking, but associations have been made with her and other prominent symbols, for example even Israel. (Thus her difficulty in communicating with her father relates to Israel's leaving and coming back to God in the Old Testament, a major allegiance with which Shakespeare was concerned as is indicated, for example, in his extensive use of the Book of Jeremiah in *Hamlet*, for which see Rossky.)

Even if the Christian story is introduced in this pre-Christian setting (Shakespeare himself presumably being a believing Christian and also capable of some anachronism), Cordelia need hardly be thought of as directly related to Christ. Let us consider an example. Several years ago, during a discussion following an MLA paper which argued that Cordelia was a Christ figure, I heard a feminist respondent assure the others that the King's daughter was instead a *Mary* figure. That would still hardly make her capable of lying, at least if the orthodox stress upon the Immaculate Conception be borne in mind, but it gives more "ambiguity" to her makeup anyway. My own inclination is to believe that Shakespeare would not have intended consciously to have the connotation of *a lie* present in her very name, the anagram being clearly not an obvious one and quite at variance with established etymology, but he certainly left ample room for such an effect to be present regardless. Not all Shakespearean feminists would be pleased with this effect, but then the same kind of ambivalent reaction has been found with regard to the final effect of *The Taming of the Shrew*, which has been both denounced as an example of "bad" Shakespeare (for which see Charney) and extolled as ending with a true sense of mutuality. The same kind of ambivalence resulting in a restored ending is present in *King Lear*. Hence a certain decoding appears in order.

True, sometimes decodification and reference to anagrammatic formations conjures up the anti-Stratfordians and their eccentricities. Yet I have found plenty of evidence even of partial anagrams in Thomas Coryate's *Odcombian Banquet*, which was set up by the same head of a printing press who supervised Shakespeare's *Sonnets*, Thomas Thorpe.

It would appear, therefore, that even the highly controversial dedication to the *Sonnets*, starting off "To Mr. W. H. All. . . ," invites name-play on W(illiam) Hall. (This appeared in my first Shakespeare book, one devoted solely to him, and was corroborated fairly recently for me at a meeting of The Shakespeare Association of America in Cleveland.)

After this essay was originally published, Thomas McAlindon came up with some new viewpoints, which deserve at least passing mention:

> There is an etymological pun on the word "cordial" [in Cordelia's name], since it derives from the Latin *cor* (declined *cordis*, *cordem*), which means both "heart" and "feeling." The pun is very relevant to both *King Leir* and *King Lear*. . . . For the hero of the old play talks about his "throbbing" and "panting" heart; and in addition there is a heavily overt pun on "cordial" linked with a similar play on the name of Cordella: "Ah deare Cordella, cordiall to my heart" (line 709); "And thou, poor soul [i.e., the weeping Cordella], kind-hearted as thou art" (line 2236)(177).

# CHAPTER IX

## CALIBAN'S NAME AND THE "BRAVE NEW WORLD"

It is a commonplace that Shakespeare invented the name of *Caliban*, most probably influenced by Florio's translation of Montaigne's essay "Of the Cannibals." The name is not found elsewhere, to anyone's knowledge, and no definite overall source of the plot of *The Tempest* has emerged. F. E. Halliday writes that the dramatist's debt to Michel de Montaigne "is most patent in *The Tempest*, where Gonzalo explains how he would colonize the island (2.1), the passage being taken from Montaigne's essay . . . , describing an ideal community in America" (321). Still, the romance is also credibly thought by many scholars to have its setting in the Mediterranean (there just having been a wedding in Tunis), so that the native involved would appear to reflect or refract an Old World or, even better, Third World, not a New World, cannibal. On the other hand, the "still-vex'd Bermoothes" (1.2.229) clearly refers to Bermuda, and "brave new world" (5.1.183) alludes, in customary terms, to the New World.

An analogous, textual problem of great concern to Shakespeareans is whether the familiar "base *Indian*" crux in *Othello* (5.2.347) conjures up an Indian of the Caribbean (where pearls, also cited in the immediate context, could be found) or an *India* Indian, in spite of the fact that the British East India Company was in operation a number of years before the tragedy was written and so presumably only poor fishermen in the Indian Ocean area would have been incognizant of the value of their riches (see Ch. VI). Clearly major parallels in the travel literature of the time support the American connection, albeit in this case the immediate context (and parallels in Shakespeare's other works, notably *Love's Labour's Lost* 4.3.216-20), point to the Near East.

The matter of Caliban's name comes up in Alden and Virginia Vaughan's recent book and in several positive reviews thereof that I have seen, notably John Reichert's. As might be expected, the Vaughans disagreed, or were skeptical of the connection between Caliban's name and his final intent to "seek for grace" (see 297). They have questioned whether *Caliban* was chosen as an anagram of *can(n)ibal*: "Would Shakespeare have chosen an anagram of 'cannibal' for a savage who did not practice what his name preached?" (30). What is more, a definite "stumbling block to the acceptance of the 'cannibal' explanation is its late emergence in print. It can be dated quite precisely to the 1778 edition of Samuel Johnson and George Steevens's annotated *Tempest*" (30). Consequently, the Vaughans prefer the "geographic link—'Caliban' as a variant of the name for a New World region connoting mystery and incivility" (32), though they concede that this correlation is also unproven. In any event, Reichert's review then has the following comment: "Or was Shakespeare perhaps familiar with the hindu word *Kalee-ban* (a Hindu Satyr)? Of the Gypsy word *cauliban*, or 'blackness' (Prospero calls Caliban a 'thing of darkness')? Or was it *kalebon*, an Arabic word for 'vile dog'?" (Reichert 32). But these are merely flighty speculations, in my judgment.

One piece of proof that has not been given due credence hitherto is that the "garbling" of *can(n)ibal* in the form of *Caliban* could easily have derived, in part or indirectly, from Shakespeare's cognizance of the logs of Columbus, or Las Casas' transcriptions thereof, phrases from which were generally popular at that time. According to J. H. Trumbull of Hartford, as cited in *OED* (s.v. "Cannibal"), "*1, n,* and *r* interchange dialectally in American languages, whence the variant forms *Canibs, Caribs, Calibi*," whereby "Columbus' first representation of the name as he heard it from the Cubans was *Canibales*." *OED* then adds that "*Calib-an* is apparently another variant =*carib-an*." In a word, Columbus' locution of *cannibals* in some form derived from his misreported transcription of the name of the offending tribe as *Caribs* or *Canibs*, though the problem may actually have originated from the Taino tribe, as Columbus heard it, or from Las Casas' own transcription of Columbus' daily journal of his first voyage. In a paper initially entitled "Columbus Was a Cannibal: Myths and the First Encounters," William F. Keegan, Associate Curator of

Anthropology, Florida Museum of Natural History, University of Florida, provides the following arresting account: "*Carib* is a Taino word. Columbus arrived . . . looking for *Caniba*, literally 'the people of the *gra Can*' [Grand Khan]. Columbus came to believe that the *Caniba* were enemies of the Taino. Columbus did not believe that the *Caniba* ate human flesh. The Taino belief in *Caniba* anthropophagy came from the failure of Taino captives to return after they were taken by the *Canibs*." (My citation is from the paper originally delivered for the conference *The Lesser Antilles in the Age of European Expansion* at Hamilton College, 11-12 November 1992.)[1]

That Shakespeare could have been aware specifically of this distorted effect (insofar as what Columbus reported could have become widely known then) can be seen from *OED*'s further comment that the Carib people of the West Indies "are recorded to have been *anthropophagi*," a term that also happens to appear in *Othello* (1.3.144) and, in a variant form, in *The Merry Wives of Windsor* (4.5.8). This corroboration would tie in with the notion that the kind of cannibal alluded to in the name *Caliban* was meant figuratively only, the argument being that if Shakespeare had meant a man-eater specifically, he would have used the longer term. In fact, *OED* provides a figurative usage of *cannibal* (whereas many modern lexicons do not and so may be misleading in this respect if consulted): "Cannibal," 1b, refers merely to a savage or primitive person, not one necessarily involved in anthropophagy. Arrestingly enough, a citation given for this usage is again from Shakespeare: "cannibals, / How sweet a plant have you untimely cropped" (*3 Henry VI*, 5.5.61-62). The point is that the Vaughans may well be correct in contending that Shakespeare had no bloodthirsty cannibal in mind when he thought up Caliban's name; but that did not preclude his associating such a name with the figurative meaning of the derivation just the same.

Further support for the position that the dramatist could have been aware specifically of the linguistic confusion suggested here might be in his allusion to Frederick, Count of Mömpelgart, again in *The Merry Wives*, as "garmombles" (cited only in the Q version). After all, one garbled account would parallel similar verbal playfulness elsewhere. Although this particular variant form was obviously derivative of the alias the Württemberg dignitary traveled under (*Count Mombeliard*), it still represents a graphic linguistic mix-up of the original surname. As with the analogous metathetic name-change from *Fastolfe* to *Falstaff* in the Henry plays, the shift from *can(n)ibal* to *Caliban* could well have been deliberate, but not wholly or arbitrarily as if it was ultimately a product of what had been taken as Columbus' own quirkiness. In positing this approach, we need not disagree with the Vaughans, who have made room already for it with the following qualification: "A close alternative explanation is that 'Caliban,' as an extended anagram of 'Carib,' suggests that Shakespeare meant the monster to be a New World native but not necessarily a man-eater" (27).

Curiously, as William F. Keegan points out in his fine paper for the collection of articles on Columbus cited earlier, the purported cannibalism recorded in Columbus' log may really in part derive from the so-called "mythic cannibalism" described by members of the Taino tribe; in a similar enough manner, Caliban's supposed cannibalistic origin or tendencies, at least etymologically speaking, are defensible as "mythic" in another, more modern, sense. Thus one feminist reading has it that he is basically a creature which "refigures . . . incestuous, self-consumptive desires" (Boose 37). Likewise, because he would "seek for grace" at the end (*The Tempest* 5.1.296), it is arguable that his eventual acceptance of orthodox Christianity (as evident from the Catholic Italians participating) bespeaks that of a sublimated form of cannibalism, at least in part, involved in the partaking of the Holy Eucharist.

At a meeting of the Ohio Shakespeare Conference at Cleveland State University,[2] I broached this latter subject to a Jesuit who had been recently then involved in a production of *The Tempest*, and he concurred that it was viable enough (at least on the psychological, if not perhaps so much so on the purely theological, level). Because the issue was raised then in public forum, I feel I can report it here with impunity. It is of further incidental interest that, as Keegan told me, the cannibalism sometimes associated with the Tainos was sexual in nature.

The same form of conversion-to-be can be found in Act Four of *The Merchant of Venice*, during which Shylock's penalty is to accept Christianity and thereby, ironically, to receive the "pound of flesh" he has been after in the form of the Body and Blood of Christ. But the most curious or ironic matter of all to end on is that, as Keegan points out, it was Columbus himself and his men who were initially identified as *Caribes / Canibales* because they carried off Tainos from their villages. Doubtless Shakespeare was unaware of this facet.

Now, it has been argued that to stress "seek for grace" in Caliban's case is simply too subtle, but I find this viewpoint anti-intellectual. Granted, Caliban's expression of someday seeking for grace sounds a bit tenuous, but it is present nonetheless.

NOTES

[1]At the time it was announced as due to appear in a collection of essays from this historical gathering to be published by the University Press of Florida (1994). I quote with permission of both the Associate Curator and the Director of the Conference (and co-editor of the volume), Robert Paquette.

[2]Cleveland, Ohio, 25-27 March 1993. Worth comparing is Zacharias P. Thundy's article "The 'Divine' Caliban in Shakespeare's Postcolonial Discourse: A Re(De)Construction."

## CHAPTER X

## ON FETCHING CALIBAN'S "YOUNG SCAMELS"

Caliban's promise to fetch "young Scamels from the Rocke" (*The Tempest*, 2.2.168) has not been fully explored. The standard gloss is that he had a form of sea gulls in mind; thus the von Schlegel (Tieck) translation reads "Vom Felsen junge Möwen."[1] The *Variorum* indicates that the following interpretations have been forthcoming over the years: shamois, stannels, scams, samols or seamars, samphires, squirrels, scalions, sarcels, and sea-owls; as well as sea-malls, or sea-mels, or sea-mews (all terms of the sea gulls).[2] The editor of the *New Variorum* himself opts for scams, which are a type of shell-fish better known as limpets (with "scamels" a proposed diminutive). One learned view is that the term derives from old Norse *skama* (meaning *shell*, hence skamels or scamels being little shells).

It has been reported a number of times that the term *scamel* has actually been used for the female Bar-tailed Godwit; the only trouble is that this bird is not a rock-breeder. A respectable notion is that Shakespeare got the term from one of his sources and that the closest approximation to such a word in his source material would serve as the best explanation; consequently, most editors have pounced on the sea-mews mentioned in William Strachey's *A True Reportory* (c. 1610) as most helpful. These creatures are described in the following terms:

> Our men found a prettie way to take them, which was by standing on
> the Rockes or Sands by the Sea side, and hollowing, laughing, and
> making the strangest out-cry that possibly they could: with the noyse

whereof the Birds would come flocking to that place. . . .[3]

There are, however, certain problems with this identification. First of all, the bird was called a "Sea-Meawe" by Strachey, and that word is a far cry from "Scamel" even given the possibility that the "c" was a misprint for "e." The other term for sea gull, *seamel*, is considerably closer to Caliban's word, but it is not used by Strachey. Second, the further description of the gulls in *A True Reportory*—

our men would weigh them with their hand, and which weighed heavi-

est they tooke for the best and let the others alone—

does not tally with Caliban's promise to procure "young" scamels only. The present essay is to submit that the term *scamel* was Calibanese for *mussel* (often spelled "muscle" or "muskle" then). It is entirely appropriate to think of his obtaining these bivalve mollusks from the rocks around his island. That his formulation of the name for mussels is strange is paradoxically not so strange at all in terms of Caliban's own state of mind at the time, of Shakespeare's propensity for playing with words (as with the name *Caliban* itself), and the many different changes which the word *mussel* had undergone over the course of the years. Deriving from OE *muscle* and Late Latin *muscula*, the term underwent the following spellings (in singular and plural forms) as registered by *OED*: 1374 *musculis* (Chaucer), 1387 *muskle* (Usk), 1393 *muscles* (Langland), 1420 *mustuls* (from the *Liber Cocorum*), 1485 *muskollz*, 1529 *muscull*, 1555 *musculs*, 1603 *muskles*. The spelling *mussels* was very unusual before the nineteenth century, though interestingly enough the one usage of that form cited before then was by Shakespeare in *The Tempest*: "thy food shall be / The fresh-brooke Mussels . . ." (1.2.463).[4] It is employed by Prospero, who could easily have taught the word to Caliban, who then got it mixed up in his inebriated state.

That he is intoxicated when he utters the word is clear from the stage direction for his very next line: "sings drunkenly," He then sings a song in which he utters a strange variant of his own name: "*Cacalyban*" (2.2.179). This is nowadays transformed into *Ca-Caliban*. Since his very name was already a kind of anagram, Caliban's own drunken wordplay when added to his anagrammatic name results in an odd distortion indeed. It is also, ironically, a mildly humorous one in that Caliban utters the word in a sing-song manner, preceding it with "'*Ban*, '*Ban*"—which hints at the monster realizing that he needs to be banned, thus anticipating his promise at the end to "seek for grace" (5.1.296). In any case, if *Cacalyban* represents an anagram that has been further distorted, there is no reason why *Scamels* could not stand for much the same: an anagram for "muscles" (mussels) with the "a" taking the place of the "u." These two vowels would come together anyway in terms of the schwa sound.

The reader may wonder why no one has so far proposed such an anagrammatic reading, yet the *Variorum* does refer to Bulloch, who in his *Studies in the Text of Shakespeare* (1878) argued that "'Scamels' is more likely to have been a coinage put into the mouth of Caliban than anything else" (140). Bulloch's own idea that the word stands for *scambles* is overdoing it. Moreover, Frank Kermode in the Arden edition of the play notes that *"Cacalyban"* (modernized then to *"Cacaliban"*) possibly "indicates intoxication" (69n184). So such hints have been available right along.

The aesthetic effect of Caliban's getting "young Scamels" or mussels for Trinculo and Stephano also should not be bypassed. His awareness of the beauty of the island is already one of his saving graces, and the delicacy of young mussels provides a particularly captivating marine reference for the reader. Shakespeare's love of the sea is well known, but the description provided by Rachel Carson in one of her popular volumes, *The Edge of the Sea*, gives us a pleasant insight into what fascinated Caliban and the Elizabethan audience:

> I can imagine the young mussels creeping in over the damp rock
> while the tide is out, spinning their silk threads that bind them se-
> curely, anchoring them against the returning waters. And then in time,
> perhaps, the growing colony of mussels gave the infant barnacles a
> foothold more tenable than the smooth rock.(106)

Although Carson is anachronistically a twentieth-century commentator rather than a Renaissance writer, her sensitivity to Shakespearean nuances may be seen from the headnote from *The Tempest* that she has used for a chapter in *The Sea Around Us*: "A sea-change / Into something rich and strange" (1.2.401-2)—slightly altered in the chapter-heading. For "muscles" underwent a verbal as well as figural sea change in being transformed into the Calibanesque delicacy called "scamels."

Another relatively modern writer is also worth citing in this connection: Jules Verne. In his *The Mysterious Island*, when the castaways examine their food resources, they come upon two forms of it at the same time: curiously enough, sea-mews and mollusks, which are first taken to be mussels (23). Such a description serves as an admirable naturalistic gloss upon the relative merits of these two foods. The mussels are seen as vastly superior to the sea-mews: the narrator tells us that "gulls and seamews are scarcely eatable, and even their eggs have a detestable taste" (23). This would be a good reason for Caliban's not getting young sea-mews. Immediately afterwards the castaways come upon the mollusks:

> Herbert who had gone forward a little more to the left, soon came upon rocks covered with sea-weed, which, some hours later, would be hidden by the high tide. On these rocks, in the midst of slippery wrack, abounded bivalve shell-fish, not to be despised by starving people. Herbert called Pencroft, who ran up hastily.
>
> "Why! here are mussels!" cried the sailor; "these will do instead of eggs!" (Ch. IV) (23)

Although it turns out that what have been found are not really mussels but lithodomes, the shellfish are eminently edible. Verne scarcely had Shakespeare in mind, but his awareness of the same kind of setting as in *The Tempest*, with its own castaways, and his knowledgeable understanding of the natural world make his account all the more credible. Kermode's finale to his long footnote on the crux in the Arden edition enlists a certain wry humor: "It is not yet impossible that this tedious argument will be settled by evidence that *scamel* is after all a shellfish" (68n172).[5] Yet properly "muscling in" on the crux by showing how these delicious mussels have been bypassed by scholars and editors down through the years may detract from the tedium by adding the required zest.

Although it could be advanced that Shakespeare's previous reference to "Mussels" in the play reveals the modern spelling of the word and so would not be of much help with an anagrammatic reading later (based more on the variant spelling m-u-s-*c*-l-e-s), the point can validly be made in defense that Prospero, in his allusion to fresh-water mollusks, is using a more educated form of the word whereas Caliban's less educated usage relates more to an antiquated variant. In any case, Shakespeare's awareness of both fresh and salt water varieties of such mollusks would prove him to be the true naturalist—not just the gourmet.

NOTES

[1] See *Der Sturm* in *Shakespeares Werke* (51).

[2] Furness 138-40.

³Bullough VIII, 284.

⁴Shakespeare refers to a "mussel-shell" elsewhere (*The Merry Wives of Windsor*, 4.5.28).

⁵Kermode also observes that *OED* "does not give much credit" to the word *scamel* appearing in Wright's *Dialect Dictionary* as a synonym for *godwit*.

CHAPTER XI

ON RETAINING *M. ARDEN OF FEVERSHAM*:
THE QUESTION OF TITULAR RESONANCE

Although the original title of the often-called "best of the apocryphal plays" (Muir 3) relating to Shakespeare was, in fact, *The Lamentable and True Tragedie of M. Arden of Feversham in Kent*, this label has, for reasons mainly of economy, been customarily shortened in print to read simply *Arden of Feversham*. Further, the title-page contains two other descriptive sentences, ones which could well be construed as original subtitles, and these have been deleted as well (yet are unnecessary for us to reintroduce here). Because the locale in England nowadays has the spelling of *Faversham* (*Feversham* being the variant but found in the main source, Holinshed's *Chronicles*), the drama's title has further evolved to be in accord with modern-day orthography, both in Wine's and White's fairly recent editions, for example. True, most Renaissance buffs appear to be undisturbed by this additional, seemingly minor orthographic shift, but a good case can still be made in support of the original nomenclature, including even the preceding initial. Whether this position is then strong enough to bolster present-day return to a purportedly outdated formula for the stage is a different matter, though not necessarily supererogatory here.

The case in brief is as follows: hints in the original full title suggest, in terms of authorial awareness, possible topical allusion and titular resonance, elements which need not be cavalierly discounted from the start as being ungermane, for they ought to be weighed with much care. Too easily may such consideration of incidental name-play give a trivializing initial impression, but though this is a valid caveat, it is here simply more of a critical than historical concern.

As a starter, the introductory letter "*M.*" before "*Arden*" might easily signify various factors upon first reading. The obvious choice is between an abbreviation and an initial, one being plausibly denotative in effect and the other connotative. If the isolated letter be taken straightaway in the most obvious manner, it would surely imply the common use of the initial of a Christian first name, as would be standard practice then as today; yet here it clearly must stand rather, or first of all, for *Master* (as then spelled out in the title of Wine's or White's modernized edition). On the other hand, let us pause to consider that *Master* was often enough abbreviated then as "Mr." (notably in the Dedication to Shakespeare's *Sonnets*). Moreover, the text of the play refers to the main figure merely as "Arden" (indeed already at the start of line one). But insofar as we should know that historically his full name was referred to as *Thomas Ardern [sic]*, that he was officially a "Gentleman" and therefore, in this context, a "Master," the "M." would have to *de*note "Master," whatever else it may thereafter *con*note validly in addition.

But has this brief analysis of "M." meanings been for nought? Not so, once we consider a deeper resonance also likely to be present—if not for most actors, readers, and spectators, possibly still for one of the most important persons involved nonetheless, namely William Shakespeare himself. The clue is that because, as has so often been argued, for instance in the reputable survey by Wine (lxxxvii), the man from Stratford could have been so readily attracted, for obvious familial reasons, to the name of *Arden*—not to forget other names in the play relating somehow to his, such as *Will*, whose friend was *Shake*(bag)—he therefore just as easily could have taken a step further and been also prompted by the preceding isolated letter.

For why not? The Arden in his own family, his mother, likewise had an "M." as the first initial of her forename: *Mary* Arden. Aesthetically, the relevance of exact etymology at this juncture is beside the point at issue. What counts instead is that whereas the "M." in the title had the *general* effect of being a simple abbreviation and not an initial, still it could have been attractive to, or even chosen by, the playwright because, on the psychological level of *private name-play*, as it were, it just happened to initiate the Christian name of his esteemed mother, deriving from an old, very venerated Roman Catholic family. This raises the inevitable question for us once again: Did Shakespeare have at least a hand in composing this intriguing apocryphal drama?

In answer, let us deal with an animadversion first of all. Were it not for other onomastic connections concerning the Shakespeare name here, such an "initial" concern (no pun intended) might at first appear miniscule at best. Those who would posit Marlowe as author, and his candidacy *has been* seriously and fairly recently suggested, could then make something also out of the setting of Kent, which likewise just happens to appear in the original full title of the drama, thereby incidentally singling out their candidate's biographical Kentish connections. But we can now abruptly dismiss that as avoiding the issue, if only because the manner of the disposal of the corpse in the play indicates that the author(s) was (or were) totally unaware of the actual historical circumstances of the murder in that district in England.

If the play was the work of a Kentish man, presumably he would have wanted to appear cognizant of all of the basic facts. Besides, the very appearance of the name *Kent* in the full title could, by the same token, look ahead to a further *Shakespearean* linkage as well, thereby anticipating the Kent name as found again in *King Lear* (this time that of a character). A further point is that that tragedy has at least one other, similar, topical allusion, as has often been evinced, in that the name of *Cordelia* relates to another, real-life Cordelia, one involved in a law court case that Shakespeare, many think, may have known of, where the female involved was known as *Cordell*—a variant spelling (see Ch. VIII). So we may dispense with the rivalry of Marlowe here as inconsequential—at any rate in terms of any convincing Kentish connection.

Now undoubtedly further examples of name relationships with Shakespeare's background can be adduced in the Arden play, for example the characters *Greene* (not necessarily hinting at the playwright Robert Greene but Thomas Greene) and *Will* (pointing not necessarily or only at Shakespeare's own abbreviated first name, as in the *Sonnets*, where it is personally cut short, but at that of his acting associate Will Kemp, especially if they were known for having acted together, though doubtfully so in this particular play). For Will Kemp's salutation "My notable Shakerags" in his *Nine Daies Wonder* certainly appears to be name-play on his friend *Shakespeare*, particularly because of his citing the story of one "Macdobeth" (most probably standing somehow for Macbeth, or for "doing Macbeth") in the same account. If so, *Shakerags* might well represent a further pun on the near rhyme *Shakebag*, the name of the prominent figure in the Arden play whose role is much bigger than in the sources. He is accompanied by Black Will (shortened to Will in the line assignments, so that line after line next to each other regularly cite *Will*, then *Shake*, then *Will* and *Shake* again, etc.). One suggestion is that if Shakespeare took the role of Shakebag, Kemp could have taken that of Will, the former's boon companion. Still, this is a bit of a long shot because it does not fully tally with evidence that *Arden* was associated with the Queen's Men (not Kemp's company, though Shakespeare may well have been in that group).

As I have pointed out elsewhere,[1] the leading names in this early domestic tragedy, as well as subordinate names, parallel ones in *The Merry Wives of Windsor* indeed so closely that it stands to good reason that Shakespeare was pretty familiar with the earlier work and most likely had at least acted in it, particularly owing to the similar rascally connotations of *Fal-staff* and *Shake-bag*, the former signifying a devious cutpurse (in robbing the King's men) as was the latter. It is useful to recollect how the Falstaffian association with *Gadshill* in *1 Henry IV* is anticipated in this apocryphal drama (17.13).[2] In both plays this locale is connected with robbery. Most interesting of all, the name of *Shakebag* is again to be found even on the title-page of the Arden drama.

Obviously it can be countered that psychology in some respects opposes a valid Shakespearean connection apropos of name-play if only because why should a sensitive playwright correlate the name of the notoriously greedy titular victim (or, in particular, that of the adulterous and murderous wife) with the maiden name of his own *mother* before marriage? Why indeed? On the surface, such a demurrer is well enough taken. Even the purported biographical connection of the *Arden* forest in *As You Like It* may be open to some question in this regard. Still, it is well to remember William M. Jones's article on how the character of William, appearing briefly but significantly in that comedy, has also links with the life of the playwright. In any event, in the new *Oxford Shakespeare* the spelling of the Forest of Arden's name reverts back to the original French, there spelled *Ardenne*, almost as if to try to cancel any autobiographical intrusiveness; yet the point is that it would have had to be somehow present first in order to be ripe for such cancelling out by an editor.

We might all too easily get bogged down in some kind of biographical fallacy here admittedly, and, in any case, the Ardenic association does appear rather speculative to some readers. The main rationale for withholding negative judgment altogether is that if indeed Shakespeare was big enough to avoid casting characters to type, as most of his *aficionados* think he was, he likewise need not have indulged in having the names of his characters reflect any *undue autobiographical* resonances of persons on whom the names could in part be based. Thus just because of punning links between Fal-staff and Shake-speare, such inherent nameplay hardly would have to imply that the "Sweet Swan of Avon" was himself in any way also a drunkard, robber, fornicator, glutton, or liar. Nonetheless, there is still a great deal of Shakespeare in Falstaff at least in terms of creativity. Likewise the "*M.*" in *M. Arden of Feversham* reverberates in relation to Shakespeare's family at least on the most obvious level, that of an "echo."

Finally we come to the other change in the title of this fascinating domestic tragedy. If we do not care to revert back to the original spelling of *Fever*sham, as some now prefer not to, we all too easily can miss out on more of the purported title-play involved in the drama. For mention is made in the plot of there being "A great fever" (10.56), to which the exclamatory response then is: "A fever? God forbid!" (10.57). But, paradoxically, the effect of the *connotation* of "fever" is for us *not* forbidden. Whereas the immediate context, Susan's illness, is not especially important here, if the reference is seen in terms of a larger (or mediate) context and applied as well to the titular locale, that of *Fever*sham, then more aesthetic, onomastic interplay is forthcoming.

For instance, the hidden notion of obtusely "shamming a fever" could be intimated by the title subtextually, suggesting thereby not only playing sick, or malingering, or hypochondria in general (comparable to Falstaff's playing dead, to bring in the analogy with *1 Henry IV* again), but commenting thereby on something else that is more notoriously "-sham" here, nothing less than the numerous sick attempts on Master Arden's life by the renegades Black Will and Shakebag, ones which are bound to fail because these ruffians are so hilariously inept. (In fact, Mistress Arden has herself to help out in the end.)

This is further supported by the name-play involving Fever*sham* and *sham(e)* as well: "towards Feversham to shame us all" (9.138), paronomasia evident even more in the spelling given in the Scolar Press edition ("Fevershame"). Further, immediately after the "fever" wordplay comes analogous name-play: Michael states that Susan's fear of a fever is "of a lurdan, too, as big as yourself" (10.58), and Wine glosses *lurdan* as follows: "'loafer' (with word-play on *Fever-lurdan*: the disease of laziness [*OED*])" (94). In any event, no doubt the name of the locale was originally assigned because the swampy terrain made all too easily for feverous conditions, and if that recollection is not especially inviting, let us say to present-day citizens there, that is no reason to avoid it in terms of its relevance to the play.

Now it might be contended that such close reading all too obviously would call attention to itself and for that very reason might best be avoided. At the same time, though, would a defender of the modernized *Faver*sham reading be willing to claim that the positive hint of "Favor," let us say obliquely implied in the modernized spelling ("Faver-">"Favor"), offsets the negative quality of something being "-sham"? Hardly so.

In any event, the only Shakespearean nexus with either spelling would involve the "-ham" effect by itself. True, it might appear to be going rather far to consider that the playwright's son *Ham*net was in any way here recollected. But, still, does not the tragedy nominally look forward in some respects to that of *Hamlet*? In terms of the long, proverbial delay involved in doing away with the eventual victim, it would certainly appear that way.[3] Yet then is *Arden* ostensibly also an early form of revenge-tragedy? Not in terms of the way the author(s) took pains to devise it (whereby it becomes, instead, more like *Titus Andronicus*, a horror play), if only because of the "decision to leave out other examples of Arden's covetousness found in Holinshed" (White xii). In other words, in real life, Arden, in many respects, had it coming to him, but not so much so validly in the play.

In actual life Arden's overweening greed on St. Valentine's Day, of all days, might, for instance, help account in part for the vengeance pronounced against him. But in the play the murder at that time can be thought of, in America at least, as a forerunner of the notorious "St. Valentine's Day Massacre" in Chicago, a major difference being not in the number of victims, but in the veritable gang of murderers bent on doing away with a single victim. Enough also "gang up" on Arden in the play.

All in all, then, to restore *M. Arden of Feversham* as the working title of this drama can have its historically beneficent textual results, especially for the advocates of at least partial Shakespearean authorship. The meaning of the title would then in part be that it sets up (or implies) a deliberate contrast: M. Árden of *Feversham*, that is, is to be thought of somewhat in contrast with M. Arden of *Wilmecote* (later of

Stratford). We readily may think as well about how the Stratford Bard was prone to employ the preposition *of* in titles of his plays (more so than many of his contemporaries) to the extent that that idiosyncrasy may be considered even a kind of syntactic signpost of his. Majority opinion still holding that his authorship, in whole or in part, cannot be ruled out (Tieck's famous ascription having been then endorsed, for example, by Goethe),[4] let us not ignore a textual hint or two of this assignment already in the older form of the title, even though, granted, the final authorship may still have been composite in that different stylistic effects in the plot suggest various hands at work (possibly making the tragedy what has been termed an "actors' showpiece").

As a side note, it has to be admitted that the biggest technical problem in relating *Arden* to Shakespeare is in reconciling its apparent affinity with the so-called "Pembroke" group of plays (including Kyd's *The Spanish Tragedy*, and *Soliman and Perseda*) with its being "echoed" later (seen with the reappearance of Black Will) in a play belonging to the Queen's Men, namely *The True Tragedie of Richard III*. The point is that Shakespeare is now often thought to have been initially linked with the Queen's Men, not Pembroke's. One way of reconciling this disparity is that Pembroke's Company could have had simply an off-shoot in the Queen's Men. In any event, it appears most probable that much of the Feversham play drew upon the works of Kyd (even *Soliman and Perseda*, which has striking parallels with it, is still at times attributed to him, as in the recent *Dictionary of Literary Biography* entry) and, to some extent, Marlowe (the echoes of *Edward II* being very strong, notably in one case where a Kyd parallel, however, also happens to be inviting [1.185-86]). This correlation is not so unusual in itself perhaps in that Kyd and Marlowe were known to have shared chambers in 1591 (at least according to Kyd). Yet, be that as it may, it would hardly have prevented still another up-and-coming, ambitious playwright like the young Stratford "upstart" from polishing it up, transforming what they started, and in the process introducing some of his own effects. It is, after all, a virtual commonplace that Shakespeare took over material later from Kyd in writing *Hamlet*, and his general use of Marlowe elsewhere hardly needs supportive evidence here.

In conclusion, with regard to a titular allusion to a woman, at least connotatively, in the titular phrase "*M. Arden*," it is at least worth mentioning that the famous ballad based on the play also stresses the female Arden and again does so

72

titularly. Further, for the Ohio Shakespeare Conference at Bowling Green University (March, 1992), I was permitted to present a paper for the session "The Problem Of / In *Arden of Feversham*" (notice again the retainment of the old spelling) dealing with the authorship issue and pointing out a few new aspects of the argument, notably how the Queen's Men produced the play in Feversham in 1591 and how various playwrights (ones cited by Jonson in his familiar eulogy on Shakespeare) might have been somehow involved along with the Master. Such concern was particularly apposite for the 1992 meeting insofar as the year marked the quatercentenary of the first publication of the play in 1592. So we have now at least four ways in which the title of the *Arden* play, considered in its complete form, may be resonant of the leading (or possibly revising?) playwright's family nomenclature: (1) in terms of the maiden surname of his mother, as has often been felt; (2) in terms of the "initial" effect of her first name; (3) in terms of the first syllable of the name of his son Hamnet figuring in the last syllable of the locale's name; and (4) in terms of his own surname's first syllable in the name of the rogue Shakebag (not to forget Will). As a very last point, something might again be said of the mention of the name *Kent* in the full title as an onomastic riddle somehow anticipatory of Kent in *King Lear* (curiously so insofar as Kent himself is disguised later as Caius). It might still be contended that such an overall hypothesis as here proposed, though valid, is "psychological" mainly and thus not conservative enough. Perhaps so, but my main textual point has been extremely conservative, namely in order to retain the original wording of the title (because loss of it could interfere with the validity of a biographical interpretation altogether). It is, after all, a commonplace that authors, consciously or subliminally, are prone to write something about themselves into their works, human as we all are. This factor can hardly be fully negated.

NOTES

[1]For lengthy discussion (but not incorporating the main points in the present essay), see my *Shakespeare and the Matter of the Crux*, Ch. 9; also consult papers of mine in the *University of Dayton Review* and the *DLB*. In p. 199 of the book, I make a passing, oblique allusion to Swinburne's quibbling reference to *Black Will Shakebag* in *Arden* as hinting at Shakespearean authorship (as I also do directly on p. 220), but elsewhere refer to the main character in question simply as George Shakebag.

[2]Quotations from *Arden* are from M. L. Wine's edition unless otherwise indicated (the name *Faversham*

there being changed back to *Feversham* also).

[3]Kenneth Muir's familiar criticism that *Arden* "does not resemble in style or theme any of Shakespeare's acknowledged plays" (3—cited by White xvi) does not take into account this factor. The *other* "Black Will" play (on Richard III) definitely was a forerunner of *Hamlet* (for which, see Shaheen in *N&Q* 32-33), so why would not this one also be?

[4]See the lengthy consideration of the authorship problem in Wine (lxxxi-lcii) and White (xiv-xvii). In an announcement of a fairly recent production of the play in Seattle (directed by John Russell Brown), this statement was made: "Scholars seeing the play will seek the influence which this early popular play may have had on Shakespeare. There are those who think that it may be one of Shakespeare's early apocryphal plays" (*The Shakespeare Newsletter* 41.3 [1991]: 37).

# CHAPTER XII

## SHAKESPEARE'S TITULAR PARONOMASIA

"What's in a name?" asked Juliet (2.2.43). But her question was by no means merely rhetorical. Indeed, one of the best answers to the anti-Stratfordians—who point to *Hamlet*, claiming Sir Francis Bacon is in effect a little ham, thus the author—is that the most famous comic character has a name that puns on Shakespeare's. For if the speare Will Shake, cannot the staff Fal[l]?

That Shakespeare deliberately made use of numerous puns, in his comedies especially, is well-known (though *Hamlet* has the most). But so far there has been little or no attempt to see if puns of merit exist in the titles of his plays as well. Perhaps the most famous suggestion along this line has been the finding of a *nothing / noting* pun in the full title of *Much Ado* (that is, if we eliminate *Love's Labour's Won*, which I have indicated elsewhere could very likely have been the original main title for this comedy). But this view has been advanced rather tentatively and has not been taken very seriously (that is, even for a pun). More interesting perhaps is that it was first registered in 1600, so that the variant spelling of *Ado* there, namely *Adoo*, might suggest the very year: A. D. [16]00.

There is something in the *nothing / noting* business, but the exact formulation of the kind of play involved appears too nebulous to demand fuller treatment. The problem is partly whether the "noting" concerns the making of musical notes or the taking of notes in the sense of eavesdropping or even both. Some critics think sex is involved.

Likewise the subtitle of *Twelfth Night* has been thought of as a kind of vague thematic pun: its *What You Will* supposedly reflects the various kinds of "willing" found in the comedy. In any case, its paronomasia should not thereby be confused with *As You Like It*, for, in the Epilogue of that comedy, Shakespeare definitely tells his audience that he wrote what he thought would "please" the spectators and evidently meant that by his title; consult the phrase "as please you" (12-13).

Since much of Shakespeare's punning revolves around Falstaff, it would not be so strange to find wordplay in a title of a drama concerned with this fat knight. In *The Merry Wives of Windsor*, the name *Windsor* seems to contain the most playful possibilities: it breaks down into "Wind" and "sor." The second syllable easily links with "Sir," Falstaff's official title. "Wind" then might describe a notable characteristic of this knight, namely his penchant for telling tales as the *miles gloriosus* (thus being full of hot air). The Merry Wives, in effect, are not only their husbands' spouses but the surrogate "Wives" of Sir Wind. The point then of the comedy is to show that Falstaff cannot claim his wives, and so the staff falls impotently.

Whereas Sir John attempts to make love to Mistresses Page and Ford, in *The Tempest* Caliban tries to seduce Miranda and likewise does not succeed. The name has been linked to "can[n]ibal," since Shakespeare was presumably influenced by the Montaigne essay on the subject. But what about the title of the play he is in? Surely it can allude to the *temp*ering of the *pest*. Since Caliban is a bit of a nuisance for Prospero to have around, and since he has a habit of calling for the plague and assorted winged insects to help him revenge himself against his magician-master, he associates himself, psycholinguistically, with the "pest" idea. At the end of the play, he announces that he will "seek for grace," presumably indicating that his rebellious nature has to be tempered. That there happens to be an actual tempest in the play—only in the first, short scene—does not detract from this motif.

Falstaff and Caliban can make us revert temporarily to *Twelfth Night*. Because of the subtitular pun on *Will* there, might there not be also a hint of a "Willful" sprite in the main title? What about the *elf* of *Twelfth*? Since the comedy was written to be performed during the Christmas season, we may be all too *will*ing to read into the hidden pun in the main title a suggestion of the elves associated in folklore with old Saint Nick—just as Malvolio (again with nameplay on *volio* as *Will*) has been called the veritable Scrooge of the play. (One alternate title for the comedy on record happens also to be *Malvolio*.) Notice that the title of the play in the First Folio is spelled *Twelfe-Night*. Certainly the presence of fairies in *A Midsummer Night's Dream* and the pseudo-fairies at the end of *The Merry Wives* proves that Shakespeare had his "elvish" moments.

*The Winter's Tale* contains the most notorious stage direction in Shakespeare, "Exit, pursued by a bear," followed by the news that it has consumed Antigonus. Is black humor on this topic already evident, proleptically, in the title? The hint would be in the last word with its *double entendre* on *tale* and *tail*, alluding in a throwaway manner to the final appendage of the animal. Shakespeare was well aware of such sly, uncouth humor; consider "thereby hangs a tale" in *As You Like It* (2.7.28), *The Taming of the Shrew* (4.1.49-50), *The Merry Wives of Windsor* (1.4.133), and even *The Two Noble Kinsmen* (3.3.41—as cited in the Riverside ed.). Hence the bear effect in the wintry romance may well be thought of as itself laying bare further titular innuendo.

PART II:

NINETEENTH-CENTURY ENGLAND
(AND THE EDWARDIAN PERIOD)

# CHAPTER XIII

## *DROOD* THE OBSCURE: THE EVIDENCE OF THE NAMES

Although any complete solution to Dickens's *The Mystery of Edwin Drood* has, in spite of the novel's references to race and racism (apropos of the titular figure's racist remarks to the Ceylonese Neville Landless), defied critical analysis, a veritable plethora of proposed solutions has indeed been put forth. The most recent so-called "Droo-id" (a term for an analyzer of the Droodian mystery) has gone so far as even to state that "*Drood* fascinates, in part, *because* of its very incompleteness" (Frank 150), namely its status as a fragment because Dickens died before it could be completed. That argument is reminiscent of the commonplace that romantic literature can be pleasing particularly because of its open-ended, organic quality. On the whole, there has been considerable subjectivity in the various arguments about what Dickens had in mind, some scholars whimsically preferring one reading over another. It is astonishing that with all this to-do, very little attention has been paid to the import of the novel's nomenclature. Having published a translation of Richard Gerber's research on names in mystery stories, side by side with one of the installments in a most unusual and intricate study of the *Drood* problem by Nathan Bengis, essays which elicited controversial responses, I should like here to apply the onomatological measuring stick to *Drood*.

To begin, it is especially surprising that there has been no serious interpretation of any magnitude on the import of names in this novel, because Felix Aylmer published a working list of names that Dickens used in composing the work (found the villain Jasper actually innocent) and because the import of Dickens's names is universally recognized as one of his outstanding aesthetic features. George Newlin's three-volume *Everyone in Dickens* is a thorough examination of the multitude of characters throughout Dickens's "Universe" (as the current expression has it) but does not go into onomastic depth. Touching on the possible significance of Dickens's working list of names as one of his marks of genius, Aylmer has this to say about *Drood*:

> This list is arranged in two columns, and it is easy to see what Dickens is at. He is preparing to christen his two leading men. None the less, there is an odd thing about the list. It lies in the aptness of the word "christen." The names are all, on the face of them, Christian names. Like most Christian names they are found occasionally, some frequently, as surnames, but we should not recognize them at first glance as having the unmistakable surnames flavour of, say, Pumblechook [in *Great Expectations*]. (41)

There is, as I shall suggest now, more to this use of "Christian" names than Aylmer implies. He deals particularly with the name of Jasper:

> If, on our first meeting with a character, we hear him always referred to as "Jasper," we may easily get it into our heads that this is his Christian name. The act of later correcting this first impression may well put us on to the very scent Dickens wants us to avoid. (42)

In his notes made in preparation for this novel, Dickens added the appellation "Mister" to Jasper and underlined it, viz.: "*Mr.* Jasper." According to Aylmer, the original use of a Christian name like *Jasper* as a surname here underscores the absence of an original surname. He infers that Jasper was born out of wedlock, and this theory becomes a cornerstone of his own unusual treatment of Edwin Drood's mystery.

The trouble is that he goes on to say that Jasper is really Drood's half-brother rather than his uncle , because Jasper is only six years older than Drood—an odd fact for an uncle-nephew relationship. Still, Aylmer does show that Dickens's name for the novel suggests such a kinship (the Inimitable had selected as a tentative title *The Mystery in the Drood Family*), although hardly conclusively. We are on safer grounds in sticking with the text of the novel as it has come down to us and then considering the thematic import of names in the novel *per se*.

Aylmer's deductions are cited only with some trepidation because they show how far scholarly ingenuity can lead readers. But to glean important meaning from Dickensian nomenclature is hardly over-ingenious in itself, for it is common knowledge that Dickens mulled his names over and over in his mind before putting them to paper. Jasper's name is indeed of much interest because it recalls semi-precious stones found in the Near East; the word is of Hebraic origin; the stone is cited in the last book in the Bible, the "undecipherable" *Book of Revelations* or *Apocalypse*, in reference to the face of God: "And he who sat was in appearance like a jasper-stone and a sardius, and there was a rainbow round the throne, in appearance like to an emerald" (iv:3). Thus, initially, the connotations of Jasper's name may not be evil at all, even though it became "a stock name for wicked baronets in melodrama" (42n). Perhaps, then, there is more to the meaning of Jasper's name than has met the eye. For his eye is evil. How? Let us now see.

The color of the jasper stone happens to be *blackish*-green—a point of possible significance in light of the novel's concern with racial matters. The greenish hue may account for the eerie quality associated with Jasper, but the blackish effect then relates to ethnic considerations. Neville Landless is also described as dark, for he is Ceylonese, and the key point of the plot is whether or not Drood's disappearance has anything to do with the racial incident involving him and Landless. We recall that Drood makes a racialist slur about Landless's darkness of skin. This episode is then used by Jasper as a means of characterizing Landless as the probable villain since Landless presumably decided to take revenge on Drood. Yet Jasper himself, as his name implies, could be of a dark-complexioned race, so that if he is to blame, his argument would work against him too. For there is a well-known theory that he belonged to an Indian group involved in thuggee, that such background may explain his interest in the occult (notably in animal magnetism), in opium, and in disposing of Edwin Drood, whose concern for the same woman that Jasper is interested in accounts for the rivalry.

Yet the thuggee theory is extremely conjectural, conjuring up Wilkie Collins's *The Moonstone* more than *Drood*. True, it has often been pointed out that a kinship may exist between the work of Dickens and Collins especially in terms of this novel; I find, however, a more interesting connection between it and Collins's "The Policeman and the Cook," in which a murder is also pinned on someone because of his skin color, "a Creole gentleman from Martinique." But that is another situation.

My principal inference is that this mystery can be solved through the clues offered by the Dickensian names, that the novelist at least unconsciously provided these hints before he had a chance to finish his story. Whatever the ultimate ending would have been (or was in his mind), it could hardly have been psychologically contradicted by the meanings already invested in character names. Compare, for example, Dickens's other stories in which villains have gruesome-sounding surnames: *Murdstone* (in *David Copperfield*) conjuring up murder and gravestone, *Gride* (in *Nicholas Nickleby*) hinting at both greed and pride, *Hortense* (in *Bleak House*) connoting the French villainess as a tense whore type. I submit that Jasper's name also fits into this haunting category.

For this reason, at least, Aylmer is on the wrong track in thinking that Jasper is innocent. Designating a semi-precious stone, the Jasper name conveys a materialistic meaning; it is indeed more than a "stock name for wicked baronets in melodrama," as Aylmer reluctantly indicates (then ignoring this evidence, or thinking that Dickens used it ironically), for the novelist was able to transform such nomenclature for his own purposes—not by changing the convention altogether, but by investing it with greater subtlety. Certainly Aylmer set himself apart from the great majority of other Droodists in fancying Jasper innocent. Indeed, his claim for shifting the emphasis away from this dabbler in mesmerism is clearly outrageous, the novelist's own special interest in mesmeric powers notwithstanding.

As the late Noel C. Peyrouton sums up "The Aylmer Case" in his review-essay intriguingly entitled "Thus Spake the Sphinx: Riddle of the Egyptian Boy," "Perhaps the most difficult part of the Aylmer thesis to accept is that centering on Jasper's innocence" (105). I submit, therefore, that the Near Eastern associations in the Jasper name suggest not only the stone, but the Egyptian *asp*. The very swish of these letters in his name suggests the hiss of the poisonous serpent so often associated with, for example, the death of Cleopatra. The point then is that the disappearance of Edwin Drood, who is also closely involved with Egypt because of his ambitions, is somehow linked with the "asp" of Jasper.

It is time to turn to Drood's own name. Although some connotations are also ghost-like, mysterious, haunting, they are not altogether that way. In any case, there seems to be a hint of his disappearance already in the surname, as we shall see. The main question, however, is whether the name has more positive or negative associations. Etymologically, it can easily be traced back to Celtic roots, to the *Druids* (mentioned in an actual early stage of the novel), but that meaning should not be taken very seriously here. At the most, it simply conjures up druidic folklore involving vanishings, shape-shifting, and other such curious elf-like events. One critic who has touched on clues in the name, Richard M. Baker, says:

> There is something about the youth's very name that suggests his
> untimely extinction. Edwin Drood: the dull alliterative recurrence of
> the "d's" is like so many clods thumping down on a plain wooden
> coffin; the odd surname holds a brooding sense of doom, a sugges-
> tion of dread and death. . . . it is rather significant that the noun
> "droud"—similar in sound if not in spelling to Edwin's family name—
> is Scottish for "a codfish; a dull, lumpish fellow."(138)

Rather significant? How with regard to the solution to the mystery? Except for his
insensitivity in making fun of Neville's complexion, Edwin is hardly to be described
as a "dull, lumpish fellow"—even his presumed racism might be designated lively
enough in its arrogant ignorance—though his girl friend does make fun of him, and
the reader may not be overly attracted to his personality. It is difficult to ascertain
what kind of a personality he does have; we simply do not get enough of a description of him to know much of what it is like.

Yet if we take some liberties with Baker's suggestions we might find more
in his *codfish* reference than he apparently has thought of. Since a traditional symbol of Christ has been the fish, and since "codfish" obliquely relates to (rhymes
with) this meaning (God / fish), the droud / Drood combination points perhaps to
Drood as somehow eventually a *Christus* figure. What is more, part of Drood's
name hints at the Crucifixion; it includes r-o-o-d, suggesting the old linguistic formulation for Christ's cross, the holy rood. His first name is reminiscent of that of an
Old English King of Northumbria (617-633), a firm believer in the holy cross. Ironically, therefore,even though Drood's actions do not reveal any particularly Christ-
like tendencies—and his racist reaction to Neville is certainly anti-Christian—his
fate may be spelled out in his name. He is destined to be a scapegoat, to be sacrificed
even as Jesus of Nazareth was.

The Christian allegory takes on additional meaning when Drood's name is
related to Jasper's. As the poisonous asp, let us say, Jasper is responsible for the
death of man (like the serpent in the Bible). But there may also be a hint that his evil
will not fully succeed and that Drood, like that other sacrificial figure some twenty
centuries ago, namely Jesus, will return from his supposed disintegration. For man
is thus reborn through Christ. The novel does not make clear what is to happen, but
given Drood's un-Christ-like behavior toward Neville, my final resolution is that he
probably does not deserve such a resurrection. Thus, if Drood is at all a Christ-

figure, he is not to be reborn, at least not here on earth. (I am no so-called "Resurrectionist" in this context.)

Nonetheless, there are some *mythic* parallels between Drood and Christ that deserve at least momentary attention, even if some of them may not be wholly convincing. It might be recalled that Jesus too was represented as a believable man, as well as God, according to orthodox belief; he also had a human nature, including presumably some human frailties, along with a divine personality. Dickens, I believe, pointed out these facets of Jesus's character in his retelling of the Christ story for his children, what has come to be known as *The Life of Our Lord*, but I shall show that this was not quite the title he gave it. (A better one is *The Little Testament*.) The most obvious example of Christ's humanity is often taken to be His exclamation on the cross: "My God, my God, why hast Thou forsaken Me?" Although it is commonly believed that He was quoting a psalm and hardly calling into question His Divinity, these words clearly express a poignant sense of dereliction. Now, to some extent, Drood's remarks to Neville Landless can be related to Christ's humanity, though hardly to those particular words on the cross. For Drood is intemperate toward Landless just as Christ is sometimes said to have been when He somewhat peremptorily emptied the temple of its money-changers. The motivations are totally different, naturally, but although this discrepancy detracts from Drood in terms of any *mystical* representation of Christ, it does not detract from our considering him at times as a *mythic* one.

The point is that both Drood and Christ believe in the *basic* brotherhood of man and thereby in self-abnegation, for in spite of his indulgence in a racial slur, Edwin's intent is to help people in Africa by traveling to Egypt and working for disadvantaged people there as an engineer. In a somewhat similar manner, at any rate, Christ's appeal for missionaries, His command that His followers traverse the ends of the earth, baptizing those who would be saved, provides a parallel. Christ "engineered" a church; Edwin, as a would-be engineer in an African country, is a potential "missionary." Another parallel, though hardly a momentous one, is that Edwin and Jesus remain unmarried, though both share a certain interest in the female sex (Edwin in Pussy, Jesus in Mary Magdalene, for example). A final parallel may be enough to vindicate the entire analogy symbolically: Drood disappears on Christmas Eve. Although ghost stories have been traditional at this time of year, symbolically speaking it especially is important for Dickens; far from making Drood a reversal of a Christ-figure, his disappearance on the anniversary of the night that Christ first made His appearance links him finally even more closely to the Savior, the point being that Christ's whole purpose in appearing was to disappear, to die so that sinful man could be reborn.

Let us now turn to other names in *Drood*. There are added correlations between name and behavior which very strikingly support the two parallels thus far set up. For instance, at the end of Chapter Four Jasper confronts Durdles to discover why he is known as *Stony*. At this point Dickens involves himself directly in the matter of etymology. Various reasons are proposed for the name: that this nickname derives from *Tony*, from *Stephen*, or from the name of his trade (that of stone mason). But if Durdles does not help very much in providing an answer for Jasper, does not explain what is called "the fact," can *we* be any closer factually? Perhaps we can. Let us bear in mind that Dickens revised the ending of Chapter Four. It had originally ended with a sulky response from Durdles to this effect:

"How does the fact stand, Mr. Jasper? The fact stands six to one side to half a dozen on t'other. So fur as Durdles sees the fact with *his* eyes, it has took up that position as near as may be" (see Cox 34-35).

My inference is that Dickens deliberately removed an obstacle to the discovery of the significance in his names when he deleted Durdles's reply in the later version. Curiously, in the succeeding chapter, the problem of nomenclature emerges again: Jasper asks Durdles the name of the boy stoning him, and the mason replies, "Deputy." This name strikes Jasper as an odd one, as it indeed is. "Is that its—his—name?" he inquires. In the case of *Deputy*, the meaning is obviously comic. Since a deputy is normally linked with a servant of the law, not a breaker, the effect of the name on Jasper is that of incongruity. Given Jasper's own devious nature, however, the overall effect is even more incongruous because of its irony. Thus Jasper's criminal tendencies are already being arrested, anticipated by a moral policeman, a "deputy."

A comic interlude like this recurs elsewhere in the novel. Edwin's betrothed's name is Rosa Bud, shortened to Rosebud by some, but then wholly converted into Pussy by Edwin. Mr. Grewgious responds to the last nickname by asking, "Do you keep a cat down there?" Edwin appropriately states that "Pussy" is, literally enough, a "pet name"; then he conflates the nickname with her Christian name by calling her "Prosa," another example of Dickens's liking for portmanteau nomenclature. The effect is primarily comic; however, since the rose symbol is so often thought of in religious terms, its import should not be ruled out here. If Drood at all stands for the rood, his Rosa or Rosebud might represent the "mystical rose " associated with the woman closest to Christ, namely His mother Mary. (Any association with the other Mary, Mary Magdalene, seems irrelevant here.) Since Rosa and Edwin do not marry or presumably have relations, their close attachment may best be explained in terms of a love that is essentially Platonic or asexual. There is nothing mystical, however, about the relationship between Rosa and Edwin. It is fundamentally more *misty* than mystic, although in more symbolic terms it is *mythic* too.

The surname *Landless* is also discussed in the novel. Mr. Grewgious suggests that it implies that someone bearing that name is separated from his homeland (hence literally landless). Since the Landlesses hail from Ceylon, they are indeed without their land in England. If, then, Neville Landless's cognomen is indeed a characteristic (and not merely a representative) name, what of his first name? Offhand, the connotation may be *without a city* (thus no *ville*), but the linking rhyme with *devil* would relate more to Christian symbolism, the point being that *Neville* is close enough to the diabolical to raise the question, at least for Jasper, of an implicit association; at the same time it is different enough to clarify for the reader that Neville is precisely *not* a devil (ne [de] ville) if it is Jasper who functions as the asp. The subtlety is deliberately teasing.

Dickens played with other names too, such as that of Mr. Chrisparkle, a portmanteau cognomen combining *Christ* and *sparkle*. Since he is the Minor Canon, it is fitting to imagine Christ shining through his very name. The mysterious opium lady is called The Princess Puffer, whereby the connotation of puffing at opium is evident enough. Dickens definitely had the import of name-calling clearly in mind from the early stages of the novel when he wrote of Cloisterham: "It was once possibly known to the Druids by another name, and certainly to the Romans by another, and to the Saxons by another, and to the Normans by another; and a name more or less in the course of many centuries can be of little moment to its dusty chronicles" (Ch. 3—the actual source for Cloisterham being Rochester in Kent). Although the name of Cloisterham is said to be "of little moment," paradoxically it is of some interest to the linguistic sleuth because it represents a form of metathesis. All the letters in *Rochester* are found in *Cloisterham*, a point I have never seen made in print before.

Other names are of moment too, though often only playfully so. The sprightly owner of the Seminary for Young Ladies is Miss Twinkleton—a feminine counterpart of Chrisparkle. More name-play is evident in Chapter 11, where the curious initials P. J. T. are introduced, and there is quibbling over whether the meaning is "Perhaps John Thomas" or "Perhaps Joe Tyler." The name which reflects the character in the most stentorian way is that of Honeythunder, the philanthropist (suggesting thereby the sweetness of honey), remindful of the boisterous Boythorn of *Bleak House*. But names can also be misleading (as we have already seen in the Neville / devil suggestion). Thus Baker writes:

> Mr. Duffield says: "One of the most prominent characters has pinned
> upon him the grotesque title of 'Tartar,' a name as redolent of the
> East as a whiff of hashish." . . . As to his title, I can myself suggest a
> way in which Dickens might have created it which is as English as
> roast beef. First Lieutenant Tartar, late of the Royal Navy? "Tar" is a
> common synonym for "sailor," short for "jack-tar." Double the common synonym, and you have "tartar," a name which has a whiff of
> the sea. (75-76)

So Baker puts the cart before Pegasus, for in the light of the racialist suggestions in the novel, surely the connotations of the East are more meaningful than what is merely "as English as roast beef." But there is not much of a hint that I can detect in the name of Datchery. There is no clue in the nomenclature regarding whether Drood returned disguised as Datchery unless the name itself is so disguised as to suggest that. Dickens deliberately cut out Chapter Eighteen, as he had originally written it, in order to fit his novel into the proper format for serial publication, and in so doing he eliminated a section indicating that Datchery was unfamiliar with Cloisterham; this missing chapter provides evidence that Datchery was not Drood in disguise, as is often believed. Obviously since Drood was a native of Cloisterham, he could not have been Datchery unless we think that he was as good a feigner as Sherlock Holmes. See Cox (36) for discussion of the deleted chapter.

In sum, then, the other Droodian names do support my main thesis that Dickens had the import of nomenclature in mind when he wrote this novel and was thus providing clues for the reader. There are a few exceptions, but they do not detract. The only pattern I can detect is the Christian, although there are a few other categories like that of animal imagery. Along with the asp and cat images already cited, Jasper is linked to "a wild beast" (Ch. Twenty-two), even to a charming cobra;

Deputy to an ox (Ch. Twelve); Mr. Grewgious to a bear (Ch. Nine); Mr. Sapsea to a jackass (Ch. Four). On the whole, the animal imagery does not appear as striking and as closely linked to the plot as in *Bleak House* (with Mr. Vholes as the vampire bat, and so forth), with the exception of the allusions to Jasper, but it is still significant particularly in terms of Dickens's own interest in animal magnetism (or mesmerism).

That this power was central to the mystery of the novel has been pointed out some time ago by Boyd (on file in the Droodiana Collection in The Dickens House, London), and the overall effect of animal magnetism upon Dickens's work is the subject of a book by Kaplan. In terms of my present topic, little more can be added except that Jasper's asp-like name provides a link to his interest in animal magnetism, his "charming" Rosa with his cobra-like qualities. The celebrated image of the canker or worm in the rose, utilized by Shakespeare in his sonnets, by Blake in "The Sick Rose," and by numerous previous writers, is reflected in the asp of Jasper trying to worm its way into the rose of Rosa Bud.

It is ironic that whereas Drood bore within his surname a hint of the rood—his cross—so Dickens, in failing to finish the novel, had then to endure his own cross by dying. As a Droo-id has put it, although too skeptically I would now say in light of the internal evidence: "whether or no Jasper killed Drood—it stands to reason that Drood killed Dickens" (Edgar Rosenberg 73). Yet it is important not to end on an ironic, facetious note in discussing this novel. For the story of Edwin Drood is fundamentally a Christmas mystery, another in Dickens's list, and as such has its own ghosts but also its implicit, if mythic, relationship to the Christ story. Thus the strong undertones of Christianity that Paul Gottschalk has recently discerned in *Drood* as a Yuletide tale, specifically one as related to the "Resurrection and the Life," point to a way in which the Christian nomenclature lent itself to a theme that was then subsumed by the novelist himself, as is especially notable in Jane Vogel's *Allegory in Dickens* (about the only major work I have come across that goes into depth on the import of Christian nomenclature and its meaning in the novel, coming to many of the same conclusions that I have).

# CHAPTER XIV

## DROOD RENOMINATED

Some years ago in *Dickens Quarterly* (1984), The Journal of the Dickens Society, Everett F. Bleiler published a provocative two-part literary onomastic study on the wordplay in the Droodian mystery. Although his work has a few intriguing etymological points suggestive of at least coincidental rhyme, on several key issues his inferences can be sharply brought into question; in fact, some appear to be flagrantly incorrect. However arresting a few of his verbal associations may be, certain additional facts need now to be enlisted. Hence the present rejoinder once more.

Bleiler acknowledges my own main previous study of Droodian names ("*Drood* the Obscure" in its original format), but he explicitly dismisses my symbolic analysis, namely any inherent Christological overtones. Thus, it turns out to be a little ironic that the first part of his study appears in the issue of a journal which also happens to list in its comprehensive Dickens Checklist some of my research on Dickens's creative reworking of the Gospels for his children (see Ch. XV). The same issue also provides, as its leading book review, an analysis of Andrew Sanders's useful work with the resonant title (as derivative of the novelist himself) *Charles Dickens: Resurrectionist*. Indeed, Sanders, though finding Dickens "insistently undogmatic," still calls him "devout" (37). But, all irony aside, the key question is this: Can Drood's very name be cogently thought of in the extended terms of "Christian mysticism and the death of Edwin Drood" (Bleiler 88)? In brief, to accommodate a whimsical but thereby apt Dickensian twist, "Do I over-Droo-id?"

In answer, first my research on Dickens's purported work *The Life of Our Lord* has raised the pertinent question of whether he did actually invent that designation. Clearly the expression "Our Lord" is one especially revered by (though hardly limited to) Roman Catholics; yet Dickens was admittedly critical enough of aspects of the Roman Church, as is well recognized. The main point is that a good many Protestants at least do not automatically interrelate the Savior with the Father as being, let us say, one (except of course in Spirit). Although, true, the "Lord" is petitioned often enough in Protestant hymnology, there the referent is mainly or tonally the Father image. It appears rather more likely, as I chanced to point out a few years ago in a first draft, that the novelist's son, Henry Fielding Dickens, bestowed the "Lordly" title upon his father's retelling of the Christ story than that Dickens himself went in for that, if only because the son had had a Catholic marriage, even though he himself (and *his* sons), were not especially Romanist, at least in the ordinary, practicing, church-going sense (see Ch. XV).

But, in any event, if Dickens would scarcely have accepted a title for a work of his that would be suggestive of Catholic dogmatics, he was clearly no less of a bona-fide Christian in spirit. Why else, to put it bluntly, would he have become so commonly and warmly venerated during the Yuletide season?

Now, secondly, with all due respect, Bleiler in his essay critiques me a bit out of context. My express purpose was not to foster righteously anagogic interpretations of the Drood story—rather exactly the opposite; for I specified again that the hero's name phonologically calls forth the conception of a *rood* (that is, *cross*), a point emphasized by Jane Vogel in her book, but only again ironically. In other words, Drood was truly meant to die and not reappear on earth at the end of the completed novel. But that hardly would mean that he was not to be reborn in heaven. It is scarcely requisite to be reminded of the title of the Old English dream-vision "The Dream of the Rood" to cope with this obvious clear-cut word link-up.

Yet, at the end, my rationale turned out to be the same as Bleiler's: Edwin the hero, in spite of his presumed missionary zeal with regard to matters Egyptian, is too snobbish, even insufferable, in his outward behavior to be thought of as acting in a truly Christ-like manner, Whereas Bleiler charged him merely with being "rude," an all-too-evident or coarse onomastic pun, Edwin's reactionary attitude toward Neville Landless may more accurately be here characterized as *racist*. Agreed, Neville, in turn, admits to having a temper, and the altercation between him and

Edwin was, to be sure, occasioned by his Uncle Jasper's spiked drink, but purportedly these clues are merely side-effects, misdirections inserted to keep us on the alert. (We remember, after all, that Dickens was also an amateur conjuror.) But what I find perturbing is that Bleiler went so far as to substitute a colloquial and profane etymology for what might be a religious hint, finding the surname *Drood* to be simply a startlingly abrupt conflation of *damned* and *rude*. Mildly diverting though such a spanking new reading may appear, it is simply not good Dickens. For, as a Victorian gentleman, the staunch Inimitable was clearly above such low-brow antics.

For the record, an earnest Dickensian, or Droo-id, who has observed the etymological "echo" of *rood* in the name *Drood* (along with the old standbys of *dread* and *Druid*) broached her views in print actually some time before I did: Jane Vogel so described the novel aptly enough as about the "Mystery of the (D)rood or Cross" (64). This constituted a reading that we happened to arrive at independently (no "mysticism" being in that), yet her own implied inference that Edwin's supposed death, like Jesus's, points actually to "a death not a death" may conflict, for some, with the so-called "survivalist" view of the last novel which is hard for many specialist readers to share. (Survivalists, as their name implies, believe that Drood did not die at all.)

Charles Forsyte, for instance, in his article "How did Drood Die?," gives an inspired "anti-survivalist" reading. In any event, that divergence hinges on disparate interpretations of the end point of a novel which Dickens was unable formally to complete; so, to restate the dilemma, the apparent dispute between Bleiler and me was virtually not one. We did not really, in essence, disagree—only went our somewhat different ways. For, in truth, how can one truly dissent over what simply does not exist to begin with? Although Forsyte has his circumstantial points, it still must be admitted that if the "survivalist" view can be demoted because of Dickens's professed intent, his initial meaning here is still susceptible to alteration, hence pointing to *final* as well as *original* forms of intentionality. Yet, in any case, Vogel's entire book, not her views of *Drood* alone, provide more than ample evidence that a veritable plethora of Christian overt meanings and connotations permeate Dickens's novels. Regrettably, her study has been given short shrift by some terse reviewers, but it warrants more attention, as is already implied in my chapter on "*Drood* the Obscure" (with its titular nod also to Hardy).

Some of the problems regarding Drood's fate involve our re-examining the supposed evidence concerning his death. It is well known, for example, that illustrator Luke Fildes had Jasper finally situated in what has come to be signified the "Condemned Cell." David Parker, in his "Drood Redux," assuming a "survivalist" position, feels that Drood is not to die at all, however, for various reasons. The most compelling factual evidence he offers is no more than one of the titles which Dickens perhaps "toyed with in notes" (187), namely *Edwin Drood in Hiding* (see his Appendix A, 218). Still, all really implied there is that his whereabouts are to be secret, not that he has to be truly alive in the biological sense.

In brief, numerous other clear pieces of proof exist to dispute a view of Drood's survival, as Parker also happens to point out, most notably Dickens's biographer John Forster's familiar statement: "The story I learnt . . . was to be that of the murder of a nephew by his uncle" (Parker 187, citing Forster 808). Granted, Parker does reveal a latent contradiction here in that Dickens likewise told Forster that the length and breadth of the story was not, in fact, a "communicable" idea; however, any such overall generalization need hardly refer *per se* to the question of whether he meant Drood to die. What is more, the novelist's well-known response to his son Charley about Drood's having to be murdered (notably then with the off-hand, give-away caption "of course") should not now be dismissed in a cavalier manner.

Parker's subtle suggestion that Dickens meant somehow to be evasive in this matter of Drood's fate is also open to some dispute. Then, too, Jasper's familiar long scarf that Fildes claimed the novelist said was meant to strangle Drood must be taken into account. Parker's adding that Fildes's claim was only "uttered thirty-five years" earlier than was reported, and so should scarcely be taken later as monumental, amounts to a relatively superficial disclaimer, in my estimation.

Then the notion that there could, in fact, have indeed been a murder in the offing—but not necessarily of the protagonist himself—involves only a lame conjecture. At the tail end of his study, Parker himself has finally to concede that it is plausible that "biographical evidence suggesting Edwin is dead" is definitely "right" (195). To state simply, then, that Dickens's death before he could finish the novel must mean that "we shall never know" avoids the notable facts designated, in technical terms, as a familiar enough *omen-nomen*: that is, the hint of a nomenclatural factor involved in the novel's basic literary hermeneutics.

The point again is that hidden *Christian* overtones could well indicate that

Drood was meant to return somehow and that he might have had to die first for this to occur. Such an argument tells against Parker's own haunting position that Drood finally does not die at all. But what stands out at the end is that Dickens himself is definitely on record for having been attuned to, and as having believed in, the ideal of the Christian Resurrection, which is a commonplace throughout Victorian prose.

Allied to the Droodian mystery is that of Neville Landless. Bleiler here arrived at the anomalous verdict that "the racial composition of the Landlesses is unclear, since the number notes do not indicate whether they are half-castes or simply dark English who have absorbed Indian ways" (92). Yet evidently Dickens wanted to have his readers believe that the Landlesses were *ethnically* rather more than Caucasian. Otherwise Edwin would scarcely have said so crisply to Neville: "You may know a black common fellow, or a black common boaster, when you see him (and no doubt you have a large acquaintance that way); but you are no judge of white men" ("*Edwin Drood*" 74). Such a passing slur was presumably directed at a member of another ethnic group, not merely at "dark English who have absorbed Indian ways." If the author had not meant it as such, would he not have been violating a basic principle of verisimilitude and incidentally thereby the reader's clear expectations? He was indeed ahead of his time in the extent to which he recognized the evils of racism, as his criticisms of attitudes toward blacks in his travels to America confirm (for which, see my "Dickens on Slavery"). Granted, he did later oppose Jamaican uprisings.

Bleiler, moreover, sets forth the view that if the Landless name indicates a loss of land or a sense of being dispatriated, no further evidence for such dispossession is extant in the novel. Yet Vogel has so cogently shown how the very first name of *Neville* also conveys this signification, which is obviously further proof: *Ne-ville* (no city or home town). She affirmed that brother and sister here symbolize in their surname the "land-less" as those being outside the Judeo-Christian pale: the dispossessed whom Christ will include among the Elect (or, as Dickens expressed it so nostalgically elsewhere, "God Bless Us, *Every One*! [italics added] ). In this respect the *Ne-* prefix may convey double connotations, an ironic enough twist (*new* or *neo* as well as *no*), Thus the final meaning of *Ne-ville* still may connote hope of a *new* city, say the biblical City of God, a New Heaven and Earth (eventually, let us posit, somehow through the intercession of the Reverend Crisparkle?).

Further, Bleiler's daring attempt to press for strong sexual innuendoes in the

names of Edwin's girl friend—*Rosebud* (i.e., Rosa Bud), but especially *Pussy*—
must be stalwartly resisted here. ("No Sex, Please," as the title of a drama not so
long ago reminds us, "We're British.") For him to insinuate that Dickens of all
people wanted such a definitely commonplace and pet name to become automatically "a slang term for the female genitals" is debatable, regardless of what in general the notorious Eric Partridge has already very loosely catalogued in his
*Shakespeare's Bawdy*. Hence *Rosebud* could suggest instead an undeveloped rose of
the world; *Rosamond* would imply "rose of the world." The Rosebud name should
also not be bandied about with that of Helena, who, as Bleiler and others have (perhaps improperly) inferred, was based on Dickens's sometimes presumed mistress,
Ellen Ternan. Incidentally, his bald implication that Helena disguises herself as the
male detective Datchery (89-90) is clearly now *passé*.[1] Among other things, it is
implausible that a lady already known so well in Cloisterham could walk about in
broad daylight disguised as a retired buffer and not be apprehended. Dickens, moreover, wrote W. H. Wills (30 June 1867) to the effect that he heartily disapproved of
the hackneyed device of "disguised women or the like" (Lehmann 360). The device
goes back at least as far as Shakespeare (one easily remembers the effect of Rosalind
in *As You Like It*), but that may be all the more reason why the novelist wanted to
steer away; it was an overdone implication. Further, Helena would scarcely be expected to possess Datchery's familiarity with the "old tavern way of keeping scores,"[2]
with which the novel abruptly ends. In short, is it not to confuse Drood with James
Bond, of all people, to overdo *Pussy* (as, say, Galore)? We *do* over-Drood that way.

Yet we need not insinuate that Dickens was essentially prudish, nor even
that Drood was. The commonplace that Rosebud's feline nickname was respectable
enough can be gleaned from such a recent collection as *My Darling Pussy*, Lloyd
George's letters to Frances Stevenson, edited by A. J. P. Taylor. This collection appeared much later than *Drood*, which is scarcely a deterrent because at that time the
questionable nickname *could* have seemed more acceptable. For would the eminent
Lloyd George have appropriated such a pet name for his beloved if he had seriously
entertained the notion that it conveyed the gross, and not merely sexual, innuendo
nowadays all too often associated with it? Scarcely so. For that matter, William
Randolph Hearst likewise dubbed his childhood darling "Pussy" without having
anything uncouth in mind (for which, see my essay "The Germination of 'Rosebud'
in *Citizen Kane*" 283; rpt in Ch. IV of my collection *A Rose by Another Name*).

Comparable, for that matter, is Harriet Beecher Stowe's allusion in *Uncle Tom's Cabin*: "'What do you think, Pussy?' said her father to Eva"—as duly cited in *OED* ("Pussy," sb. 3). In brief, the pet-like name derived from *pussycat* has been accepted often enough down through the years for a young female—especially when the nickname "Puss" commonly enough given a girl by her mother is any indication— although it is also one that she is naturally expected to want to outgrow. In point of fact, Edwin and Rosa are fully aware of this exigency when he promises that he will henceforth refrain from calling her by that pet name any more.[3]

## NOTES

[1]Among noted Dickensians who have recently stressed these points is Arthur J. Cox, editor of the Penguin edition of *The Mystery of Edwin Drood*, but see also Robson 1246, 1259.

[2]In his second installment, Bleiler argues *against* Helena's being Datchery, but gives no explanation for why he earlier thought she would be disguised (142, 89). He also curiously finds the name *Neville* to convey sinister meaning (141), but any connotation of *devil* could presumably be negated by the *Ne-* prefix.

[3]Cf. also my "Sherlock Holmes Confronts *Edwin Drood*."

## CHAPTER XV

## DICKENS'S *LITTLE TESTAMENT*: SPIRITUAL QUEST
## OR HUMANISTIC DOCUMENT?

With the Christmas season, we normally think of Dickens's Yuletide tales such as "A Christmas Carol," "The Chimes," or even "The Haunted Man." Ebenezer Scrooge has acquired a mythic resonance akin to that of a gruff Santa Claus (for, after all, the old miser *is* finally converted). Somehow the Christian and pagan meanings of the season play hand in hand in Dickens's works, notably the age-old association of the telling of ghost stories during this reverent time of the year. That commercialized symbol of heathen adoration, the Christmas tree, became apotheosized as a mythic image in Dickens's own little-read work on that subject. Few readers, however, may be aware that his ultimate Christmas story can be considered his retelling of the life of Christ. This leads to the question of its title. Although it has come down to us as *The Life of Our Lord*, there is no evidence that Dickens himself used that label, that he used a title at all. As the former Curator at the Dickens House Museum in London has written me, the MS. copy of it made by Georgina Hogarth for Mark Lemon's children has been place on indefinite loan in the Dickens House. Georgina evidently had neither a title to copy, nor any advice from Dickens. I am indebted to Dr. David Parker there for this information.

Of course since he composed this narrative strictly for his children, such a relative lack of scholarly awareness is not surprising, but the resurgence of interest in his writings these days warrants reconsideration, especially to see what title best fits the bill. My contention is that his gospel account should be accepted now as a work of *belles lettres* as well as a unique condensation of the history of the roots of Christianity. As such, it would have a bearing on other works of his, novels as well as tales, that have plausibly Christian themes. Thus, in *Hard Times*, he refers to "the gospel according to Slackbridge," and it may not be too condescending to label his own retelling of Christ's life *The Gospel According to Dickens*. (For more on this matter, see my note "The Title *The Life of Our Lord*: Does It Fit the Dickens Canon?")

To begin, recently several efforts to probe the Christian element in his works have met with hardly unilateral acclaim. The most current and ambitious attempt at the time of my original writing, Jane Vogel's *Allegory in Dickens*, a surprisingly low-keyed title for its subject and style, has been deplored by reviewers as an exercise in special pleading. Critics have castigated her for piling far-fetched Christian analogy upon further-reaching Christian analogy to "the point of self-cancellation of meaning" (Samuels 112), for being "quite mad" (Barfoot 566) (which may, though, be a tongue-in-cheek Dickensian compliment of sorts), and, most flagrantly, for being even "just around the righteous corner from fascism" (Hornback 54). Just for the record, it should be known that Professor Vogel is Jewish. True enough, danger may indeed lurk in our making, let us say, Procrustean Christian mangers out of literary works (if taste permits this analogy); in any case, I find much of such criticism of Christian interpretation intemperate. Let us see how now.

Vogel emphasizes two works in particular, the gospel story, posthumously entitled *The Life of Our Lord*, and *David Copperfield*. True, I reject the first title. Though obviously "Establishment-oriented," a title like that suggests a much more orthodox acceptance of Christian formulae than Dickens clearly approved of. It was chosen by the publisher after the novelist's death as a label which would appeal to most Christian, specifically Anglo-Catholic, readers. Since we have no evidence that he himself used the label, we might better dispense with it as uncharacteristic. Of the variant designations that have come down to us, the most modest of them, *The Little Testament*, is probably still the best. For if Dickens was not always a modest man in other respects, for example in his dress, he expressed a suitable sense of humility when he considered the Bible.

A leading question is: To what extent can the Dickensian gospel be accepted seriously as a literary Christian document? Since he did not try to have it published, he may not have thought of it as typical of either Christian teaching or his own work. On the other hand, he did allow it to be used not by his own children alone, but by those of his friend Mark Lemon, who was to become editor of *Punch*. It also was meant as more than a mere children's fable in that he concerned himself with retelling the life of Jesus in what he took to be commonsense terms. But that still leaves its spiritual import up in the air. He did not de-mythologize.

A principal task, in assessing the book, is determining whether it is, in effect, a Unitarian document, the label used for it by the novelist's chief biographer, Edgar Johnson, but which has come under assault notably by Noel C. Peyrouton, editor of *Dickens Studies*.[1] Because the Peyrouton criticism is basic to our coming to terms with *The Little Testament*, it is imperative to reconsider it in detail, for it is one of the few reasonably close readings of the work available. In addition, a study of *Dombey and Son* looks at that novel from a Unitarian perspective as well, notably because it was composed about the same time as the gospel story,[2] and Vogel takes the same approach to *Copperfield*, though deeming that a confessional autobiographical novel more orthodox than Unitarian because of its having been written in strict accompaniment with his reading of the Bible.[3] Such a conflict in verdicts underscores the problem of just how orthodox Dickens's ultimate Christmas story actually is.

Before approaching *The Little Testament* head on, let us revert temporarily to Drood, in which both Vogel and I have found Christian themes operative to some extent. She suggests in part that the mystery of what happened to Drood, whether he is finally alive or not, conjures up a Dickensian "Mystery . . . of Christ, the death not a death" (64). She calls him a "shy" Christian because he was not known as much of a churchgoer and has been dubbed a "closet Christian" (Samuels 113). That label is hardly disparaging in spite of the wordplay, for it suggests that he prayed in his closet and thus was truly conscience-bound in a manner which does not convey the possibly derogatory overtones that, say, "closet drama" suggests in implying one limited to the library rather than made for the theater, It is hardly blasphemous to suggest that he reinvested Christian symbolism with his own sense of creativity— far from it, such an attitude points to the Romantic concept of God as the eternal "Becoming," as found in *Faust*.

Now Edwin Drood is a kind of divine scapegoat, but one with a difference. The "druid" effect of his name emerges with the commonplace that English folklore linked mystery and ghost stories with the Yuletide season. But is Drood both druid-like and the kind of "Christ figure" that Vogel makes of him? Granted, she has a striking parallel in the case of Stephen Blackpool of *Hard Times*, though his stature has also been considered ambivalent. Yet Edwin is unlike Jesus in one dominant respect: he is a racist in his slurring remarks to Neville because of the dark skin of this visitor from Ceylon. This is true regardless of whether Neville is truly non-Caucasian or simply a Caucasian who adopted Ceylonese ways. How can a man with a lack of brotherly charity be construed as a symbol for Him whose whole life was based on love for His fellow man?

The "survivalists" claim that Drood will be physically "resurrected" (that is in the unfinished part of the novel) to separate the sheep from the goats, to reveal Jasper as the culprit, as the fiend who tried to do away with him presumably by having him covered with lime. Yet if Drood would return as a kind of vindictive spirit to take revenge on Jasper, he would rather fit the pattern of pagan revenge ghosts than the spirit of Christianity. So I submit that he represents a counterfeit analogy with the resurrected Christ, though with God all is possible.

But let us get more directly to Dickens's understanding of the New Testament as such; in so doing, Peyrouton's commentary needs close attention. It was he, after all, who is to be credited with having described the novelist's account of Jesus's life as "The Gospel According to Dickens" as well as his "ultimate Christian book" (103,112). Helpfully he provides the other "official" designations as well: *The Children's New Testament*, *The Little History of the New Testament*, and, best of all, *The Little Testament* (102-3). The copy bestowed on Mark Lemon's children bore this long-winded heading: *The Children's New Testament, An Abstract of the Narrative of the Four Gospels for the Use of Juvenile Readers* (104). This is scarcely accurate since the work "abstracts" also from the *Acts* of the Apostles.

Peyrouton's main, commendable purpose was to rehabilitate Dickens's gospel story, to point out that it amounted to more than a mere potpourri of Unitarian ideas or was a sentimentalized cutting of the Bible. He felt that it had to be itself resurrected from the impression of eccentricity, that it was fundamentally orthodox. His point was that the novelist's form of Christianity was to be taken simply as refreshingly undoctrinaire, not as essentially innovative. But he went too far in his zeal. It is not without some trepidation that I elect now to debunk some of his points, ones which are off-target. His heart was surely in the right place, as much as Dickens's own was, but it would be a critical disaster if his article were to be considered as the definitive study of the novelist's Christianity. At best, Peyrouton's work represents a prolegomenon only.

For example, let us return to the subject of nomenclature, since even Adam began with naming things, and see what Peyrouton comes up with. He asserts that Dickens "never" called the protagonist of his gospel anything other than "Jesus Christ" (106), thus in full regalia. But this is formalistic nonsense. It may sound official in a Victorian kind of way, but it represents an idiosyncratic formality which is itself eccentric. Let me digress for a moment to such an analogy in onomastics. I recall asking a fervent Dickensian during the Dickens Year in England (1970) whether he ever heard the Inimitable referred to as "Charley." His response was similar to Peyrouton's: "Never." But Sinclair Lewis, who was vastly indebted to Dickens (may even be called the American Dickens, to avoid the racism sometimes associated with Mark Twain), did not hesitate using the diminutive. So, regardless of whether the full appellation, Jesus Christ, sounds like an echo of the full name Charles Dickens, or whether the double name has a stalwart Dickensian "flavor" to it, the fact is that Dickens, in *The Little Testament*, also called his hero simply Christ and Jesus. Reverent it may be to give Him both names at once, but I suspect Peyrouton was carried away with the charm of his rhetorical flourish.

On the other hand, Dickens also liked to use the full phrase "Jesus Christ" upon occasion, perhaps even preferred it. Peyrouton does not examine the rationale. A possible explanation is that Dickens knew that Christ, the name, meant "the anointed one," the Messiah, and that Jews have traditionally believed that their Messiah would be a worldly leader—not thereby a scapegoat or martyr. Hence for Dickens to refer to Jesus as Christ only would have seemed unfair to Jewish folk, even as for him to refer to the Savior as Jesus alone would have seemed wrong to true Christian believers. So the happy compromise he hit upon was the initial use of the full term. Such a compromise is, of course, essentially not a compromise at all, but a rationalization, yet at least if it is nonsense it is Dickens's this time and not Peyrouton's. It becomes a parody of psychology trying to overtake theology.

Another aspect of nomenclature in the Dickensian gospel can hardly be ignored: *The Little Testament* has come in for Jewish criticism as being anti-Semitic largely because of the use of the generic term "the Jews," thereby ostensibly giving the impression to innocent little children that the Jewish people *en masse* were killers of Our Lord. When we recollect the furor generated by his description of the monetary Fagin in *Oliver Twist*, such criticism ought not to be shrugged off. Yet it unduly ruffled Peyrouton's critical feathers. For instance, in alluding in passing to Dickens's *A Child's History of England*, he felt compelled to state that we ought to bear duly in mind that, after all, *The Little Testament* was hardly intended, in turn, as Dickens's *A Child's History of Israel*! Possibly so, we might add, but the Dickensian gospel is not without some Pentecostalist leanings, and one aspect of even such belief has been that Jewish people will now be permanently reinstated in Israel.

Evidently enough, Dickens felt that he had the privilege to make use of certain conventionalized Christian expressions. Hence he felt no qualms in employing the cant phrase "the Jews" but without deliberate generic intent. At least he had no religious meaning in mind. For we know that when he was accused of calling his villainous Fagin Jewish, he responded that, to him, "Jew" had a racial and not a religious significance—an unfortunate disclaimer in the light of what has happened in the next century, but Dickens himself can scarcely be blamed, because he did not know any Jews. His attempt to vindicate himself by creating a good, if sentimentalized, Jew called Riah in *Our Mutual Friend* has been judged not entirely satisfactory. In any event, since he did not revise *The Little Testament* for popular consumption—as he did *Oliver Twist*, deleting the epithet "the Jew"—he ought not to be charged with misrepresentation. Had he effected a revision, he most probably would likewise have changed the allusion to the idea that all or only "the Jews" were responsible for the Savior's death, so that not only would Jewish readers not be adversely affected, but readers in general would not be contaminated with a misleading expression.

Another problem is that of oversimplification. Since the title indicated he was writing for his children, he naturally saw fit to make the gospel message easier to understand; so he omitted mention of technical theological expressions too complex for their ears. Peyrouton points out this tendency well enough. Dickens had ulterior motives also, since he was a staunch believer in St. Paul's doctrine that "the spirit" takes precedence over "the letter." In this respect, he definitely was more a follower of the New Testament than of the Old, more of a bona-fide Christian than many would-be ones. He studiously avoided reference to the Holy Ghost, *per se*, because he found the abstract concept of the Trinity not only too difficult for his children, but unbiblical. Such revisionism need not imply Unitarianism as such, for he had a precedent in another famous writer's dismissal of Trinitarianism: John Milton. As a Puritan, Milton may be considered a heretic, by some orthodox believers, but hardly Unitarian. Dickens followed suit, the end of *Great Expectations* following the ending of *Paradise Lost*, as is well known.

Perhaps more difficult is the problem of why Dickens avoided referring to Christ's title directly as the Son of God. True, he did attend some Unitarian services for a short while. Comparison of Milton's so-called "Arianism" is also germane. Yet I should like to propose only that Dickens did not want to confuse his children. The point is that Christ is referred to in the Bible likewise as "the Son of Man." In ambivalent terms, Dickens allowed for God's loving Christ " *as* his own son" (107).[4] Peyrouton, however, makes too much of this ambivalence. For the use of "as" hardly rules out the hint that the Father loved Jesus because the latter was God's only begotten Son. Certainly it is perfectly possible that Dickens meant that Jesus, like all men, was made in God's image and was thus "as his own son" in that sense. But one meaning need not rule out the other.

Dickens does describe the descent of the dove upon Jesus, and he may well have felt that the phrase "my beloved Son" uttered by the Lord identified Christ with God's Son. Peyrouton thinks so. On the other hand, it is possible to interpret "Son" simply metaphorically. It is a commonplace that the phrase "son of God" had other theological meanings, one being the traditional expression for an angel (as in the Book of Enoch). In this connection, it is worth pondering that Dickens felt no hesitancy in his gospel in describing little children as becoming angels in heaven when they die—in itself scarcely a theologically "correct" belief, but one rampant enough in folk tradition (as even in the Catholic tradition whereby an "Angel Mass" is said for a child which passes away).

He did not worry his children with the dogma of Mary's being virginal and referred to her as one of The Holy Family only. Although Peyrouton finds this omission unorthodox, it need not be. For Dickens did not apodeictically state, after all, that she was not a virgin. Interestingly enough, *The New English Bible* and some other modern exegetical tracts (including a letter I recall to the editor of the *TLS* by T. S. Eliot, but one which I cannot trace now) point to the possible confusion of the Hebrew for *maid* with the word for *virgin*, but that issue is after the fact and beside the point: The traditional Christian view has always been that Mary is to be honored not because of virginity but because she was the mother of Christ. Dickens was thus orthodox enough, especially if he remembered that the standard *Ave Maria* happens not to contain any mention of virginity.

What was his attitude toward formal Christianity in terms of the Church? Here Peyrouton lapses by condescendingly alluding to "all this stuff about the true church" which he contends would never have entered the Dickens head, nor his children's. But let us seriously reconsider the designation "one true church": It can mean "unified true church" (and not just in the Unitarian sense) and not merely "only true church." A truly unified church—this is, true, in a sense, because it is finally unified—would also be opposed to rampant sectarianism. Dickens surely was that. We easily recall that one of the more disconcerting aspects of Coketown in *Hard Times* is that it has no fewer than eighteen religious denominations, in effect all vying with one another—a veritable religious bureaucracy.

Is it going too far to suggest that Dickens intuited a modern understanding of ecumenism? Perhaps so, but more to the point is that he was following Christ's own injunction that His bona-fide disciple is bound to follow the lead of a child-like, not childish, faith. He scarcely meant to justify simple-mindedness as a basis for belief in God, to claim that the biblical bidding "Except ye . . . become as little children, ye shall not enter into the kingdom of heaven" (Matthew 18:3) meant that adults should regress. Still, he deserves due credit for taking that statement literally enough to believe that an adult could not be truly like an infant without knowing, say, how to write for one. More than a testament for his children, then, the aptly entitled *Little Testament* represented a confessional statement of his own. Aesthetically and morally, it deserves comparison with the work of others who have followed his child-like lead in their own charming ways, notably Dylan Thomas in his memorable "Child's Christmas in Wales."

Another critic who has broached the subject of Dickens and religion was Theodore Maynard, who published a provocative piece in a Jesuit periodical entitled "The Catholicism of Dickens." Evidently using Dickensian wordplay in his own manner, thereby alluding to *catholic* in the sense of *universal*, Maynard then made a leap from the mental to the extra-mental order, choosing to find the novelist Roman Catholic *in spirit*. His account of Dickens's dream about a lady in blue is presented almost as if it was meant to recall for us Bishop Fulton Sheen's familiar saying "lovely lady dressed in blue, teach us how to pray." This apparent vision was reported by the novelist in a letter to his biographer Forster,[5] can be recapitulated as follows: While traveling in Italy, Dickens dreamt of a blue-clad lady whom he identified with someone called Mary. So far so good. He asked her what the true religion was. (If he had asked about the one true church, that would have been a different matter.) When she was hesitant to respond, he plied her with a further query: "Do you think as I do, that the form of religion does not so greatly matter, if we try to do good?" Such a question might even have been asked by a devout Anglican intent on avoiding "formalism" in church worship. Still receiving no response, he put a further question to her, that of whether Catholicism was not the best in that it made one think of God more often and more steadfastly. Mary replied, in true Dickensian fashion it might be added, "For *you*, it is the best." (Maynard casually omitted the italic print.)

Now what would such a dream tell us of Dickens's own faith? It might mean that his conscience bothered him about being, in imagination and in deed, something of a rascal. (He certainly invented some of the most lovable rapscallions in English fiction.) Mary's response was abrupt, the kind that might be made to a naughty child in a Dickens novel, one who asks too many silly questions. So I find the dream itself a creative experience—vintage Dickens. But the dreamer himself was deeply moved by what happened. Characteristically, he identified Mary first as Mary Hogarth, who had died some year before in his arms and would presumably be in heaven. Then his travel through a Catholic country came to mind and made him reflect on whether Mary might not stand for Jesus's mother. Afterwards he questioned the nature of such a "vision."

Maynard, however, pulls out all the stops. He notes that the novelist took what might be called a pro-Catholic position when he wrote of the Gordon Riots in *Barnaby Rudge*—quite ignoring Dickens's criticism of Catholic mores in *Pictures from Italy* and the *Child's History of England*. But Dickens was simply against any oppression of people in general, whether by Catholic or Protestant or non-Christian. Mary's response is actually amusing in a Dickensian sort of way because instead of asserting that the Catholic Church is the true religion regardless of the individual conscience, she affirms that it is best only in terms of the dreamer and, in effect, his conscience. In other words, she is allowing for a Protestant conscience's acceptance of what was Catholic. Such an approach may be acceptable to some Protestants but would hardly represent orthodox Roman Catholic teaching. Certainly Dickens opposed rigid religious dogma. His biographer Forster reports that when Dickens was editor of *Household Words*, he saw fit to publish a story of the nefarious misdeeds of a certain Father Rocco. In itself, such a publication would be considered no more anti-Catholic than, say, some of the so-called anti-clerical writings of Dante, Boccaccio, or Chaucer; it is a sad faith which cannot afford some self-criticism. But the appearance of the story incensed Harriet Martineau, who said that she would no longer contribute to the journal. "The last thing I am likely to do," she pouted, "is to write for an anti-Catholic publication."[6] It seems that she may have gone overboard.

Still, Peyrouton dutifully reminds us that Dickens's only attractive clerical figures are Anglican: Rev. Frank Rilvey of *Our Mutual Friend* and Canon Septimus Crisparkle (whose name reflects his Pentecostalist nature) of *The Mystery of Edwin Drood*. Moreover, as is well enough known, Dickens was strongly resistant to papal control in impoverished countries, to which his letters especially attest. We may think again of Milton, who was also critical of the Roman church. But, in spirit, Dickens was no more anti-Catholic than he was anti-Jewish; he belonged to "one true church," which we may christen The Christian Church, and *The Little Testament* fitted the bill. Although in some respects he followed the stern hebraism of Carlyle, to whom *Hard Times* is dedicated, in his Christmas writings certainly (as the conversion of Scrooge intimates) he stressed the New Testament. As the *New York Times* reviewer of *The Little Testament* put it, "Never was Dickens so completely in earnest as when he filled these pages"[7]—evidence of spirit-filled authorship, if hardly the best literary acumen on the part of the reviewer. He compared the Dickensian gospel to "the mono-syllabic rhythms of the King James Bible"—under the circumstances a remarkable compliment. If anyone should be credited with revealing a style reflective of the Authorized Version, however, it might better be Dickens's friend Carlyle.

The novelist's rewriting of the gospel was influenced not only by the Bible, but by another biographical account, the *Life of Arnold* (father of the poet Matthew Arnold). Peyrouton does us a valuable service in making a point of this debt (109). For example, Dickens is on record for having stated to Forster, "Every sentence that you quote from is the text-book of my faith."[8] Taken literally, such a remark would put the *Life of Arnold* in fierce competition with *The Little Testament*, but actually the comment is ironic since Dr. Arnold saw fit to declare Dickens's work as child*ish* rather than truly child-*like*. Matthew's father was a stern headmaster and might be expected to have overdone his Victorian reaction to Dickens's ludic spirit. In the light of Dickens's acceptance of Arnoldian hellenism over Carlylean hebraism, at least in the gospel narrative, we might rather see the parallel as not so much with Dr.

Arnold's life as with that of his son.

That Dickens's concern for the poor and disadvantaged, as exhibited through-out his works, influenced his story of Jesus goes without saying, though the opposite can also be claimed: that his personal acceptance of Christ influenced his more creative writings. But the problem is where to draw the line. Would Sam Pickwick, the *naïf*, be a "wise fool" akin to Dostoevsky's Idiot? Surely his falling through the ice is resonant neither of the Crucifixion nor of Christ's descent to the netherworld (Dante's use of ice in the *Inferno*, it might be added, notwithstanding). Is Little Nell a female Christ figure, a Christ*ine* if you like? Her being sometimes coupled with Cordelia, a valid enough comparison from the point of view of William Macready's production of *King Lear*, is no excuse for taking her a step further and terming her a female Christ. Cordelia, incidentally, has been called a Mary figure as well as a Christ figure (as I heard it discussed at an MLA session in New York), but that would not make Nell one. She relates much more to fairy tale figures in nordic folklore.

As for Dickens's personal acceptance of Christ, much can be said. He is known for having opposed a formally Christian, in this case specifically Anglican, catechism being required reading in the English "Ragged Schools" because it was hard enough being ragged. Again *The Little Testament* comes incidentally to mind, especially the ending, where he stressed love as the very basis of Christianity. He appended several prayers, one of which specified that love of neighbors has a direct bearing upon love of God.

To what extent, however, was his gospel narrative authentic? He mainly followed the Lucan account of Christ's life. Why, rather than the first (Matthew), the most spirit-filled (John), or the earliest and hence perhaps most historically reliable (Mark)? The answer is easily forthcoming and wholly in keeping with common sense. He evidently appreciated Luke's account as the most chronological, thereby the most suitable for a biography, and also because Luke was a physician and so might be expected to have been the most factual. On the other hand, the effect of *The Little Testament* is of less interest in terms of facts than in terms of the spirit. If Pickwick is hardly a Holy Fool type, Dickens still interested himself in this concept in his own way. We may think of Sissy Jupe and the circus atmosphere of *Hard Times*. Or, better, we can call to mind how he edited the memoirs of Grimaldi the clown, who, in a delicate pre-Rouault-like manner, is comparable to Christ. If we relate Paul's characterization of Christ as Holy Fool (1 Corinthians 3:18, 4:10) to Dickens's Christ / Grimaldi concept, we have a basis for reconsidering the Holy Fool Motif as operative in his novels, notable even in characters like Barnaby Rudge or Mr. Dick of Copperfield.[9]

As a final caveat, let us say that *The Little Testament* in a modest way, as its title suggests, permits us to look at Dickens's work anew in terms of a heightened Christian sensibility, yet it should not be used uncritically. The humanistic element is quite strong in his writings, and the most fascinating aspect of his faith is that it plays in counterpoint with his aesthetic and social conscience.

## NOTES

[1]See his explicatory notes in *The Dickensian*. Edgar Johnson in his leading biography speaks of Dickens's "consistently Unitarian emphasis" here (Vol. II, Part 7, Ch. 1, p. 1).

[2]See Samuel Pickering's study of Dickens's so-called "Unitarian Period" in *The Georgia Review* but also his book on *The Moral Tradition in English Fiction*.

[3]Her Copperfieldean deductions are, at times, most illuminating, dealing with Old as well as New Testament "echoes." To me, however, the most exciting debt is to Shakespeare (see n5 below), a subject which she also broaches, though in a somewhat different manner. That connection was the subject of my NYU doctoral diss. See also Valerie Gager's recent follow-up.

[4]Peyrouton's reference is to *The Life of Our Lord: Written for His Children during the Years 1846 to 1849* (14). All references in this chapter to *The Little Testament* are to this edition, usually by way of Peyrouton.

[5]For a full account, see my *Dickens and Shakespeare* 13-14.

[6]Martineau's autobiography is given as cited in *The Dickensian* 75 (1979): 28-29.

[7]See P. W. Wilson's review (15 May 1931)—as cited by Peyrouton (107).

[8]Cited by Peyrouton (109) from Forster's *Life*, ed. J. W. T. Ley.

[9]Cf. Robert M. McCarron's article on Dickensian wise fools.

CHAPTER XVI

TESS OF THE D'URBERVILLES AND
GEORGE TURBERVILLE

Because the noted Hardy scholar Carl J. Weber has observed that Rebekah
Owen related her reading of *Tess of the d'Urbervilles* not only to the Dorset town of
Bere Regis but also to her discovery of "a 1570 edition of the *Poems* of George
Turberville,"[1] it is worthwhile to consider whether any connection between the names
can be documented. As a starter, we should note that the same edition of Turberville
poems is cited in the *Dictionary of National Biography* as being in the British Museum (the only copy there) and that Hardy had the *DNB* in his personal library (Cox
194). It seems reasonable that he would have looked up "Turberville, George" there
particularly because he knew of the mansion of the Turbervilles, demolished in 1832
(Kay-Robinson 82, 96-97), The last acknowledged members of that family had died
in the previous century. Because the Turberville name is unusual enough, might he
not have thought back a century even earlier in order to "echo" some traits of the
noted Renaissance student of Boccaccio when he wrote of *Tess*? If such a supposition appears on the surface to be a bit pedantic, it is not without its few points of
interest, as we shall see; because linguistic boundaries are crossed, the literary
comparatist should also be interested.

   To begin, in Chs. 34 and 52 Hardy by implication treats the name *d'Urberville*
as if it were originally a variant of *Turberville* (191, 324), or vice versa, which it was
(see again Kay-Robinson 82, 92-97). Further, *Tess* harks back nominally to the Re-

naissance in several respects, Roger Ascham being cited in Chapter 15, for example (86). George Turberville (?1540-?1610) wrote on sports, as did Ascham. (Whereas Ascham wrote one on archery, Turberville composed two books on hunting.) What is more, *Tess* is replete with both hunting and bird imagery, probably the dominant metaphors of the novel.[2] This association at least provides some circumstantial linkage, which would corroborate Hardy's comment that "the Jacobean and the Victorian ages were juxtaposed" (*Tess* 16). He was doubtless aware of the wordplay involved in *The Noble Art of Venerie* (the sport of Venus), the title of one of Turberville's treatises, and may have appropriated it in *Tess* subliminally.

Both Hardy and Turberville also took a strong interest in agrarian subjects and the use of dialect. At the same time they had frequent recourse to classical subjects. Hardy cites "Artemis, Demeter, and other fanciful names" (115) in Angel's reference to Tess, and Turberville models himself on Mantuan, Ovid, and Mancius. The most arresting phrase in the novel is probably at the very end, with its reference to "the President of the Immortals, in Aeschylean phrase," having "ended his sport with Tess" (354). Thematically, a Turbervillian phrase may even furnish a gloss for the novel: "A hatefull thing is Love (God wotte). . ." (Turberville sig. D1v). This adage, which comes from one of his pastoral translations, suggests the tension between love and hate so operative in Tess's story: it recalls oxymoronic treatment of these abstractions in *Romeo and Juliet*, also cited in the novel (189). The *DNB* makes the point that Turberville was found to be a "translator only of the passion of love," not of its spiritual side.

What is more, Turberville's use of the *Faust* tradition (that is, of Job) in his eclogues bears upon a thematic undercurrent in *Tess*: the theme of seduction in stark Mephistophelean terms. For example, when Tess first encounters Alec, he is smoking (30), suggesting hellfire. Shortly afterward he says to himself, in a casual oath, "I'm damned" (34). When Tess is violated, the narrator asks flatly, "But, might some say, where was Tess's guardian angel?" (63). A leading irony of the novel, and further evidence of Hardy's intense onomastic interest, is that her angel—Angel Clare—turns out to be anything but angelic, again suggesting the dangers of the Faustian alter ego.

Floral imagery interconnects as well. Turberville wrote of the fading of flowers and women ("beauty's buds like fading flowers do fall") (Craig 45), recalling for us the despoliation of Hardy's heroine. In the same context, much is made of "the cowslip in the midst of May" even as the novel tells of May Day festivities, of flower imagery to the extent that Tess's own mouth is compared with a "mobile peony" (8). Yet her darkening sun—a prime image—makes flowers wither. The tragedy of her story recollects Turberville's own interest in *Tragical Tales* of 1587.

According to Michael Millgate, Hardy "gave much attention to the naming of his characters and was particularly happy in the combination of the Norman-sounding d'Urberville, which also manages to suggest the urban origins of the *nouveau riche* family by whom the name has been appropriated, with the uncompromisingly rural and plebian Durbeyfield, which none the less sounds like an authentic 'corruption'" (284). True, but in telling how "the fictional d'Urbervilles had declined to Durbeyfields," Millgate also in the same breath cited "the historical Turbervilles" (294), though their own specific decline ("to Troublefields") is relevant only analogously. In any case, even as Tess's first name connotes her need to undergo a test or moral trial in maturing, so her appropriated last name harks back in part to that of George Turberville, whose own agrarian as well as amatory interests are reflected in the "-field" of her demoted maiden name.

In sum, Hardy's use of names bears looking into more, even as his Jude Fawley had the original, manuscript name of *Hopeson*, the ironic connection being that St. Jude is known as the patron saint of hopeless cases. Hardy even cited "Jude the saint" in correspondence about that novel (for which, see my essay "The Name *Jude*"). Further, the "T" and "e" of Tess's Christian name may derive from *Tryphena*, the double "s" from the beginning and end of *Sparks*. Awareness of Hardy's secret love for his cousin Tryphena Sparks is now a commonplace. The contrast of the religious and secular is not so surprising given his notable ironies. But there is also some room for a Renaissance Turberville, however incidentally. It fits his historical nature.[3]

NOTES

[1]See Weber 75, 79. Also Robert Gittings reveals numerous instances of Hardy's debt to the Renaissance period, notably to Shakespeare, e.g. *Othello, The Taming of the Shrew, Romeo and Juliet*, and *King Lear* (40, 60, 80, 84). Cox shows that, through the works of the Avon genius, the Renaissance is well represented in Hardy's library.

[2]Notable animal imagery is found on 44, 46, 48, 106, 244-47, 295, and 351. For critical treatment on

114

this subject, see Holloway 243. Hardy's animal imagery here probably owes something to Shakespeare as well. See Griesbach's diss. See also my "*Lear* and Polanski's *Tess*" (3, 7).

[3]This paper was originally presented, in somewhat different form, at a literature conference at Wright State University in 1985, then published in a first draft version in *Names* (1989).

# CHAPTER XVII

## "HYDE AND SEEK": THAT LONG VOWEL ALSO IN DR. JEKYLL'S NAME

"In the law of God there is no statute of limitations."
"If he be Mr. Hyde, I shall be Mr. Seek." —R. L. Stevenson,
*The Strange Case of Dr. Jekyll and Mr. Hyde*

Whereas it has become commonplace enough to categorize Robert Louis Stevenson's Gothic characterization of Dr. Jekyll and Mr. Hyde as a literal kind of "Case" study in the split personality, such pragmatic cubbyholing can be ultimately unsatisfying; hence a new, verbal approach may now be worth investigating. The once familiar, modish term *Doppelgänger*, as ultimately derivative of the mystery story writer E. T. A. Hoffmann, is also fairly vague to apply inasmuch as a technical distinction would thereby need to be made between schizophrenic and schizoid personalities, whereby symptoms only of the latter type can be seen prevailing in this novel. In a word, the two titular characters actually are separated from a single person, as it were, rather than simply subsisting side by side; in so being, they reveal more acute differences than similarities and hence would technically be schizoid, not split, personalities. In this connection, the long-held critical verdict that, at the tail end, Dr. Jekyll merely demolishes the Hyde within himself should be seen as all too elementary, thus hardly in full accord with the novelist's professed purpose, as we shall shortly observe. It is, finally, rather misleading to contend that the presumed variant signification, "Je-kyll," is relevant here, thereby supposedly representing in symbolic terms the French pronoun *je* ("I") combined with an archaic or, if one prefers, a stylized spelling of the English verb *kill*. In brief, for M. Miyoshi, for one, to affirm flatly that Dr. Jekyll turns out to be "the most thoroughgoing '*je*-killer' of them all" (473),[1] although a clever turn of phrase, ultimately is to pay scant homage, let us say, to such historical ego-downplayers as Samson and Socrates. More on this later. Evidently Miyoshi's view in the end is too simplistic.

Further, the presumed Anglo-French onomastic connection here is unconvincing on the whole not only because it represents ultimately a strained bilingual conjunction, but is one detracting from the novelist's own pointblank statement of intent regarding the correct pronunciation of the name he created. For he is on record for having specified that the physician's surname was meant to be enunciated with a long "e," thus not the clipped vowel sound as in French *je*. Speech therapists have for a long while, moreover, effectively established that a long "e" sound can be characteristically pleasant in tonal terms and so should be given its due here (though at the same time not overstressed). Stevenson's insistence on this long "e" may have been élitish too; it was made to a San Francisco reporter in 1888, as Furnas reveals (304), probably then not taking into due account the long, drawn-out "e" (namely the Scottish variant) sound, an effect which the reporter, in this context at least, would not so readily comprehend.[2] Nonetheless, Irving Saposnik has found the Stevenson insistence on this long vowel rather irritating insofar as "the mispronunciation of Jekyll's name" in our day and age has simply become "annoyingly persistent" (88). What is more, Stevenson happened to have insisted also on avoiding any French pronunciation even of his own middle name, *Louis* (Furnas 297)—any Francophilic effect thereby amounting to an affectation, as he saw it. In any event, because comparable enough is the familiar British pronunciation of the male name of Ēvelyn, clearly *Jēkyll* also can be acceptable.

Although such an authorial revelation about proper enunciation may momentarily perturb critics used to the present, popularized, more American sound of the name, such a matter of phonics turns out to be a "strange case" of Dr. Jekyll indeed, even as the sound effect can validly be thought of as affecting the story's overall meaning, What is more, Stevenson scarcely would have unconsciously allowed for a short vowel effect in the pronunciation (the "*je* kyll" thematic coincidence notwithstanding), even as what is audible represents at least something physical, hence objective on that score, thus not merely some psychological happenstance.

Thereby the correct version could be in conflict with what might be designated the "suicide" reading. According to standard theories about the origin of individual speech effects, termed *parole* (as distinct from the general concept of *langue*), as technically observed in Leonard Bloomfield's standard authoritative reference tool, *Language* (and then complemented by the well-recognized linguistics of De Saussure), sound has to take a certain immediate precedence over sense in human behavior. So evidently Stevenson had something rather diverse in mind in creating his Dr. Jekyll, was not merely providing a simple portmanteau label symbolically then to be linked with the "death urge" principle. In sum, he was playing his own word-game with the name.

Clearly if a supposed connotative, all-too-obvious interpretation like Miyoshi's *je*-kyll theory, turns out to be at definite odds with any professed oral intent of the novelist, it should be discountenanced. The only allowable exception might be if a psychoanalytic critic would prefer to ensconce the author himself on a couch, so to speak, a procedure which would traverse the bounds of ordinary literary criticism as such and, in any event, is inherently unpersuasive when the subject is deceased. Hence not the *je*-kill but the *Gee*-kyll formula becomes preferable. Such an apologia is, at any rate, of some import because any view which claims that the Stevenson novel is not truly in the main concerned with morbid self-slaughter is apt to elicit raised eyebrows from the start. Yet such is the provocative proposal of the present essay.

Given the corrected pronunciation now, we may still determine that the Stevenson game of "Hyde and Seek" is eminently playable, even with a certain critical impunity. For with the re-established long "e" effect in *Jekyll*, a hitherto unnoticed archetypal, even Jungian,[3] signification emerges: his presumed hidden affinity with no other than the sacrificial scapegoat image (as opposed then to the suicidal figure). On the surface, admittedly, to infer that the introductory syllable of the surname would obliquely connote that of, let us say, the Divine Scapegoat, namely *Je*sus, may appear to be remote, yet let us examine this very proposal.

As is commonly understood, the "Gee" sound can happen to represent, often enough, a popular-culture euphemism for (or a simple shortening of) the name of the Second Person in the Trinity (as so commonly evident in the abbreviation "Oh,

118

Gee!"). Comparable then would be the analogous "Joe" effect with William Faulkner's well-known fictional figure of Joe Christmas. For, at the very outset of his *Light in August*, we are duly apprised that if the inner light in Joe's name could be truly shed, we would be capable of predicting the moral (or religious) outcome of his story. With that popular analogy as a hint, comparatively speaking both Jesus and his earthly father, Joseph, would readily come to mind in this context. Consider this parallel: "Joe" links with "Christ-" (the full Faulknerian surname being *Christ-mas*) in being similar enough to a shortened, euphemistic form like "Gee," even as a modern, popular-culture, Christ-figure might easily enough be christened "Joe Christ." Lest such onomastics seems a far cry from what Stevenson meant or as seeming to be only "after the fact," recall now that the idea for his novel admittedly did occur to him, after all, in a nocturnal dream. Thus some kind of pre-conscious activity was perforce invoked.

Hence the secretive connotation of *Je*(sus) in *Je*(kyll) should readily alert the reader to the romanticized notion that the climactic destruction of the mythic Jekyll/Hyde syndrome was wont to evoke nothing less than a veritable Death-of-God archetype: in short, the seeming destruction of the divine element in man, through the self-sacrifice of the Savior, but then its eventual salvation. Should such a pro-vocative overtone seem a bit *outré* at the start for some traditionalist Christians, may they also be aware that the novel's very generic mode—that is, its being in the Gothic tradition—lends itself easily enough to such an archetypal proposal, a some-what medieval one at that. Let us consider how.

It appeals to the Gothic sense of the gargoylish, for instance, as found so often in the elevated romantic imagination. So, instead of inspecting some stereo-typed haunted castle or deserted mansion, the up-to-date modern literary sleuth ought to be capable of ransacking the inner recesses of his creative psyche for a fit method to discern the *mystique* inherent in Stevenson's mystery fable. Further, the very notion of the Gothic likewise has to convey its Christ-like overtones, deriving from the medieval period. Analogously, Umberto Eco's bestselling translated novel *The Name of the Rose* happens to deal with seemingly sacrilegious effects, notably with perverse goings-on in a medieval monastery, but then presumably for an ultimately moral purpose (that is, especially from the ethical perspective of the religiously faithful Adso, or Dr. Watson type, if not finally so much from that of the cynical or nihilistic William of Baskerville, a name also derivative of Edwardian fiction).

With such proposed symbolic name-play cautiously in mind, the curious Jekyll/Hyde duality can now be experienced in a novel light. "Originally written as a fable of Victorian anxieties," Saposnik claims, this novel "has been distorted into a myth of good-evil antithesis, a simplistic dichotomy rather than an imaginative exploration of social and moral dualism" (28). That is well taken, as far as it goes, but let us now reaffirm, in part at least, the age-old philosophic distinction between mind and body that has functioned throughout western man's cultural heritage, however distorted that dichotomy may appear to modern man. Sometimes called "Cartesian," the split more basically (thus biblically) recalls the celebrated Pauline "warfare 'twixt flesh and spirit," that time-honored caveat so dear to the hearts of the Victorians. By the same token the surname of Hyde connotes the need to sequester (or simply points to what is hidden), in short the gross, inchoate forces of Mother Nature before they have been brought securely under man's conscious, moral control. As one of Stevenson's most celebrated Victorian contemporaries, Alfred Lord Tennyson once notably inquired of his Age: "Are God and Nature then at strife, / That Nature lends such evil dreams?" (*In Memoriam* LV, 5-6). Hardly a mere rhetorical question, this, when one ponders the effects of evolution, especially on some religious mentalities.

His name likewise connoting the bestial animal *hide*, the good Dr. Jekyll's lively counterpart harks back to Nature but to its inchoate state, whereby this doctor would himself stand for the divine spark of the Creator in mankind. Thus, if the "dreaming up" of the character of Mr. Hyde by Dr. Jekyll had the final *effect* of evil (or, let us say, of a drug), at least the initial spark of creativity was Godlike, akin to Dr. Frankenstein's production of a new, half-human being. In showing how social respectability can serve as a convenient but perilous shield to disguise the inner reality of blatant self-contradiction, we can see that Stevenson's story invites the discerning reader to detect thereby *his own* latent Hyde slyly secreted within. For he, too, ought to be able to size up inner bestiality from its appearance—even as Dr. Jekyll should have medically discerned the telltale symptoms in the countenance of Mr. Hyde.

Failure to grasp the import of such a monstrous inner capability can lead to dire results like, say, adhering to the so-called "future shock" of totalitarian forces outside of man's conscious control. So, when Dr. Jekyll feels compelled to accept a sacrificial death to purge the Mr. Hyde within, his action represents, in effect, a modernized variation on the theological dogma that the Savior erstwhile conquered sin through a mode of self-destruction. Clearly such exegesis was not beyond the novelist's ken.

True, some hardened Stevensonians might like to object now, pointing to the net effect of the mystery as leading the protagonist rather to perdition, scarcely to eternal bliss with Jesus (albeit He too descended into hell first). But does that truly represent the Stevenson "Case"? After all, like other similar, romantic experiments, this *Strange Case* does have those implicit, open-ended Gothic qualities. Should it be debated whether to associate Christ's sublime act of atonement with apparent self-destruction represents an outrageous parallel, let us recall young Werther's similar self-immolation in Goethe's celebrated novel, one which also has been interpreted, at least of late, in terms of such romantic Christology, for Werther happened to be in love and at heart did mean well; his death thus represents a sort of apotheosis. That he may also have been overzealous is, in this context, beside the critical point.

Theologically, certain key issues arise that we can now cogently confront. For instance, in being one with the Father as the Son of God, Christ *could* have descended by Himself from the Cross—had that been His will—and not have suc-cumbed almost like a common criminal. By declining formally to resist, like Socrates, He was in effect electing what would later be designated the "Right to Die" protocol rather than openly having to fight miscreants, or having Himself slain by those who would decline to accept Him. It may be of some help here even to enlist the "Death of God" conception—not in the modern or atheistic sense to be sure (that being essentially a misinterpretation of Nietzsche's views),[4] but rather in terms of the pro-totypes as outlined in Frazer's *Golden Bough*, where the scapegoat is recognized anthropologically in folk tradition, notably apropos of the cult of Osiris in ancient Egypt. (On Frazer's himself happening to have been a keen reader of Stevenson, consult Crawford 169.) Granted, for the pedestrian churchgoer, self-immolation may not relate enough to what has been too often stereotyped as "The Comfortable Pew" to be accepted exactly with pious alacrity, but that does not leave it out of the picture for Stevenson.

His novel having been notably celebrated on its recent centenary, a leading article thereon in the London *Times Literary Supplement* by Richard Alter deserves some reappraisal now. It serves a useful purpose in analyzing various analogies to the novel, probing its psychological depths, and emphasizing its relevance to the current world. Among the literary analogies of interest uncovered are, as might be expected, Hoffmann's melodramatic "Die Doppelgänger," then Nabokov's *Lolita*, Poe's "William Wilson" story, but, most conspicuously, Hogg's *The Private Memoirs and Confessions of a Justified Sinner*. Of further archetypal value would be the biblical Cain and Abel story (to some extent also that of Jacob and Esau), which represents in effect a reversal of the Jekyll/Hyde syndrome insofar as the bad personality overcomes the good. For that matter also worth comparing, at least in passing, is the modernistic retelling of the Cain-Abel legend in Hermann Hesse's novel *Demian*, wherein a stronger man overcomes a weaker one (considered valid psychology before the advent of the Decalogue), Hesse having been himself an avowed Jungian, and his work, notably the more famous novel *Steppenwolf*, being certainly related to the Jekyll/Hyde mode.[5]

With regard to new thematic insights into the Stevenson novel as such, Alter writes that "Calvinism may reinforce the imagining of doubles and splits but it could hardly be their ultimate source" (1190). In other words, the effects of primal sin are indeed a basic consideration, yet only in certain respects, for seeing the novel likewise as a satire on puritan hypocrisy can hold its own as well. In any event, the New rather than the Old Covenant appears more pertinent here, hence the relevance of the *Christus* story. Part of the reason for this may be the very sexlessness of the Jekyll/Hyde description, which indirectly points not only to Christ's own bachelorhood, but to His apostle Paul's follow-up that "it is better to marry than to burn" (1 Cor. 7:9), here meaning "better not to marry, if possible."

The point is: Do we have any indication that Hyde represented at all a sex fanatic? To be sure, our first description of him is of his sadistically trampling on an innocent little girl, but even that atrocity does not make him out to be necessarily a Jack-the-Ripper, or even sexist, type,[6] for, as Alter has put it, Hyde's hidden inclinations were instead to eradicate "suppressed rage and frustration of the self." Reasonably Alter refuses to allow Victorian *prudeur* to take the blame for this. His most suggestive focus is then on imprisonment imagery in general and how that finally can relate to the Stevenson syndrome. Yet when he goes on to state that the climactic effect comes not with the expiration of Hyde himself, but with the bashing down of his door, thus elevating the image of incarceration over and above sacrifice, he goes rather far.

Yet does he also sometimes not go far enough? For example, in citing the

122

analogy of Poe's story "William Wilson," he finds the second self there "not satanic but, on the contrary, the embodiment of conscience." Perhaps that is right, though the same point can be made of Dr. Jekyll and Mr. Hyde in a valid sense: their split happens to be one also involving the conscience, which then resides only in the former rather than in the second self. Alter claims that at the end Dr. Jekyll, and thereby the novelist himself, foresaw the self as dividing into not merely two but numerous parts: "It is a moment of haunting prescience. Those multifarious denizens look forward to versions of the protean or serial self" (that is, in much of modern fiction). Still, such a viewpoint might look askance at pluralism in contemporary culture. Thus, lacking a spiritual or moral basis for his analysis, Alter resorts to a kind of critical showmanship which, although arresting enough, fails to convey a truly convincing final message.

In a more recent essay, Joyce Carol Oates provides touches of data on the novel not known to the common reader, such as in regard to Stevenson's own biographical connections with his work. But unhappily, like Alter, she neglects to come to terms with the fundamental religious message here, her vantage point being mainly only on the psychological, not at all the theological, level. So we might largely bypass her view. For the record, my own modestly meant submission was for the Stevenson centennial (namely that of the novel), happened to appear in a Doylean journal and involved Holmes, Dr. Watson, and none other than the Frankenstein monster again, then finally, as a sort of *deus ex machina*, Dr. Jekyll.[7] That pastiche concludes when the sick doctor (in contradistinction to John Watson as the sane one) discovers the Hyde counterpart warily secreted in, of all things, another alter ego, this time in Mary Shelley's monstrous creation come to life once more. The perspective relates the alter ego effect to a renewed understanding of Victor Frankenstein's monster, the old veteran sleuth Holmes then being called in to bridge the gap with his customary finesse. The verdict turns out to be that one monstrous evil actually can, in effect, cancel out another. The basic notion is that, with such a haunting thought, perhaps eventually the diseased alter-ego image itself may self-destruct. The Jekyll/Hyde effect turns out to be much more penetrating than, say, the seemingly analogous Jack-the-Ripper syndrome, based as the latter is only on isolated episodes in nineteenth-century British history. Saucy Jack does not vie with Jekyll/Hyde any more than a rascal can compete with modern sick society: they simply emerge as divergent manifestations of civil unrest.

Then a word should be put in for yet another exploration of the Jekyll/Hyde syndrome, an operatic production I chanced to witness on stage in Ithaca, New York.[8] This modernization of the novel was consciously based on the writings of Nietzsche, and Freud as well; it consisted of a series of *tableaux vivants*, including a very ritualistic scene in a make-shift church with celebrants ominously intoning the phrase "*dies irae, dies irae*." Whether such symbolism betokened a kind of Black Mass, as one reviewer in fact proposed,[9] or manifested instead the religious nature involved in the Jekyll/Hyde split itself, becomes a matter of dispute. In any event, as the reviewer sensitively then put it, "There is something of vital moment struggling to be born."

So let us no longer allow Jekyll and Hyde to degenerate into mere types. Stevenson's explicit key to enunciation alone—that long vowel sound effective in the physician's surname—duly informs us that he had in mind something far more individualistic, and perhaps even more anagogical, than can be recognized in a modern, psychological, stereotyped version. It is worth recalling here that his most familiar poem has been his "Requiem," a minor yet pious creation. Comparable also are allusions to "eternity" in his "Alcaics: to H. F. B.," which I found in the British Library. And, although his personal religious instincts were not especially formalized, they still ought not to be totally discountenanced. After all, he did once compose an essay on Monsignor Ronald Knox, and his letters to the Reverend Dr. Hyde (note that name again ) on the subject of the maligned Father Damien have been termed a remarkable defense of a flawed man (for which see Stevenson's *The Lantern Bearers and Other Essays*).

Curiously, Leslie A. Fiedler contends that perhaps the basic trouble was that "Stevenson, unlike his characters, did not really believe in Hell" (292). Then, with reference to Dr. Jekyll, Fiedler quotes Stevenson himself to this exclamatory effect: "He is bound upon my back to all eternity—to all God's eternity!" But this critic does not take into due account Protestant mysticism here, as in Jakob Boehme's conception (so apparent already in Blake, Coleridge, and other romantics) of evil as being the Dark Side of God. That Boehmean viewpoint does not obscure a basically Christian or optimistic message, even as it also may be closely tied to aspects of Hebraic mysticism.

Everyone who has thought long enough about the Jekyll/Hyde revelation can conclude that the book has lived well enough up to its title: above all else, it has turned out to be a strange case indeed. As if to enliven this very strangeness, Stevenson's little clue to pronunciation, the long "e" in *Jekyll*—in direct complementation, as it were, to the long "i" in *Hyde*—offers us the most fascinating piece of factual evidence there is in favor of a new and lasting (and not merely self-annihilating) interpretation. The symbolism behind the vowel clue provides added resonance both in sound and meaning, a sort that is fundamentally of Christian import, thus intoning for us even the name of *Je-sus* Himself. In short, what really "Hydes" in the novel is ironically then to be found in Dr. Jekyll's very nomenclature pronounced as Stevenson wanted it to be.[10] In recognizing this, we can find that his name-game, "Hyde and Seek," may be suitably replayed. For, by calling attention to the vowel effect also in Hyde's designation, as in the wordplay "If he be Mr. Hyde, I shall be Mr. Seek," Stevenson is making sure that the reader is cognizant also of the inner sound and meaning of the Doctor's vital surname, *Seek* rhyming with *Jēk*. Hence my own title.

NOTES

[1]The point is also made by Irving Saposnik; he traces the "je" theory back to Joseph J. Egan (30). Also Jean-Pierre Naugrette's onomastic approach is of interest.

[2]For criticism of this reading, see n10 below. In brief, it is too hypothetical, forced.

[3]Given the respective birth dates of Stevenson and Jung, this correlation is not merely universal but fits in with the intellectual history of their time period.

[4]The complexity of Nietzsche's *Gott ist tot* affirmation in his *Also Sprach Zarathustra* has been overlooked in terms of its context by those who impute the God-is-dead, amoral syndrome to him personally or find the philosopher (rather than his chauvinistic wife, Frau Förster-Nietzsche) a harbinger of the Nazi movement. The noted authority Erich Heller, in "The Importance of Nietzsche," wrote that this major thinker did not scorn Christ by any means, but instead only the saccharine counterfeit of Him too often evident in modern life. "'Caesar with the heart of Christ!' he once exclaimed in the secrecy of his notebook" (Heller 12). If such a link-up appears dubious (even though Will Durant has devoted an entire book to *Caesar and Christ*), we might still ponder its possible creative effect upon someone like G. B. Shaw, who then took over the Nietzschean superman ideal in his popular play *Man and Superman*.

[5]Again the distinction between the terms *schizophrenic* and *schizoid* becomes germane, on which see in particular E. Fuller Torrey, M.D. (158-61).

[6]Intriguingly, the centenary of the Stevenson novel was celebrated close to that of Jack the Ripper, not to mention the anniversary of Conan Doyle's *A Study in Scarlet*, which led to my pastiche (see n7 below).

[7]Emerging formally during the centennial of *A Study in Scarlet* (1987), the pastiche appeared in the inaugural issue of a Sherlockian journal. The connection between Stevenson's *Strange Case* and the Holmes stories has been made earlier (see Egan). Cf. the plausible influence of Stevenson on Conan Doyle in general and their most probably having met while in Edinburgh in that they were at the University together.

[8]This musical version was an adaptation by James Magruder and Lisa Peterson with music orchestrated and directed by Helen Gregory (The Hangar Theater, August 1989).

[9]Willmer 24.

[10]Pursuing the notion that Stevenson, by the long "e" sound, meant simply an extended enunciation of a short vowel is of little help. First, bringing in the Scottish pronunciation is neither here nor there, Jekyll's name not being particularly Scottish; second, any extension of the short vowel could introduce the connotation of "jackal," a predatory effect which Stevenson surely wished to avoid with the physician. The name of Hyde is also not Scottish; cf. Hyde Park in England.

## CHAPTER XVIII

## THE ONOMASTICS OF *SHERLOCK*

*The Sign of the Four* is replete with recondite allusions to the etymology and origin of Sherlock Holmes's name. A study in what is called the science of deduction (though concerned more scientifically with induction, now designated abduction), the first chapter starts off with a reference to Holmes's interest in "the most abstruse cryptogram," his "genius for minutiae," wordplay on the name *Sherlock* in various guises, and then ends with this curious statement of misdirection: "I have no recollection of the name." Although the name in question here is that of Mary Morstan, such a pronouncement after so many hints on onomastic matters have preceded it is indeed a puzzle. Let us consider the nomenclatural points now in detail.

The first clue to the name-play is found in the cryptogrammatic allusion; we are led to wonder whether Sherlock's own name may have had that meaning for Doyle, and some evidence exists to that effect; however, since onomastics is concerned not merely with the author's own intent but with what others have made of half-conscious reverberations, let us keep an open mind. The ultimate significance of *Sherlock Holmes* may well be more on the mythic level than anything else. However we formulate our quest, the fact that Conan Doyle himself claimed that he borrowed Sherlock's name from a player of a game, cricket, provides a precedent for the name-game itself. For did he not take his form of gamesmanship seriously?

Shortly we hear Sherlock's off-hand remark to Watson, "Ah, that is good luck." After a few short sentences, he speaks of a "shocking" habit. It is altogether clear that the connotations of *luck* and *shock* could have been combined at least in Doyle's unconscious to generate an association with *Sherlock*. Certainly they have done so, let us submit, for Sherlockians since then, for they have led to various pastiche (and parodic) names, notably *Sheerluck Jones*, considered a "refreshing and capital travesty of the Doyle / Gillette monodrama," *Sherlock Holmes*.[1] Independently, I came across another travesty with the sleuth designated *Sheerluck Holds*.[2] There might be many more. Indeed, at a Sherlockian conference I happened to co-direct, one of the participants automatically thought of "sheer luck" as a parodic form of *Sherlock*.[3] "The luck of the Irish," we might add, remembering that Doyle had his own Irish heritage. So let us keep the memory of his name also green.

As for *shock*, surely we must think of *Schlock Holmes*, the name of whom invites the verdict that much pastiche and parody, mostly the latter, has taken the form of *Schlock* (or *Kitsch*) art. The numerous examples in the fairly recent compendium *Sherlock Holmes in America* provide much evidence of this tendency. But of course the connotations of *schlock* would have been too late for Doyle himself. More relevant historically would be Jon L. Lellenberg's comment that too many publishers of take-offs today "seem to believe that a story must have some shock value or a gimmick to make it attractive to the masses."[4] Thus the connotations of *shock* too are built into Sherlock's name, at least for the uninitiated. The true reader of the Canon would see that the detective would have been much too reserved to ponder such a meaning in his own cognomen. Indeed, the very passage cited from *The Sign of the Four* containing the term "shocking" indicates as much. But it would appear that unconsciously Doyle anticipated what would happen with some modern trends.

One other connotation of the Sherlock name is deployed in the opening chapter: it is found in the paragraph about the key-hole. Although ostensibly about a lock made by a drunk (a rather far-fetched ploy, to modern sleuths), the very notion of a *lock* being brought up has its hidden implications again. For is Sherlock so called because of his ability to have criminals *lock*ed up? This assumption is hardly new with me (having been advanced, for example, already even by our late family handyman), though the transformation of *Sher-* into *sure* (for him to "sure lock" them up) seems more comical than cogent. Not to be forgotten is that the *-lock* suffix *could* also relate to a possible connection with the name of Shylock. For both Shakespeare's Jew and Sherlock were men of justice in their own right, even "shysters" to the extent that they take the law into their own hands at times to gain their ends.[5] Owen Dudley Edwards's book which emphasizes the Scottish background of Doyle, even to the extent of claiming that London settings in the stories had their antecedents in Edinburgh, makes an issue of *Sherlock* being the name of the dumbest boy in Doyle's class there.[6] Perhaps so, but a connection with the familiar Scottish word *loch* (as in watery "Loch Lomond") may also be present, just as easily. Compare the name Sherrin*ford*, Sherlock's original formal designation.

Edwards's views have been criticized in the *TLS* review on the grounds that Conan Doyle had other acknowledged sources for his names;[7] indeed there was a cricketplayer named Sherlock, and since the author was such a sportsman (having, for instance, introduced the sport of cross-country skiing even into Switzerland), such an etymology may appear more likely than a remembrance of such an old school chum. The argument, however, is that Doyle would scarcely have admitted getting the name of the brightest of detectives from a flunky, so to speak, even if he originally had a private joke in mind. That he would not have been against such an odd switch might be seen in his naming his arch-villain with an Irish surname (*Moriarty*) when he himself was of Irish descent. He simply was not that sensitive about his own heritage. For that matter, as has been pointed out, *Sherlock* may derive, in part, from Sherlockstown in Ireland.[8] See also D. Redmond.

Steve Lauria has summed up the etymological studies on "The Name Sherlock" by pointing to Baring-Gould's belief that the Master Detective Story writer's father "insisted that the boy should be named William Sherlock, for [he] had long been an admirer of that seventeenth-century theologian and author";[9] Lauria himself, however, favored an association with the shearing of locks of hair. Citing the Old English derivation (*scortlog* meaning short hair), he noted that Maundy Thursday was traditionally known for the "custom of shearing or shaving the beard" and deduces from this connection that Holmes was born on that day, though the exact day has now been disputed.[10] Surely we have no urgency in believing that the origin of the name related to the day on which he was born.

Is there anything new that can now be added? I should like to pose several ideas, which may have occurred to others but not in any of the material I have come across. The first is that even as Holmes refers to the "most abstruse cryptogram," so his first name can be understood that way, but not in terms of Doyle's intent. (Cryptograms are cryptograms, it is said, regardless of intent.) The puzzle could here take the form of an anagram. If so, a simple transposition of the first letter to the end tells us that Sherlock was named after his mother's esteem for his curly hair; hence it meant "her locks." From a Freudian point of view, such a reading would hold, since a basic insight of the founder of psychoanalysis was that a child is attracted from infancy to the opposite sex especially. (Shades of *The Seven Per Cent Solution*?) That would perhaps explain why the adult Sherlock then had so little to do with other women. Although he called Irene Adler "*the* woman," the real woman in his life was the one who gave birth to him. If this view seems a bit remote, it is at least no more so than many other such source studies, and it is a truism that unconscious emotions and their rationale are different indeed from common sense. Elsewhere[11] I have studied the origin of the related name *Shylock* and have concluded that it too was a "homesy" word, having an English rather than a Hebrew origin, possibly one relating to the recusant Richard Shacklock (since Catholic recusants compared their plight to that of Jews). It is, in fact, more likely that Doyle would have heard of the recusant's name than that Shakespeare would have, so I would not totally rule out a Shylock-Shacklock-Sherlock correlation, thus a "combination lock." But, in any event, when a man's last name already connoted home territory (as with *Holmes*), we have all the more reason to suspect that his first name did too.[12]

Last, but certainly not least, mention should again be made of Donald A. Redmond's learned study "On the Name of Sherlock." This extensive treatment of the name in terms of historical etymology (e.g., as plausibly deriving from Cheshire as well as elsewhere) is too complex to consider further here; granted much is still guess work.[13] In any case, if *Sherlock* connotes a "sure" thing (that is, *sure* with a Scottish burr), then *Watson* by the same first syllable token connotes the everlasting questioner, the stooge, the man who does not know, namely "What?" Yet now I am trying to be psycholinguistic. Instead of "Is it Hoyle?" in any case, let us ask now "Is it Doyle?"

## NOTES

[1]See Stanley MacKenzie's review of M. Watson and E. La Serre's *Sheerluck Jones* in *Baker Street Miscellanea*.

[2]I have disclosed the source of this tidbit in my critical essay "Sheerluck Holds Out? A Piece of Promiscuous Parody" in *The Baker Street Dispatch*.

[3]The original "Homing in on Holmes" symposium was held at Central State and Wright State Universities (November, 1981). The commentator here was Charles Dean (Central SU).

[4]See Jon L. Lellenberg's "Sherlock Holmes in Parody and Pastiche, Part II: 1930-1981" (32). He also discusses on this page Robert L. Fish's parodies about Schlock Homes of Bagel Street.

[5]I discussed this view in my paper "*The* Woman is only *the* Woman, But a Well-Stacked Calabash is a Smoke." This was graciously accepted by a feminist Sherlockian journal.

[6]*The Quest for Sherlock Holmes* 116. For some reason this proposed etymology strongly appeals to my students. Donald A. Redmond, in his book, cites Doyle's own modest claim that he got Sherlock's name from a bowler ("L'Envoi" 303). The London *Times*, in the review of Edwards's work by Julian Symons, cited Fiedler's view that *Sherlock* was a "grafting of Doyle's original [Sherrinford] and a sudden 'emergence in his undermind of the Jew Shylock,'" to my recollection, but I no longer have access to it.

[7]Patricia Craig, in her review of Edwards in the *TLS*, calls Edwards's book "a fairly eccentric pursuit": "Even Agatha Christie's Poirot never sparked off this obsessive ferreting on the part of his admirers." But some scholars may simply" be anti-onomastic. What she appears to overlook (deliberately or not) is that such obsession with minutiae is simply typical of Holmes's own methods.

[8]The point was raised in Philip Gerber's "Namen als Symbol" in *Neue Rundschau* (1972), which I have translated in *The Armchair Detective*. Gerber also went extensively into the Sherlock-Shylock connection, as has Leslie Fiedler. I was informed that his article also then appeared in *Das Grosse Sherlock Holmes Buch*, which I have not come across.

[9]See "On the Birthday of Sherlock Holmes," which was originally read at "Holming in on Homes" (see n3 above).

[10]See Raymond L. Holly's response to Lauria.

[11]See Ch. 1. The view that Shylock's name came from the Hebrew (for *cormorant*) is not cogent.

[12]It so happens that an exact anagram of the name *Sherlock* is *Schlocker* (if we double the "c" as Shakespeare doubled the "n" in relating his *Caliban* to *cannibal*), but such a neologism may best be relegated to an endnote. More germanely, Gerber finds Holmes suggesting the British term for a small island, *holm* (which may then relate geographically to *loch* or *ford* suggestions in *Sherlock* and *Sherrinford*). Curiously, J. M. Gibson in a paper called "Shacklock to Sherlock" in *The Sherlock Holmes Journal* (Vol. 14) enlists a cricket player called Shacklock again! But may not Doyle have become acquainted with the initial controversy over the etymology of *Shylock* in *The Gentleman's Magazine* and *Notes and Queries*? This is too much to go into detail on here.

[13]Worth finally considering in passing is Christopher Roden's "What's in a Name? The Genesis of Sherlock." He sees the origin in Gaboriau's *Monsieur Lecoq*: "All that he had to do was drop the first syllable and anglicize the remainder. It is a simple step from *Sher-le-cock* to Sherlock and a fitting tribute to one whose style he admired" (37). That is ingenious. (This comment is also to appear to my article, forthcoming at the time of writing, in *The Sherlock Holmes Journal* entitled "What is in Sherlock's Name Again?")

# CHAPTER XIX

## POE'S C. AUGUSTE DUPIN AND SHERLOCK HOLMES'S INITIAL

I

Following the lead of the well-known British Holmesian Roger Johnson and a letter of his in *The Sherlock Holmes Journal* (Summer 1987), I have come out with a paper arguing that Conan Doyle originally had intended Holmes's first initial to be "I." (not "S.").[1] This paper was based on his working notes for *A Study in Scarlet*, easily accessible, which contain the phrase "with I Sherrinford Holmes." Johnson had argued in his correspondence that the initial "I" here may have stood for one of Doyle's original first names which he also then dropped, *Ignatius*, and I followed suit. The editor of *SHJ* responded to him, and the matter came up concerning whether first initials were always followed by an end-stop, as was plausibly not the case here; in my follow-up paper I provided evidence that many English names dropped this punctuation. I can now provide further proof. For example, I have seen original letters by Conan Doyle signed "A Conan Doyle" (no end-stop after the initial). The use of a period was often rather after the complete name. What is more, it is scarcely necessary to go to primary source material in manuscript when the standard American edition of the Christopher Morley *Complete Sherlock Holmes* provides a facsimile (in fact four of them) right inside front and back covers.

Because this note of mine was somewhat controversial perhaps, a bit more introductory material is now warranted. For I happened to announce this "finding" to a reporter from the nearby *Dayton Daily News*, who thereafter headlined the matter in the "Metro" section as follows: "CSU prof unravels mystery of Holmes' original name" (20 March 1988). Because I happened to be interviewed on this during the annual Dayton area Conan Doyle conference, the director called me up afterwards and wanted an explanation. The point was that I had not talked about this at the main symposium itself, having indulged, in my official presentation, in deploying an original Sherlockian pastiche I had then devised (a penchant of mine at the time). The prudential director's qualms made me call up the editor of *Baker Street Miscellanea*, which had accepted my paper, whereupon the decision was made definitely not to withdraw it.

Why all this fuss? The reporter's story, which dealt with other aspects of the annual event (including whether Holmes believed in God, which also was not a topic *per se* at the conference but which tied in with the "Ignatius" identification, given Conan Doyle's Jesuitical training), was evidently written somewhat tongue-in-cheek; at least I heard it was taken as such. Second, one of my chief arguments was found rather controversial, namely that the "I" was justified as an *initial* rather than as the capitalized personal pronoun because it was preceded by the preposition *with*. The point was that the preposition happened to appear *just above* the preceding line, and the author evidently need not have been sticking to the niceties of syntax, but was putting down random thoughts and phrases as they occurred to him. Later in the notes, on the same page, the personal pronoun is obviously used, so why not also then at the outset? The fact that the sudden "I" there is preceded by a slight slash is neither here nor there. Indeed, the editor of *The Sherlock Holmes Journal*, when I met him in his Oxford residence, argued that my point about the lack of a comma after the "I" could easily be discountenanced by the argument that no quotation marks preceded it as well. Yet, what is more, it would be curious if the stress was on Sherlock as the "I" when Watson is the one who does the tale-telling in the first person.

Now before the essay was printed, I discussed the matter in brief with the editor of *The Baker Street Journal*, in St. Louis, and he concurred that the reading that I suggested was definitely possible. Moreover, Roger Johnson himself, in a published letter to the editor of the *Miscellanea* there,[2] stood up for his original position, though he preferred now the "I" to stand for "Innes" rather than "Ignatius," basing himself on the purported influence of Conan Doyle's younger brother with that first name. Apparently "Ignatius" had too Jesuitical a ring for Johnson in this context, though he admitted in his letter to the American editor that it was still a dignified one. (For the record, I might state here that the noted British Sherlockian Geoffrey Stavert had previously suggested "Innes" to me rather than "Ignatius" as well, notably in Portsmouth, Southsea.)

Lively correspondence ensued, though no more was officially published to my knowledge. Even Dame Jean Conan Doyle, the author's kin, entered the fray, standing up for the editor of the journal of The Sherlock Holmes Society of London, as might be expected, by writing me a gracious note which was waiting for me then in my London hotel. A Jesuit from Marquette wrote me an amusing letter. I received courteous correspondence from the offices of the Society in London, from Mrs. Pam Bruxner, whose only possibly relevant comment was in her postscript ("please, *not* Ms., which I consider an abomination!"). The editor of *The Journal of the American Name Society* wrote me (3 June 1988) that he would try "to squeeze a few lines about this" in the next issue. And so it went. The last I heard, during my visit with British Holmesians in London in August 1990 to celebrate *The Sign of the Four* at a good restaurant, was that my effort was taken as acceptably "lighthearted."

What now can be added to support or detract from my proposed radical thesis? First, apologies must be made for the horrible misprint for "Sherrinford," namely "Sheringord" on p. 13. That hardly got by as an ironic comment on my entire enterprise unless Loki was at work. Second, the point must be made that I never asserted that the contextual, grammatical interplay of "I" *ruled out* the effect of a personal pronoun perhaps, for in fact *both* meanings could be present in the manuscript, which after all has the effect of a Rorschach test; the creative mind is capable of all kinds of inchoate conceptions at this stage, including ferally conflated ones. In other words, Conan Doyle may have primarily meant the "I" to stand for the personal pronoun but, in some Gestaltist manner, saw it as possibly standing for a presumed first initial as well. Later he may have ruled out the second possibility but certainly not until he had at least completed the page.

II

Now in support of this argument, let us consider that he might have been influenced in this respect by the name of another prime literary detective, *C. Auguste Dupin*. Because of the generally acknowledged overall debt of the Holmes stories to Poe's earlier character, such an influence ought not to be entirely ruled out. Clearly such a formulation of the prior detective's name was not French—at any rate in the usual sense. In the same manner, the use of the "initial initial," so to speak, is certainly more American anyway than European. How then did Dupin's own name originate?

A very ingenious solution for part of this at least has fairly recently been put forward as well. In their article "The Reader as Poe's Ultimate Dupe in 'The Purloined Letter,'" Hal Blythe and Charlie Sweet have proposed that *Dupin* stood for no less than *duping*, with the final "g" left out in what might be called the Southern manner (hence *dupin'*), that omission constituting, outrageously in effect, that of the *real* "purloined" letter! The story, in other words, turned out to be a clever hoax of Poe's with the reader being the expected dupe. This could be. In a curious misprint, their learned article also makes reference to the *Collected Worls of Edgar Allan Poe* (hinting at *Whorls* as well as *Works*?) (314n), so all things may seem possible.

Further etymological suggestiveness has come to the fore. In his chapter "Capitalising on Poe's Detective" in *Nineteenth-Century Suspense: From Poe to Conan Doyle*, Clive Bloom has offered several additional onomastic ramifications of the name *C. Auguste Dupin*. For example, in stressing how the detective-aristocrat was then "reflected in the theology of a certain figure to whom the aristocrat of medieval lore is joined: that is, *the priest*," he showed how such an individual appeared "to be without visible means of support, therefore perhaps immoral," suggesting "C. Auguste Dupin a singular CAD!" (20). In my earlier *Baker Street Miscellanea* article, I had likewise likened the plausible "Ignatian" element in Holmes to his also having some plausibly priest-like characteristics, to which might now even be added that, like the Jesuits, he did happen to do something personal once for the Pope (see "The Adventure of Black Peter"), not to mention his being involved in the case with the Vatican cameos (cited in *The Hound of the Baskervilles*). Bloom then elaborated on how "Dupin's life is lived in seclusion amid his books like a monk in his *cell* (singularly appropriate in a detective story)," observing how the narrator is brought specifically into closer "communion" with Dupin, who is then able to "fathom" the former's "soul." Further, Dupin helps out a prefect "to *confess*," all of which would suggest a "new secular priesthood." What is more, in connection with Holmes's own tendency not to ask for recompense, Dupin "works just for the 'love of it,'" "absents himself from the cash nexus even as he becomes its slave" (24). In this context, Bloom noted that Dupin's name would also point to *du pain*, which suggests "some bread" and thereby monetary recompense, but such a connotation would scarcely be carried over to his English counterpart.

Still this etymology may have to be corrected in the light of a less learned but more convincing article that appeared in America's most distinguished journal on literary studies, but was overlooked. Entitled "Who Was Monsieur Dupin?," the author, W. T. Bandy of the University of Wisconsin, arrived at the amazing conclusion that the nomenclature derived from a letter written Poe by S. Maupin (30 Sept. 1840) with inner reference to M. C. Auguste Dubouchet. It is hardly necessary to rehearse the contents to point out that the *C. August Du-* part could have been attached then subliminally, at least, to the *-pin* to arrive at *C. Auguste Dupin*. Yet Bandy concluded that "indeed, it is not difficult to imagine Poe amusing himself with a little private joke, which it has taken us some time to appreciate" (510). His main supportive evidence was that the date of the letter corresponded to the time when Poe was "probably engaged in writing 'The Murders in the Rue Morgue.'" Could not then the original formulation of Holmes's first initial also have derived from a similar personal jest? Ironically, it could have been a jest by way of another jest then, if it was at all indebted to Poe. This represents my principal point.

But was the jest also on the reader, as would be the case if "*Dup*in" relates to the reader as the dupe? Was then *Sir Arthur* not the one who was having us on?

## NOTES

[1]"On Spelling Out Sherlock Holmes's Secretive Initial" in *Baker Street Miscellanea*. This led to a published letter by Roger Johnson in the same journal urging that the "I" must be intended as an initial and not an indication of the first person singular since Doyle's note in question reads: "Ormond Sacker . . . Lived at 221B Upper Baker Street *With* I Sherrinford Holmes" (his emphasis), the point being that Doyle would never have put the *object* of a statement into the nominative. He reports that Conan Doyle himself used "I" as an original initial at an early age, as reported by Dame Jean Conan Doyle to him. See n2 below.

[2]"My Correspondence has the Charm of Variety': Letters to the Editor," *BSM* no. 58 (1989): 33-34.

# CHAPTER XX

## ON THE PEDIGREE OF THE *HOLMES* NAME: APROPOS OF THE FIRST ENGLISH DETECTIVE WORK

"Backwards and forwards may you see
The print of many feet within the snow."
—*M. Arden of Feversham*, 14. 394-95

Whence did Sir Arthur Conan Doyle arrive at the surname of his master detective? Most *aficionados* would recall that of Oliver Wendell Holmes. But then that Holmes was an American whereas a British source would appear rather more apropos. In any event, because of the inherent name-play often recognized on *Holmes* and *homes* in popular culture (as in that now time-honored quibble "there is no police like Holmes"), a previous, even anticipatory play on words which could have made use of similar quibbling is at least worth taking into account. As an attention-getter, let me say that the immediate source of inspiration derives from the coincidence that a short way from where this paper was initiated a real estate agent has set himself up with the trade-name of "Sherlock Homes." Moreover, a well-known mystery bookshop I am familiar with calls itself "Sherlock's Home." As the consulting detective's brother Mycroft once put it, "I hear of Sherlock everywhere," for which see "The Greek Interpreter."

In this essay, we shall consider that the original piece of wordplay from which the quibble on the name was derived, whether considered deliberate or not, occurred actually far back in the Renaissance. The literary work involved is again the anonymous tragic drama about a certain Master Arden of Feversham, a tale which contains numerous other examples of paronomasia and of names which happen to look ahead toward later literature (see Ch. XI in this book).

Consider, for example, the nomenclature of the roguish companions Black Will and Shakebag, a combination which may hint at Will(iam) Shake(speare)'s having had at least pertinent familiarity with the play; in performing in the play he could have enacted one of these roguish roles and then perhaps touched it up. The name Black Will is also evident in another drama, one definitely connected with the esteemed group called The Queen's Men, and because nowadays scholars like the leading authority, the late Samuel Schoenbaum, concur that the newcomer from Stratford could have worked in his early career with this company, it is eminently plausible that *Arden* was also a Queen's Men's play somehow involving him. See also Ch. 9 of my crux book.[1] For the four hundredth anniversary year of the publication of the play (1992), I chanced to prepare a summarizing paper on this genetic subject for the annual Ohio Shakespeare Conference. Because it was at Bowling Green State University, known for its popular-culture interests, the paper was entitled "*Arden of Feversham* as a *Whodunit*: Was it Shakespeare?";[2] it thus comprised another quibble, but truly not a trivializing one for scholarly sleuths on the serious trail of authorship.

The issue presently is this: If we let Shakespeare in, why not also leave some room for Conan Doyle? On the level of spirit, or even Spiritualistically (summoning up, momentarily Doyle's later occultic concerns), he happens to be prophetically anticipated in the drama in onomastic terms once again, as we shall see. The play has been fairly authoritatively dubbed, for the English Association, "the first piece of detective work in English literature."[3] So why should not the stalwart Sir Arthur, with his widespread interests, have been aware of this? Evidently he did not have enough concern with real-life crimes outside his Sherlock Holmes Canon, as Peter Costello's book has shown (not without causing a little controversy in the process admittedly),[4] and indeed, for the record, the *Arden* play was also based on an actual murder case, one wherein the victim's name was actually spelled *Ardern*. For that matter, a key character figuring in it has the resonant name of the well-known British Holmesian and collector Richard Green, who then happens to have brought into question some of Costello's findings, but that would be in a different essay.

For our purposes, the key passage of interest is the tenth scene, during which a sinister individual dubbed Michael calls out merrily to the departing Master Arden: "So, fair weather after you! for before you lies Black Will and Shakebag . . . . They'll be your ferrymen to long home."[5] Thus villainous ruffians will duly escort him to his *last*, thus long, home, namely to his deathbed. The plot begins to thicken.

Could there not be more than one "home" here involved? The answer is provided in an unpublished Oxford B. Litt. dissertation by a leading Shakespearean, MacDonald P. Jackson of New Zealand, who has this pertinent (now published) gloss: "There is a quibble on 'holme,' meaning a little island in the river. Arden is about to take the ferry to the Isle of Sheppy; Michael says that the two murder[er]s will act as his Charon-like ferryman to a home / holme of a different kind" (175).[6] (Incidentally, Jackson has privately written me that he is still much interested in the plausibility of Shakespearean authorship even after all these years; he ought not to be displeased at my announcing this.) It has likewise been contended not so long ago, curiously enough, that the name *Holmes* etymologically and sociolinguistically relates to *small islands*.[7]

Hence some name-play on *ho(l)mes* appears implicit. Lest the modern or absentminded, casual reader simply passes by such punning, the anonymous playwright has (or playwrights working together have) conveniently made the very next speaker employ the sound effect once again, if in a slightly different context: "How doth my mistress and all at home?" Thus, the play provides a definite plural effect here on *ho(l)me(s)*. And may the modern reader, at least the re-creative one, not incidentally call to mind even *lanky* Sherlock as, in effect, another "long Holmes" too? This circumstance needs investigation.

Because of the seemingly quirky nature of such name-play, let us inspect it a bit more precisely under the Sherlockian lens. The now curious, prepositional phrase "to long home" (as found in *Arden*) originally came from Ecclesiastes xii. 5 ("because man goeth to his long home, and the mourners go about the streets"). In turn, Conan Doyle was himself clearly no stranger to the Bible. Further, the allusion to "Charon-" in the play in this context (one including ferrymen) would have recalled for him how classical and medieval myth and literature were somewhat mixed in the past with Christianity, as most noticeably already in Dante's *Divine Comedy*. The *Arden* play was so well known, with scholars having argued the famous authorship problem already a good bit even in the last century, that this mystery story (or *double* mystery here, if one likes) would not have bypassed his ken.

The Faversham story presents various subtle textual and thematic problems in analysis, and consideration of Conan Doyle's own possible predilection, whether conscious or not, could help spur solution to some of these. For example, the title-page calls the drama a tragedy, but is it actually not more of a suspenseful melodrama? Perhaps so, given the original, non-pejorative meaning of the term from the French *mélodrame*. Is there really any basic *moral* meaning (so much emphasis there being placed on fate), or is concern with the inept machinations of the two villains in doing away with Arden (at the prompting of the wife, Alice, who was having an affair with a certain Mosby) mainly a study in the workings and final effects of evil somehow for their own sake?

In answer, principally because of Doyle's wrapt-up Victorian heritage, the natural tendency is to believe he would have preferred a story stressing staunch *moral* purport (though at the same time it need not have been, or should not at any rate be considered as, somewhat deprecatingly, moralistic). The inherent social problem is that Master Arden has acquired and utilized abbey lands in such a self-serving way, whereupon the disenfranchised or poor people understandably want and deserve Arden's comeuppance. This very need for justice is clear enough already and especially in the leading source for the play, in Holinshed's *Chronicles*.

The point is that if revenge never truly pays, at any rate ethically speaking, it at least can provide a certain aesthetic balance, one making this so-called earliest of domestic tragedies a valid or universally retributive one in the end. In support of this, Sarah Youngblood, in her article on "Theme and Image in *Arden of Faversham*," speaks of "a clear pattern of tragic retribution" (208). Nonetheless, Martin Wine, the *Arden* editor of the Revels series, in citing this comment (along with many others touching on similar ethical considerations), states that this conclusion "simply does not fit our response" (lxxiii), claiming that Alice Arden "goes to her execution blaming Mosby for her plight rather than assuming responsibility for her actions" (lxxiv). Nonetheless, her last line is, in fact, a confessional enough one: "Let my death make amends for all my sins" (18. 33). Granted, the drama's Epilogue downplays any didactic tone, but a spectator or reader sensitive to religious issues would be obliged to take into account at least that penitential petition. Truly Conan Doyle, who had his own religious background (though he then chose to dispense with some of the religious formality of his Jesuit training), would have appreciated that kind of finale—if one were intended, as appears likely.

Numerous other "clues" present themselves in the story, ones which would likewise have intrigued the real-life detective in Sir Arthur. Most of the more fascinating ones relate then to the major (or authorship) problem. For example, was the play a *collaboration* because of set differences in style, humor, and seriousness, their being oddly mixed, for instance? Is it also actually too showy a play for Shakespeare to have composed, at any rate by himself at that very early stage of his career? So it has been suggested. Because Conan Doyle, although clearly intrigued at one time by the age-old issue of whether the Canon of the plays accredited to Shakespeare *was really* a result of the Stratford master's pen, finally applauded this so-called "upstart Crow" as the true author in the long run,[8] he would have shown, let us deign to admit, at least a minor concern with the issue of who it was who composed what has been authoritatively dubbed the very best of the "Apocrypha."

After all, it has been such a commonplace that Shakespeare's name was often pirated and applied to works which were not his in any form, a matter which concerned Conan Doyle particularly insofar as he is on record for having opposed the corollary problem of assigning the known plays eccentrically to a non-Stratfordian. True, some other strange, dramatic puzzlements then, such as the introduction of an artist who could create a painting that would poison whomever looked at it, would obviously have strained his credulity. Yet a few Roman Catholic allusions interspersed might well have caught his passing attention because of his own one-time Catholic background, notably the gruesome introduction of a poisoned crucifix, whereby he also may think of Holmes as having once done his good deed for the Pope—not to mention as well the curious case of the Vatican cameos (cited in *The Hound*). Incidentally, the poisoned crucifix has been thought to suggest Marlowe's authorial contribution; his *The Jew of Malta* might be compared (where an entire nunnery is poisoned), but we might also remember that Romeo's sweetheart herself feared the possibility of being envenomed—in this case by a friar.

In any event, suffice it to say toward the end that the dramatic incorporation of allusions to *Ho(l)mes*, however anticipatory of Sherlock Holmes's surname, can provide for us the earliest possible onomatological source or analog in this case and deserves therefore room (or should we rather say its home?) even next to Oliver Wendell.[9]

Last of all, it might casually be remarked that Jackson, in his Oxford thesis

(270), happened to allow for at least the possibility of *Arden* having been written by a certain Watson, no less. Indeed, because Thomas Watson was mentioned by Frances Meres in his *Palladis Tamia* (1598) as among the best for tragedy, he remains a candidate even though (or best because) none of his work has in fact surfaced. In contrast, Jackson's own penchant for Shakespearean authorship is cited in Wine's standard edition. My personal suspicion is that the work was an "actors' showpiece" (a view also supported in the Penguin edition of the play), but that would scarcely rule out the *partial* contribution of the precocious actor-playwright from Stratford.[10]

NOTES

[1]Ch. 9 there. A formal endorser, Michael Marsden, happened to be also from Bowling Green State University. The book also contains numerous other matters of Sherlockian concern duly documented as such.

[2]See also my paper delivered for the Ohio Shakespeare Conference at the University of Dayton in 1978 and included in the *Proceedings*, namely "'The Secret'st Man of Blood': Foreshadowings of *Macbeth* in *Arden of Feversham*." Cf. my later entry in the *DLB* and the essay on the subject appearing in *AEB*, here revised as Ch. XI.

[3]See Chapman's study in the official journal of the English Association, in England, namely *English* (17).

[4]For example, was Conan Doyle really driven around by a motor-bandit? (See Costello's discussion in his Ch. 21. But Richard L. Green has largely disproven the matter.)

[5]Citations from *Arden* are from the Revels ed., this passage being in the tenth scene (10.43-45).

[6]Although I have examined this dissertation in the Bodleian Library, I do not have permission to quote from it and so cite Wine's edition of the play (93).

[7]The point was first raised, to my knowledge, by a Swiss Jungian, Richard Gerber (Free University of Berlin); citations are from my translation thereof in *The Armchair Detective*. Gerber finds the *Holmes* / *islands* connection indicating "the isolating, locked-up quality comparable to the 'lock' element in *Sherlock*" (281); he goes further by accommodating Sherlock's original name, *Sherringford*, finding *ford* "a shallow river passage which connects the separated tracts of land with one another" (286); "*Ford* and *Holmes* are therefore exactly complementary, and together they constitute a symbol of the individual's human existence in society: made solitary and yet united" (286). After also relating *Sherri . . . f* to *Sheriff* as well as *herring*, "the fish in water," Gerber concludes as follows:

"The name of Sherringford is consequently archetypal for the human condition, in equipoise between harmony and conflict, between isolation and community, between natural freedom and organizational constraint. That Conan Doyle at first hit upon this name shows how inexpressibly normal he fundamentally was" (286-87).

[8]See my study of "Conan Doyle and the Shakespeare Authorship Mystery," which was initiated with the understanding that the excitement shown by anti-Stratfordians can on one level be much like that of Sherlockians. My conclusions differed from that initial premise, though.

[9]Richard L. Kellogg's study is a suitable one on this issue.

[10]This paper was revised twice from one originally presented for the "Names in Literature" session at the Modern Language Association of America annual meeting, Toronto, 1993, and then to appear in *Clues*. For Jackson's word on the subject, see especially his Shakespeare Association of America paper then published in *Archiv für das Studium der Neueren Sprachen und Literaturen*.

PART III:

NINETEENTH AND TWENTIETH-CENTURY AMERICA
(AND SOME EUROPEAN INFLUENCE)

# CHAPTER XXI

## IRONIC FERTILITY:
## "DEFOLIATING" THE TITLE *LEAVES OF GRASS*

One standard understanding of Walt Whitman's collection of poetry is that its title plays on foliage and the leaves of the book itself, thereby exhibiting what has been expressed in such a telling turn of phrase as "the wit of Whitman." Yet did Whitman arrive at such wordplay entirely independently? As an arch-Romantic in his own right, he was evidently indebted in other respects to the leader of the British school, William Wordsworth, who summarized his famous iconographical poem "The Tables Turned" in a concluding stanza commencing with the following familiar exhortation: "Enough of Science and of Art; / Close up those barren leaves" (*Oxford Anthology* 18-29). Thus, in following the example of "those barren leaves" in the kind of book Wordsworth was opposing, Whitman arrived at his own reformulation, "leaves of grass." Such title-play then, incidentally, lends itself easily to the notion that this way a man of wit (Whitman) found indeed his true *words' worth*— if that further name-play does not appear too neat. Thus, C. Carroll Hollis relates the Wordsworthian favorite "The Tables Turned" to *Leaves of Grass*, albeit not specifically in any titular capacity.

What are other suggested origins of Whitman's unusual label? Roger Asselineau is confounded somewhat by it, but then finds an apt vegetative metaphor: "Whitman allowed his book to grow within his mind little by little with an organic and almost vegetable growth. (In this sense the title of his book was particularly happy.)" (11). Similarly, until 1881, when it acquired its current title, "Song of Myself" was untitled and later given only stock descriptive labels such as "Poem of Walt Whitman, an American" (1856) or "Walt Whitman" (1860). Consequently, James E. Miller suggests that the frequent change of title indicates that Whitman was perhaps uncertain or confused as to its basic aura (see p. 6).

One of the most unusual etymological suggestions is that it derived from printer's slang, a supposition questioned, however, by Charles M. Adams, who finds no evidence in Whitman's writings to support it (167-68). Another curious view is that the title sprang full-blown from Sara Payson Willis's *Fern Leaves from Fanny Fern's Portfolio* (1853), which was an extremely popular collection of little sketches. This proposal does take into account the wordplay on "leaves" as suggesting both vegetation and pages of a book or, at least, a scrapbook. What is more, the collection was bound in green, tooled in designs of curling roots and so on, providing pictorial evidence as well. Still, the striking use of the "leaves" pun in Wordsworth certainly stands out more and, for that matter, Willis could easily have borrowed her pun from the Lake Poet too.[1]

A major problem with the Wordsworthian association is that some Whitman critics refuse to allow for much, if any, Whitmanic use of the Lake Poet on the grounds that the two poets were so dissimilar. Thus Arthur E. Briggs writes: "Wordsworth viewed Nature much as a communion with God. Whitman in the more modern scientific manner conceived man and Nature as not separate but of the same order and system of being" (80). Abdelwahab Muhammed Elmessiri finds Wordsworth's imagination historical, and Whitman's anti-historical.[2] Jeanne Bugliari tries to be more conciliatory but still dissociates them, finding that they shared a basic philosophic orientation but were different in form, style, personal tempera- ment, and in general ideology. So one might at first be inclined to agree with Edna Davis Romig, in her note on the roots of *Leaves of Grass*, that it is more heavily indebted to Emerson than to Wordsworth. On the other hand, Harry B. Reed finds at least a "Wordsworthian tinge" in what he calls "Whitman's Arcadian imagination" (125). Probably the best defense of the correlation comes from the poetic pen of none other than William Carlos Williams:

> Leaves of Grass! *It was a good title for a book of poems. . . . It was a challenge to the entire concept of the poetic idea. . . In a word and at the beginning it enunciated a shocking truth, that the common ground*

> *is of itself a poetic source. There had been inklings before this that*
> *such was the case in the works of . . . Wordsworth . . . . (22)*

Yet if the true source of Whitman's title and imagery in general is "the common ground," still the best *literary* basis can now be thought to reside in Wordsworth, once Whitman's title is, let us say, properly defoliated. After all, a minor but still primary clue is that the initials of the two poets were also exactly the same. Or, to put it yet another way, the Wordsworthian tables have been turned once again.

On the other hand, whereas the Lake Poet refers to getting away from pages of books in order to reach the truly fertile (or the actual) leaves of nature in the raw, Whitman cites the pages themselves as fertile and thereby desirable. Thus, if Whitman made use of Wordsworth here, he did so with a certain latent *irony*, revealing a poet's ability to modify his use of source material aptly enough. The critic's job is to be sensitive to the nature of this switching.

Finally, another romantic irony is that some critics feel naturally disposed to claim that Whitman, in his use of "leaves" to refer to both books and vegetation, was indebted to an unproven commonplace, rather than to a major predecessor, simply because his precious individuality would otherwise appear to be in doubt; but that demurrer is on the side of romantic heresy, given the fundamental obsequious nature of the human animal. In short, the title amounted to a kind of purloining. As T. S. Eliot reminds us, it is the bad poets who imitate, but the good ones who steal.

### NOTES

[1]For a discussion of the Willis connection, see Frances Winwar's note with its own punning title, "Fern Leaves and Leaves of Grass" (7, 24).

[2]See his Rutgers State University diss. in 1969: "The Critical Writings of Wordsworth and Whitman: A Study of the Historical and Anti-historical Imaginations."

# CHAPTER XXII

## AS YOU LIKE [PRUFROCK]: SHAKESPEAREAN UNDERTONES IN THE MONOLOGUIST'S NAME AND NATURE

T. S. Eliot's memorable *persona* in his earliest published interior monologue (or psychologue), "The Love Song of J. Alfred Prufrock," provides a modernized and, to some, a seemingly Hamlet-like "dissociation"—to accommodate thereby the poet's own familiar term from his highly critical essay "Hamlet and His Problems"—but it can now be shown that alternate and more cogent Shakespearean resonances had actually worked their cunning way in. First of all, let it be well recognized once again that if any debt to the dilemmas of the Danish Prince is manifest, it would more ostensibly have come rather by way of Jules Laforgue's well-known modern adaptation, "Hamlet, ou les Suites de la Piété Filiale," not merely be in terms of Shakespeare's play alone. For Eliot so demoted the drama in that essay of his as representing an "artistic failure" (if not truly then a *histrionic* one, as he had once to concede)—to some extent, it can be said, for idiosyncratic reasons. Insofar as Prufrock proclaims, in no uncertain terms, "No! I am not Prince Hamlet, nor was meant to be" (1. 111), surely it would appear somewhat gratuitous to contend, as a few critics still would, that he nonetheless reflects a genuine (or original) Hamlet-*figur*, even in spite of himself. In corroborating Laforgue's influence on the young Eliot, we might revert to the entry under the Frenchman's name in Ricks's edition of Eliot's 1909-1911 *Poems*, as duly cited in the Index a good bit there.

Second, a general but pointed reminiscence of King Richard II, at least indirectly of Shakespeare's portrayal of him, would enter the poetic picture as well, if intriguingly by way of Walter Pater's likewise sudden, introductory-sounding disclaimer "No! Shakspere's kings are not, nor are meant to be . . . ," an admission following hard upon his familiar "Irony of Kingship" proclamation in his *Appreciations*.[1] Happily, after I had initially posited this Ricardian correlation, Henry Janowitz, M. D., came to my support by professionally enlisting the tie-in by linking Eliot's medical metaphor "The whole earth is our hospital" with yet another expression of Pater's: "the whole world seemed to present itself as a hospital" (589). There could hardly be a closer fit than such a surgical one, at least on the verbal level. Pater's analysis links then to his extended description of King Richard as a debilitated monarch, being rather more so in the *Appreciations* than in the dramatist's own version. Still, more than one kind of Shakespearean conjunction may well be operative here, notably, as we shall see, in terms of a key portion of *As You Like It* (hence my title).

For even an analogous pre-Prufrockian parallel emerges with the striking character of Touchstone in that pastoral romantic comedy,[2] especially in that the monologuist's very surname bilingually relates to the familiar Germanic substantive *Prüfstein*, meaning *touchstone*, Eliot's anti-heroic evening wanderer in the poem having thereby certain Teutonic reverberations instilled in his very surname, as has often been documented.[3] This touchstone association links then with that key term's own Victorian reverberations, thus recalling Matthew Arnold's metaphoric use of the term as a critical standard in his essay "The Study of Poetry,"[4] Eliot and Prufrock being in effect "late Victorian" or Edwardian in their style, especially in terms of moralistic concerns. So when Prufrock elects at times to play "the Fool" (1. 119), as he says, Touchstone as celebrated court jester would obliquely re-enter the scene.

The underlying point is that certain key textual links notably support such an overall affinity. To begin, the names themselves come verbally together in a kind of symbolic ritual: what is *rich* (evidently connoted by the first syllable *Rich*ard) and *hard* then as a *rock* (subtly implied in Ric*hard* again and along with Pruf*rock*) would subliminally relate even to *touch*ing a *stone*, particularly should the mineral in question be a precious one and thereby, in turn, be connoting something *rich*. So if the Touchstone name links, let us posit, also with the biological connotation of *stone* (meaning testes), one accessible enough back then, would there not be in the two characters' affinity an ironic hint also of Prufrock and thus of his purported behavioral problems? Nothing off-beat sexually need be implied here; comparable are Eliot's notes on his analogously entitled "The Love Song of St. Sebastian," in which he made an issue of stating that "there's nothing homosexual about this" (for which, see Ricks 267).

To be sure, at the International Shakespeare Conference at Stratford-upon-Avon, Warwickshire, England, in 1992, bearing as its prime focus "Shakespeare and Sexuality," I heard the point made during colloquia that the very quaint name of the jester conveys some subtle biological reverberations, "-stone" in his name having even then a certain testicular overtone, as duly recorded for posterity in Partridge's standard reference work, *Shakespeare's Bawdy* (195). If such an offhand effect appears to be at all overdoing a relatively minute point in itself, it need not be so in terms of the "echo" of the Touchstone name in that of the more self-absorbed, but still biologically sensitive enough, J. Alfred Prufrock. Thus David Sanders writes that the Prufrockian "'head (grown slightly bald) brought in upon a platter' compounds his self-contempt with the exposure he dreads," and because it is cut off from the body, "as is Prufrock's thought from action and speech," it thereby points to what else but the "castrating power of fear" (46). Hence a seemingly testicular effect again emerges.

True, Sanders, in spite of his essay's subtitle, namely "Prufrock as Touchstone," tries to deflate the Touchstone-Prufrock relationship in general by finding that the jester in the play "equates 'feigning' with 'the truest poetry,'" whereas Prufrock himself would feign "by taking the form of silence and by keeping desire a private affair," thereby denying language "its social and moral force" (48-49). Still, Sanders tends to idealize the Shakespearean fool here a bit much. Rather it is Jaques in the comedy who turns out to be much more the real social critic, not so much Touchstone.

Likewise, an explicator, Ian Dunn, has claimed that Prufrock fails to operate as a social commentator in the way that Touchstone can. For a good corrective to such idealization, compare now Harold C. Goddard's clear demotion of Touchstone in his standard workbook (applauded incidentally by Harold Bloom in his *Shakespeare: The Invention of the Human*), namely *The Meaning of Shakespeare* (I, 285-91). The question might then be seriously raised that if the name of Touchstone hints at all at the bawdy meaning of *stone*, would there not also be in the Prufrockian surname, in turn, an ironic hint of some of his implicit sexual problems, ones evident by way of, let us admit, the commonplace onomastic formula of *omen-nomen* (fate being intimated by a name)? That would be with his being also after a certain "proof" of "rock" (namely a true foundation for his faith) notwithstanding. Is he also on the sly then a "pru[de]" in a "frock," as has been suggested a number of times? This is cited again at the start of Nathan Cervo's more recent explication. The more reasonable nomenclatural verdict is that he is after a sure foundation for his initially wavering beliefs, hence after "proof" of "rock" in the biblical sense: "Thou art Peter, and upon this rock [namely, *petra*] I will build my church" (Matt. 16.18).

In any event, the double syllabification and use of the "ch-" effect in the initial syllable of *Touchstone* links thus at least obliquely with *Rich*ard and Pruf*rock* too. So let us correlate the texts more closely now and observe how also Richard II and the jester surprisingly interconnect thematically and in a manner which could then anticipate what happens with J. Alfred, thereby lending more meaning to the monologuist's own singular situation. Such a broad link can help to enrich the inherent meaning that Eliot evidently had in mind with his Prufrockian figure by providing additional resonances, several of them a bit autobiographical in nature and thus of import to the biographer and so finally not amounting merely to *incidental* name-play.

Register first Richard II's deposition scene with its sense of verbal vacillation (so analogous then to Prufrock's own) as in such an ambivalent turn of phrase in sound effects like "I[=Aye], no; no, I [=aye]" (*Richard II*, 4.1.201).[5] Following this, further wordplay occurs whereby the "I" effect changes in its meaning: "for *I* must nothing be. Therefore *no, no*, for *I* resign to thee" (201-2) (emphasis added). In current editions, the first two uses of this personal pronoun in the passage are historicized so as to read "Ay" at the outset. The relevant analogy is that Touchstone, as well, plays similarly upon the *sound* of these words (and so, by verbal implication, Shakespeare does too, but also then upon their orthographic interconnections) in the Fool's familiar pronouncement upon arriving on the scene in the Forest of Arden: "I, now am I in Arden, the more foole I" (*As You Like It*, 2.4.14).

To be sure, in current texts the first "I" is spelled differently from the Folio reading, usually as "A-y" again, thereby signifying probably not an affirmation but an exclamation of slight pain, or simply an exhalation. Thus, in the comedy, the initial wordplay relates to "A-y" again along with "I"; the word *now* is used here with it, whereas Richard has *no* instead. Such an orthographic (but also phonetic) association, rather coincidental though it at first may appear to be, readily happens to anticipate Prufrock's own mannerisms in its repetitive effect (the monologuist allowing himself to reiterate words and phrases for a noticeably similar rhythmic reason), thereby underscoring well enough the speaker's first-person dilemma and indeed in almost solipsistic fashion. Recollect here his "No, I am not Prince Hamlet, nor was meant to be. . . ."

Although to imagine Shakespeare echoing his own word patterns in such a relatively minuscule capacity may seem a bit open to question, no doubt exists that the ironic effect involved in Touchstone's utterance amounts to a kind rather similar to that in King Richard's own seemingly paradoxical *AY / no* announcement. We therefore might well gloss what is said as follows: Because this court jester remains a confused anti-romantic cynic, even in such a romantically pastoral setting, he is, in short, in that respect, actually *more* of a fool; that is, he is so in not duly conforming to the nature of what we might call the green world in which he finds himself. On the other hand, his seeming ability to rise above the influence of such natural surroundings, and retain his sense of aloofness, makes him, at the same time, paradoxically, more sophisticated and thereby actually rather less foolish than the others. So he ends up being one of those so-designated "wise fool" types. Comparable, then, is Prufrock as likewise cynically anti-romantic, this time in the later tradition of Laforgue's *personae*.

Granted, Seymour Bernstein's more recent short article disputing the punning effect of "I, no; no, I" in *Richard II* can be cited, but because it did not take into account the similar collocation in *As You Like It*, the evidence he presents lacks a certain cogency. King Richard's wordplay is more self-conscious than Touchstone's but is still present; the punning effect need not suggest a lack of seriousness in this case (nor need it in terms of Prufrock's interior world). Uncomic puns, such as those relating to what is funny in the peculiar sense, abound. Bernstein has been disputed by Arthur Kincaid in published correspondence; Kincaid sensibly claims that the pun in *Richard II* here is *aural*, the understanding determined by how an actor says "I [=Ay], no." Such a verdict is reasonable.[6]

In any case, would not Touchstone's familiar line upon entering Arden have somehow been duly recorded in the recesses of Eliot's psyche? Insofar as that utterance is one of the most "touching" that the jester has—very likely even the key one that readers now remember him by—such a passing hypothesis is by no means to be ignored. But the main issue at hand is that, in terms of Shakespeare's development as a playwright at least, Touchstone himself can inherently hark back (for Shakespeare at least) to Richard, even as he does in his own comedic context; many sensitive readers of the early plays, including Eliot, could have been well enough aware of that, at least on the subliminal level.

In a similar manner, the Fool's well-known proclamation upon entering the Arden forest happens to be resonant in yet another key respect, harking back titularly to the Apocryphal mystery play *Arden of Feversham*. Some scholars now think Shakespeare, as an actor, may have had a certain hand in this work (if not in the final overall composition?), especially since it is associated with the Queen's Men, to which it is now largely believed he also at one time belonged, and the play has indeed been commonly accepted as the very best of the Shakespearean Apocrypha. Thus Touchstone's later statement "When I was at home, I was in a better place, but travellers must be content" (2.4.15-16) clearly connects, on the half-conscious level at least, with the oft-quoted "forlorn traveller" speech by the character called Will in the *Arden* tragedy (3.100),[7] this figure happening to be another lowly and witty, but buttressing, one. That phrase in the Apocryphal drama is shortly followed then by a reference to "Arden's tragedy" (3.103). Even so Touchstone's similar talk relates, if by way of subtle, extra-textual reverberation and contrast, to *As You Like It* as involving, in effect, yet another Ardenic resonance, namely that of the main setting, the Forest of Arden. So the nomenclature of the victim, Thomas Arden, in the Apocryphal work had then the surname evidently transposed to become the blander label of the woods in the later drama.

At first glance, such an onomastic correlation may appear almost coincidental—were it not for the allusion very soon thereafter, in the earlier play, to the "starven lioness" (3.110), a phrase which is almost certainly then "echoed" in the following passage in *As You Like It*: "Food to the sucked and humpy lioness" (4.3.127). What is rather more, notice that the lioness in the *Arden* work happens to be cited as also being "dry-sucked" (3.111). Now if the later, pastoral romance was truly indebted to the Feversham play, as I posit, it could have been just as easily likewise influenced by a work somehow involving the same author, *Richard II*, because of the very similar verbal, "echoing" effects there. Further, Eliot would have been aware of this, too, for he had had once his say on *Arden of Feversham*[8] and would certainly have been cognizant also of the obvious Ardenic associations relating somehow to

Shakespeare's mother, her maiden name being Arden, as pointed out earlier.

Strong irony becomes evident in Richard's outcry, when deposed, which symbolizes his being an anointed king who presumably can thereby do no wrong on the throne (or so he would imagine) and yet has to recognize his human failings in his allegiance to his associates as well as his appropriation of what they have accomplished. Another obvious irony is that although he appears in a history play, one belonging to the two major tetralogies, this odd duality could easily have been the result of Shakespeare's own ambivalent feelings regarding Richard in terms of what had become known, mainly through the familiar codification by E. M. W. Tillyard, as "The Tudor History Myth." In a word, according to this, the playwright was basically on the side of the Lancastrians and against the Yorkists, but, as a dramatist, he still would have had sufficient sympathy for a well-meaning, yet weak and ineffectual, monarch.

That same kind of ambivalence then became evident in Queen Elizabeth's notorious, well-recognized *cri de coeur*, "I am Richard II, know yet not that?," after having been accosted by hostile forces in the Essex rebellion; yet then, at the same time, as a Tudor queen, she had to defend the Red Rose against the White, thus the right to the throne of the House of Lancaster. Because all this has been common enough knowledge, it clearly could have been so as well to Eliot, thereby supporting his presumed memory of Richard's lines then in terms of Prufrock's own.

In any event, such an *ironic* correlation between King and Fool was a subtly inherent one for Shakespeare, even if he presumably did not plan it all in any such deliberate manner. Eliot, at the same time, could have become himself aware of its implications early on, when Prufrock, in his analogous, ego-centered mode, relates himself, however negatively, to royalty and then again, not so many lines later, to the capitalized "Fool" (1. 119), presumably meaning thereby again the jester type. Although some *Hamlet*-inspired readers try to invoke the figure of Yorick here as being the basis of the Fool figure, we might again revert to Eliot's dissatisfaction with what he happened to consider the relative immaturity of the Danish tragedy as a whole, not merely in terms of an overly hesitant protagonist. Indeed, I heard him actually speak of this immaturity in one of his addresses for The Young Men's Hebrew Association in New York; he said then he preferred the dramatist's "more mature" works, in other words not a presumed revenge tragedy like *Hamlet*. In sum, the overall King-Fool linkage with Richard and Touchstone serves to tie together what might otherwise appear to be merely loose strands in key source material for what is commonly taken now as the first Modernist poem. Both onomastically and thematically, then, Richard and Touchstone happened to merge in Prufrock—hardly instead Hamlet, Yorick, or even the pompous Polonius, as some think.

Finally, we might consider again the *manner* in which both Prufrock and Touchstone reflect their author's autobiography to a certain valid extent. Consider the ritual in which the jester and Audrey are to be married by a hedge-priest as plausibly harking back to Shakespeare's own unconventional wedding in the Warwickshire countryside. In turn, Eliot's very own unconscious association with Prufrock has been remarked often enough, notably of course by Ezra Pound. On a more literary level, the very names of the Fools involved are rather similar with respect to their creators' names in that even as a *stone* to *touch*, let us posit, is not very far removed from a *spear* to *shake*, so too the "stern" effect of the protracted name of *J. Alfred Prufrock* commends itself to the originator even in that he at one time had signed himself, as is well known, as *T. Stearns Eliot*. Such etymology has enriched our understanding of the characters themselves at least by duly prompting further epistemological associations for readers. It thus adds to the value of A. D. Moody's notable research, even as he himself deigned to posit a major Prufrock-Touchstone link-up (32). True enough, now Sanders would rather feel better in *contrasting* the two. Still, as has been pointed out (again by Goddard), such a severance in this context would simply serve to over-idealize the character of the jester. Eliot himself would most probably have been aware of this peril concomitantly.

### NOTES

[1]See my chapter "Prufrock, Pater, and Richard II: Retracing a Denial of Princeship," in my *Ascending the Prufrockian Stair* 97-116. Although the poem itself tells of *descending* a stair, the poem as a whole is the first step in an eventual ascent, culminating in "Ash Wednesday" and *The Four Quartets*, the arrangement showing the influence of Dante.

[2]Originally appearing as a short item, "Prufrock as Touchstone," cf. my thoughts on this subject finally as the second chapter in my book on *Prufrock* 17-18. But the bulk of the data here is new.

[3]For example, see the studies by Grimaud and Dunn, the point having been also briefly made by

Hugh Kenner. Dunn cites a previous study relating Prufrock's name Teutonically to a familiar enough collocation from St. Louis, *Prufrock-Littau*, on which consult Stepanchev.

[4]Cf. also an incidental comment by Jill Franks: "Eliot may have had in mind Matthew Arnold's poem 'The Buried Life,' when thinking about Prufrock's submerged self" (25).

[5]Citations to Shakespeare's plays are to the Norton edition of the First Folio of 1623 for textual references and to the revised Pelican edition for line references. The Pelican ed. has "Ay," not "I," with the notation "*Ay . . . ay* 'yes, no: no, yes,' but also 'I, no; no, I'" (659). The Riverside ed. has this comment: "The pun is on *ay* and *I*, which were pronounced alike; moreover, *ay* was often written *I*" (829).

[6]After this paper of mine was initially delivered at one of the American Name Society annual meetings, in Toronto (1997), the interesting point was raised during colloquia afterwards that Richard's "comfort" speeches (3.2.75-90) relate thematically to Prufrock as well. For the very latest analysis of Prufrock in Touchstonian terms, see Nathan Cervo's recent explication again, which adds a number of other links also with *As You Like It*, but does not cite earlier research on the matter.

[7]References to *Arden of Feversham* are to the Martin Wine edition in the Revels series. Cf. Ch. XI.

[8]Eliot once happened to opt for Thomas Kyd's authorship of *Arden*, a position strongly favored in the past but now disputed by the best modern scholarship. For this, see his "The Elizabethan Dramatists" in his *Selected Essays* (93).

# CHAPTER XXIII

## SINCLAIR LEWIS'S *ZENITH*—ONCE AGAIN

Scholars have long probed the problem of where Sinclair Lewis got the name of his Zenith; some have posited Cincinnati, others Duluth (actually captioned "The Zenith City" before Lewis wrote), more recently Robert L. Coard has pointed out that the name may derive from Edith Wharton's "Apex City" (9).[1] It is suggested here that Lewis was at least partly rather inspired by the community of Xenia, Ohio. First, a bit of deadwood needs to be cleared away. There is, I should think, no definite evidence that he was specifically thinking of any one American locale alone. Mark Schorer has plugged for Cincinnati on reasonable enough grounds, but even he has admitted to me that the conception was "certainly . . . an amalgam.'[2] It was natural that, after the novel was published, "the newspapers of five . . . cities—Cincinnati, Duluth, Kansas City, Milwaukee, and Minneapolis—each declared that its city was the model of Zenith" (Schorer 344),[3] but that says nothing about Lewis's intentions. It is arguable that he could have had cities like Cincinnati and Kansas City largely in mind since he referred to them in *Babbitt* (183), but the evidence can also be reversed: since he referred to them in quite separate terms in his very first Zenith novel, why should he have identified Zenith itself with any one of them?

Of course, Sauk Centre does appear as a place name in *Main Street*, and no one can reasonably doubt that Lewis's home town is the model for Gopher Prairie, but one exception does not prove the rule.

Second, it is evident that Lewis had an *ironic* purpose in mind when he invented the name of Zenith. The city, far from being a real zenith of American culture, the ideal metropolis, is in point of fact the *nadir* of true elegance, or (as a student happened to pencil in the copy of *Babbitt* I have) the "Zenith of Mediocrity." This has led to a few possibly over-sensitive souls claiming that the setting of Zenith was really perdition. Schorer writes, "Quite brilliantly T. K. Whipple made and Maxwell Geismar developed the observation that *Babbitt* is set in hell" (*Sinclair Lewis* 50), and Richard P. Blackmur has contended that "out of the same impulse that in times of less dismay produced visions of Utopia Mr. Lewis has projected an inferno" (*Sinclair Lewis* 108).

With this in mind, it might be possible to deduce a source for Lewis's inspiration in terms of his ironic intent. I have come across no city of any import that sounds at all like *Zenith* in America, except perhaps for *Xenia*, which was sometimes spelled Z-e-n-i-a (as in Thurber's "I Went to Sullivant," a story of boyhood education in Columbus, Ohio,[4] which has certain literary associations). It is also not so very far from Cincinnati and has many of Lewis's typical midwestern associations, but the literary import seems most revealing here.

For, in its connections with William Dean Howells, the community of Xenia has ironic significance. The so-called Dean of American letters settled in the vicinity of Xenia in order to establish with his father an ideal kind of communal experiment, an endeavor which proved to be abortive. Actually he settled some six miles from Xenia proper, in the township of Sugarcreek, but the standard reference works, including Cady's biography, speak of the Howellses' settlement at Xenia, and the identification has stuck—except for so many Xenians who claim never to have heard of Howells and identify their community more, anyway, with the writer Whitelaw Reid. It seems, however, that Xenia could well have had some significance for Lewis, not only because of Howells, but because Charles Dickens passed through this place en route from Lebanon to Columbus. And, as is readily admitted, the similarity in the satiric attacks of Lewis and Dickens can hardly be gainsaid. Both were outstanding critics of society.

But the Howells-Lewis association may be more significant in this case historically. This is partly owing to the irony in Lewis's use of the name *Zenith* which sounds so close to that associated with the Howellses' abortive "communitarian" enterprise (that of *Xenia*). Lewis was interested in communal living from the time that he spent in a communal environment himself when he dropped out of Yale to work in Upton Sinclair's Helicon Hall as a janitor. What is more, Lewis could easily have known of W. D. Howells's early career from at least four of the latter's books: *My Year in a Log-Cabin: A Bit of Autobiography, Years of My Youth, New Leaf Mills*, and *A Traveler from Altruria*. Howells's writings were permeated with the ideal of a fraternal society. As B. A. Sokoloff has stated, "Although the settlement at Xenia died in embryo, W. D. Howells did not give up the hope for a better society" (67). That hope was then revitalized in his later writings. He revisited Old Eureka Mills, the so-called "Xenia settlement," for instance, in writing *A Modern Instance*, and there is a suggestion of his utopian predilections in *The Rise of Silas Lapham*, in an allusion to the New Harmony project of Robert Owen's that, along with the rather evident influence of Shaker example here, had helped engender the "Xenia" experiment (71). Compare the Howells-Lewis relationship discussed by Jerome Ellison. Lewis had been requested to contribute to "a cooperative magazine based on that mentioned in Howells's *A Hazard of New Fortunes*" in 1947; according to Ellison, "Sinclair ('Red') Lewis was discouraging but prophetic.... 'It won't work,' he said" (256-57). The utopian editorial project was related to Howells's *A Serious Call to an American (R)Evolution* (259); so Lewis was doubtless well acquainted with Howells's utopian ideals.

Now, Lewis had met Howells, for which see Grace Hegger Lewis: "we met William Dean Howells, the dean of American letters" (83); Lewis's chat with Howells is given. Though the disapproval of his forebear is well-known, this negation does not detract from the relationship but lends itself more to the irony of the American dream manifesting itself creatively in both writers. In his Nobel Prize speech, Lewis stated, "It was with the emergence of William Dean Howells that we first began to have something like a *standard, and a very bad standard it was*" (see *The Man from Main Street* 14-15, with emphasis added). Compare this with Dr. Yavitch's remark in *Babbitt* that Zenithite "normalcy" has "*standardized* all the beauty out of life," then with the evil "*standardizations of thought*" in Zenith. Lewis further added, again ironically perhaps, that "[Howells's] influence is not altogether gone today" (1415). When we read that, in at least one of the Zenith novels, *Dodsworth*, "Zenith was still in the halcyon William Dean Howells days" (3),[5] the irony becomes self-evident.

NOTES

[1]Lewis acknowledged Wharton's influence to the point of dedicating *Babbitt* to her.

[2]Letter of 7 May 1969. Schorer replied to my query regarding the Xenia-Zenith correlation, saying that it "sounds most likely." He has preferred Cincinnati as the model, however. See his *Sinclair Lewis: An American Life* 301, 304. Since Lewis worked at the Queen City Club in Cincinnati when he "consolidated his remarks" for *Babbitt*, he could easily have heard of, or visited, Xenia, only some fifty miles distant.

[3]This is natural since Lewis anticipated it in *Arrowsmith*: "Every small American town is trying to get population and modern ideals. . . . they all want to be just like Zenith." Lewis saw Zenith as a city that "yet is a village." See *The Man from Main Street,* ed. Harry E. Maule and Melville H. Cane 26. Xenia, too, might be considered a city "that yet is a village"; Howells described it as a "pretty little town" in *My Year in a Log-Cabin.* Its population in 1920 was 9,110, and it was noted as a good manufacturing center. See Charles B. Galbreath, *History of Ohio* I, 352.

[4]For Lewis's knowledge of Thurber, who was writing on the novelist as early as his Columbus *Dispatch* column of 1923, see Schorer's biography 594, 618.

[5]Edward Wagenknecht, in his *Cavalcade of the American Novel*, interestingly attests that "Dr. Canby has rightly remarked that this picture of the American businessman abroad [in *Dodsworth*] is . . . like Howells" (360).

# CHAPTER XXIV

## BURNS AND FROST: FIRE AND ICE AGAIN

Current predictions of global warming cannot help but make literate modern man, especially if he is American, recollect somewhat Frost's celebrated short lyric "Fire and Ice." He could, for example, recall how 1988 had been publicly cited as *the* year of the threat of such warming in our atmosphere, yet then that that was followed by Alaska having its coldest winter yet—hence "fire and ice" even in such a curious follow-up respect. Thereafter the cold weather from up north eventually filtered its way into the southern climates. We might nowadays likewise recollect the shift from *el niño* to *la niña*. Thus, Frost's poem can even be taken as calling into question the very "global warming" warning, as it were, even as, at the tail end of his lyric, he refers to a cold ending of the world as being also one that "would suffice." Notice the cool understatement for effect there as relevant enough too.

For our present purposes, however, let us rather concentrate on other debts in the Frost lyric, more onomastic ones to begin with (owing to my interest in the American Name Society as well as Robert Frost Society symposia). The most obvious influence thereon might be thought to be that of the Bible because of the end of the world being there notably predicted—one presumably in terms of fire, just as the world, as the children of God knew it back in Noah's time, was already consumed by water with the Great Flood. Further, as a New Englander, Frost labeled himself an "Old Testament Christian," meaning one who duly based himself on the older Covenant, so was not a regular churchgoer but someone who still had a rever-

168

ent attitude toward God and things biblical, as then evidenced especially in his play-
let *A Masque of Reason*, based on the Job story; but also, at least indirectly, on
Goethe's *Faust* [this paper having been presented in 1999, a celebrated Goethe Bi-
centennial year], which, in turn, had, to be sure, its wholesome antecedents in *Job* as
well, even as the subtitle of my book on the subject published in West Germany
reveals—that is, at least in terms of intent (for which, see the bibliographical entry
here).

Still, more may now be involved than meets the retina, especially from the
nomenclatural point-of-view just mentioned. In a word, by subtly ending the lyric
on a note of ice, Frost was surely, in a broad, but perhaps half-conscious sense,
playing up to his very surname (even as a commonplace in scholarship has been that
winter lies all over his landscape). Yet in addition he may indirectly have happened
to have had in his mind the surname of that romantic whose full name truly comple-
ments his own. The obvious label that fits the bill is surely that of Robert Burns,
whereby we have two surnames (and forenames) running together in exactly the
same manner, historically and connotatively, as fire and ice *per se*.

Now because fairly recently 1996 has been celebrated as a Burns Bicenten-
nial year (he died in 1796), this association has taken on rather special significance;
we might query if such a linkage may indeed be more that coincidental, say with the
poem in question. Agreed, it is common knowledge that Frost, being partly of Scottish heritage, was a great admirer of that famous Scottish romantic, Burns, duly
citing him from time to time in public, as in a familiar tiff with T. S. Eliot, one
recounted by Thompson in the second volume of his biography (402). At that well-
known time, a special dinner get-together, Frost asked his erstwhile compatriot (originally also American but then a British citizen) whether Burns should not get some
rightful credit as a poet, thus duly looking ahead toward modern times. Eliot's mild
response, that we might grant this popular Scotsman his "modest" due, as he phrased
it, has been taken at times as even a bit snobbish, though we might readily recall also
here that Eliot was known for formally upholding the virtue of honest modesty in
contradistinction to mere self-promotion. So what he said need hardly be taken as
simply an aesthetic put-down, especially in the light of criticism of Frost himself as
a self-promoter, impolitely presented by Thompson, as is so well known—thereby
open to some question.

Otherwise, then, how do Burns and Frost share some common characteristics, that is aside from their heritage as stemming from the north of Britain (notably with Frost's mother having been born there)? This leading question arose briefly at the special gathering of Frost specialists at the University of Virginia in Charlottesville (Fall 1996), which I was privileged to attend, and one answer that was readily suggested in the parley concerned their mutual interest in nothing less than the *music* of poetry. In other words, Burns, as is well recognized, was much involved with Scottish balladry; Frost, in following this tradition, also showed some due indebtedness to similar native rhythms. After all, the New Englander strongly believed in metrics, in the music of rhymed lines and the structure following therefrom; he would not "play tennis with the net down," as he had once succinctly put it, by simply writing free verse. In this respect, he was also being classical (or formalist, as poets now say) rather than merely romantic, even more so than his so-called main poetic rival, Eliot (although the latter did use his own classical models, notably for his dramaturgy, as especially in *The Cocktail Party*).[1]

Let us now look further, this time at the subject-matter of these respective "romantic" poets, though Burns has also been called *pre*-romantic and Frost clearly given more qualified labels as well (recently "romantic modernist"). No doubt the Scottish romantic's best-known lyric has got to be his "To a Mouse: On Turning Her Up in Her Nest with the Plow." The relevant question is the following: Is such concern for a suffering fellow creature, even if outside the human veil, then also evident with Frost? True enough, he certainly took much interest in the animal kingdom, birds and beasts, though never happened to address a poem specifically to one, as did Burns. He admired suffering humanity too. It thus might be recalled, at least by the wayside here, that he honored the likes of Ridgely Torrence of Xenia, Ohio (about a mile or so from the multicultural university where I have taught for well over thirty years, Central State), knowing that the latter took pains to honor African Americans, as in his notable *Plays for the Negro Theater*, which broke ground in the development of black histrionics in this country. (True enough, many black people, however, would naturally prefer to think of their tradition in this respect as largely self-generated, and not thereby by Torrence, but that is of secondary concern.) One of these dramas, *Simon the Cyrenean*, was then given a staged reading by African American students at the three-day Frost conference our Department sponsored in 1982 with a handsome grant from the Ohio Program for the Humanities, as well as several Dayton businesses. (Torrence, in point of fact, had wanted all the characters to be played by non-Caucasians, though white himself.)[2]

Burns also, like other British romantics, loved the out-of-doors in general, and his balladic effects related to that as well. In turn, we think of Frost's admiration of Wordsworth and the elevation of nature *by him* almost to a deity ("From Nature doth emotion come"),[3] though it is well to bear in mind that Frost qualified the Poet Laureate's influence on him also somewhat, finding himself basically a romantic *realist* in the long run, not one given to, as he once put it, "that Beauty is Truth claptrap" (*Selected Letters* 141).

Now Jeffrey Meyers, in his rather controversial biography of Frost, mentions a few things about the Burns kinship which here deserve also repetition and some analysis. For instance, he notices at the outset that "Frost, who was named for Robert Burns as well as Robert Lee [*Lee* being Frost's middle name], heard his mother read aloud from the border ballads, Scott and Burns throughout his childhood" (9). This connection had also been made by Louis Mertins, with a long, direct quotation from the poet on the matter (39), and then by biographer Lawrance Thompson in his first volume (69-70). For example, the poet's mother "may also have realized that [James Macpherson] had indirectly paved the way for some of her favorite romantic poets, such as Burns, Wordsworth, Bryant, and Emerson—many of whose lines she had been quoting to her children since their infancy" (70). Jay Parini also notes this matter (16). So Frost learned of Burns initially from his mother, no less. (Comparable then is the influence now found of Eliot's mother upon Eliot.)[4]

Following this up, Frost alluded to these Scottish writers in his own verse, for instance made a careful examination of Burns's manuscripts "when he visited the rare books library at Buffalo," and even "named his eldest daughter after the heroine of Burns' 'Bonnie Lesley':

> Thou art a queen, fair Lesley,
> Thy subjects we, before thee:
> Thou art divine, fair Lesley,
> The hearts o' men adore thee" (Meyers 9).

It might be added that Lesley Frost Ballantine's daughter, Dr. Lesley Lee Francis, as a scholarly Frostian in her own right following in her grandfather's footsteps, likewise reveals such a nomenclatural debt—even in a clear capacity in her own Scottish-sounding forename.

What is the most self-evident poetic debt of Frost to Burns then? Because

Burns is romantically known so much for "A Red, Red Rose" ("O My Luv's like a red, red rose"), Richard Poirier is right in also sensing an obvious link with Frost's "Asking for Roses," which has, he notes, clear "echoes of Burns" (56). Surely another clear-cut borrowing from Burns would be his use of "the same tender, protective theme of Burns' 'To a Mouse' ('Wee, sleekit, cow'rin', tim'rous beastie, / O, what a panic's in thy breastie!') in 'The Exposed Nest'" (as Meyers [9] notes). Then it might well be mentioned that, no doubt partly because of his own Scottish heritage, Frost was "baptized in the Presbyterian church" (linked likewise with the Scots originally), albeit he "finally worshipped with the Swedenborgians" (Meyers 10). Eventually, however, religiously speaking, he became more of a loner, or, as he might put it, a veritable "peeker."[5]

Because of 1996 as the Burns centenary year, some consideration of his being critically reassessed in this respect needs to be brought in, if a bit belatedly, too. For this reason a British specialist in Romanticism, Nicholas Roe, has a leading essay in the Oxford *Essays in Criticism* on Burns that can be of some help. One of the points made at the start and considered throughout is the poet's relation with the fair sex and how that affected his overall reputation. Thus, even on the centenary of Burns's birth (in 1859), Roe says, the Scot was denounced as "a person who never loved a woman but to betray her" (*The Daily Scotsman*, 24 Jan. 1859). For this and similar reasons, Burns's social life became then an object of concern, "an obstacle for nineteenth-century commentators and editors" (Roe 195). Robert Louis Stevenson, then in his own Scottish turn, regretted that Burns had shifted from artistry to hedonistic interests involving licentious love. All this can point, we might think, to present-day (or, really, Meyers-like) concern with Frost's own personal love life, again unduly stressed at times, namely his presumed adulterous relations with his secretary, Kay Morrison, for one. Many reviewers have felt that Meyers has gone much too far (though he presumably based himself to a considerable, but unreserved, extent upon Thompson's unpublished notes and mainly on what Morrison's daughter Ann told him—rumors in part).

Another "affinity" between Burns and Frost that *may* be obliquely drawn from Roe has to do with the so-called Burns penchant for a bit of self-advertisement. In fact, the Preface to Burns's 1786 collection is said to remain "one of the canniest exercises in literary self-promotion ever penned" (200). In a strangely comparable manner, Meyers ends his biography by trying to stress Frost's emphasis upon egotism; Edmund Wilson is thus authoritatively cited as claiming (unfairly) that this poet was "one of the most relentless self-promoters in the history of American literature" (320). Again this represents a derogatory framework that has not endeared the biographer to the hearts of many Frostians, not to say others, though a few may have buckled under the strain of this stigma perhaps.

In any event, during his 1932 dinner get-together with Eliot again, involving the tiff relating to Frost's standing up for Burns, Frost whimsically pretended to compose a poem on the spot to show his adeptness, but that exercise turned out to be no more than a sort of publicity stunt, for he then recited a lyric composed long before. (This is not widely known.) The same sort of publicity exercise can be linked with his familiar recital at Kennedy's Inauguration in that the poem he seemed to have to recite—because of his inability (owing to climactic conditions) to read a new one he had composed for the occasion—was evidently really one he had prepared to present again anyway; that is, to do so after reciting his new "Introduction" to it. So he did not, in truth, show off his ability to recite a poem suddenly from the depths of his memory. Certainly such performances need not be taken as basically lacking in frankness, though they do admittedly serve to call attention, to some extent, to the poet rather more perhaps than to his poetry as such.

Clearly the leading Burns-Frost correlation happens to lie in their use of the speech of common folk, a characteristic they strongly shared with Wordsworth (who himself had drawn special attention to the Scot, probably largely for this reason).[6] Frost's own affinities with Wordsworth can scarcely be discounted, although certain critics nowadays seem to prefer to dwell rather on incidental divergencies. Certainly "The Road Not Taken" had some basis in Frost's reading of Wordsworth's "Lucy" poetry (for which, see my *Frost's Road Taken* 3-17), to which Meyers happens also then indirectly to allude (142), though it was initially cited in print by an India Indian, C. D. Narasimhaiah, editor of *The Literary Criterion*. Lastly, even as Roe brings in several times Burns's affinity with Keats (197, 214), so it might easily be recalled that Frost, too, was a Keatsian in his own way, his famous lyric "The Demiurge's Laugh" surely having been inspired, at least in part, by Keats's familiar sonnet "Why Did I Laugh Tonight?," a matter discussed in my essay in the Winter 1970 Frost issue of the Ball State University *Forum* and more recently in the Fall 1998 *South Carolina Review*. Thus, to cite this "comical" connection, by which I mean one dealing with laughter as such, is then hardly in itself to end merely on, let us say, a light-hearted note in parting. Thematically, it has its serious historical basis. And as Sandra Katz's helpful book on the subject has now shown, even humor can have its solemn moments.

In short, then, "fire and ice" here can mean thematically that seeming opposites still attract—a clearcut romantic perspective.

NOTES

[1]Also see the paper "Eliot and Frost" that William Harmon (Univ. of North Carolina, Chapel Hill) presented for the ALA a few years ago; he graciously sent me a copy. One of his points at the outset was in relating Eliot's phrase "frost and fire" ("Little Gidding," l. 4, in his *Four Quartets*) to Frost's "Fire and Ice."

[2]See also Melvin Tolson, an African American poet who was at a Bread Loaf Writers' Conference and was influenced by Frost, on which see Robert M. Farnsworth, *Melvin B. Tolson, 1898-1966: Plain Talk and Poetic Prophecy* 2079 *et passim*. Tolson happened to teach at Central State University—not my campus, however, but that in Oklahoma (now renamed).

[3]See Wordsworth's opening phrase in *The Prelude*, Book 13.

[4]Cf. Lee Oser's emphasis on this matter in his new book, which I have recently reviewed with this in mind. Yet reference should also be made to Elisabeth Däumer's essay on Eliot's mother—allusion to which was cut from my review by the editorial staff without my permission.

[5]David Sanders wrote me, shortly before the Frost conference at the Bread Loaf School of English, about the Frost-Burns connection in Frost's letter to Sidney Cox (15 Sept. 1913) and the way Burns related then to a current project of Frost's. The letter contains the line "I wonder whether [Northerners] made Burns' poems or Burns' poems made them" (see Thompson, *Selected Letters* 94). The Burns "Mouse" poem is cited in a previous letter of Frost's (1 July 1907) to Susan Hayes Ward. Burns is also cited in Cox's letters to Frost (12 July 1936, 14 Jan. 1946).

[6]This paper does not take into account certain Scottish affinities which may be found in one poet but not in the other. One quality worth momentary consideration at least is the so-called *dour* attitude, typical of Scots in many ways, a melancholy, somber approach which is evident in Frost but hardly typically so in Burns. At least this does not stereotype their relationship then. As for Burns being truly considered "romantic," he is taken as such in the *Norton Anthology* but not thus represented in the *Oxford Anthology,* though Blake is.

# CHAPTER XXV

## WHENCE THE NAME OF NANCY DREW?

In a recent essay on Dickens's *The Mystery of Edwin Drood* in The Journal of the American Name Society I cautiously felt obliged to add an endnote to the effect that the name of the celebrated teenage unraveler of crimes, Miss Nancy Drew, may derive from well-known Dickensian sources: in short, that it was a conflation of the heroine's name of *Nancy* from *Oliver Twist* along with a shortening of *Drood* from the mystery novel bearing that surname. The immense popularity of the last of Dickens's works, fragmentary only because the Inimitable died before it could be completed (thus allowing for countless sleuths to enlist their prowess in undertaking to accomplish what he himself was unable to), lends itself to this verdict.

Likewise Nancy in the earlier novel by Dickens surely represents that novelist's most famous female creation, if we dismiss a few less relevant, and certainly much older, people, ones in *David Copperfield*. Then *Oliver Twist* can be taken as a sort of prime detective novel on its own, one appealing especially to youth as well, in that Fagin has to be brought to court. Compare Russell Nye, who writes in *The Unembarrassed Muse*: "In the earlier books [in the Nancy Drew series] there were . . . aggressive Jews" (87); Fagin's reputation can be related. As for *Drood*, the first name of *Edwin* is, in effect, partially anagrammatized in the combination of *Nancy* and *Drew*, for many of its letters happen to be present in the amalgam.

Did the creator have all this consciously in mind? Perhaps not, but does it really matter here? Many influences are half-conscious. A feminist reaction worth taking into account, though, might well be the following: Does this mean that we shall next have to consider that the familiar, contemporary Hardy boys series likewise bears somehow on a complementary Victorian novelist, that is Thomas Hardy? Hardly so. (I owe this demurrer to a knowledgeable feminist employed at The New School for Social Research in New York, whose name I am not at this time at liberty to divulge.) But then Dickens was rather more popular to begin with. At least in passing it might now be mentioned that a favorite of Dickens was Wilkie Collins, whose famous mystery novel *The Moonstone* clearly had at least titular influence upon the Nancy Drew *Moonstone Castle* mystery (1963). Insofar as the series is based on the Gothic pattern as ultimately deriving from German and British Romanticism, it would relate more to Collins and Dickens than to Hardy.

The onomastic suggestions made herewith at least provide us with one last unravelment of the Dickensian mystery tale: it achieves its ending, or solution as it were, in the name *Drood* being transformed into, of all things, its diminutive. True, it might be contended that, in the same manner, *Drew* could be taken as an accommodated "diminutive" of *druid*; such an analogy is a bit arcane, but it does not diminish the Dickensian association even as *Drood* enthusiasts have been, in turn, classified as *Droo-ids*. The changeover from *Drood* to *Drew* may appear indeed a bit ironic, but hardly for that reason displeasing to readers of the Nancy Drew series. A further plausible reason behind Drew's having an antecedent onomastic origin might be seen in the fact that the name of her creator, Carolyn Keene, was also pseudonymous. This effect then is also, to a certain extent, ironic. In any case, if the female-male combination of Nancy and Edwin Drood in Nancy Drew may at first appear odd, it is useful to be reminded that the mystery series also had its origin in both the male and female: Edward Stratemeyer and Harriet S. Adams. Although the original author was Mildred Wirt Benson, it was Stratemeyer who formulated the name Drew as a counterpart to the names of his previous male characters (on which see Caprio 18). In terms of her Jungian approach, Caprio prefers to see *Drew* simply in terms of the past tense of *draw*. Lastly, for help in arriving at source material in this essay, I am indebted to Norma Pecora of Emerson College, a Nancy Drew specialist.

# CHAPTER XXVI

## SALINGER'S CAULFIELD: A REFRACTION OF
## COPPERFIELD AND HIS CAUL

Surely a major irony of J. D. Salinger's *The Catcher in the Rye* is that its
would-be hero, though openly disdaining what he calls all the "David Copperfield"
kind of nonsense even on the very first page, is in fact described in terms of the
*Bildungsroman* as stemming to a large extent from Dickens. What is more, though
he repeatedly exhibits revulsion at what he dubs the "phony" type of individual, he
himself turns out to be the biggest fake of them all. In the light of this latent irony, it
is puzzling why controversy has arisen over the genesis of his name. One former
editor of the journal *College English* writes that "even his name, one suspects, is an
ironic amalgam of the last names of movie stars William Holden and Joan Caulfield,"[1]
who, he reminds us, co-starred in the 1947 cinematic version of *Dear Ruth*.

Yet, in a rebuttal that reappeared when editor Oldsey's article was
reprinted in a collection of essays, he is taken to task on the grounds that the Caulfield
name in the Salinger stories predates the film by several years (Bhaerman 508). An
essay by Dexter Martin offers a more speculative solution: "Salinger's primary reason for selecting Caulfield is obviously the fact that it means 'cold field'; and, therefore, within the book, it signifies 'cemetery'—specifically the one in which Allie is
buried. Since Holden means 'deep valley,' it may also imply 'grave' or 'abyss'; but
certainly its primary significance is 'trying to find somebody or something to hold
on to' or 'trying to hold myself together and find somebody who will help.' Holden

Caulfield means, then, 'The boy who needs love because he's obsessed with the death of his brother.'"[2]

But is it not crystal clear that the name springs at least partly from that of Copperfield, the latter reported also on the first page, this time of Dickens's own novel, as being born with a caul, thereby betokening good luck? Both David and Holden tell their own stories and relate rather similar early school experiences (whereby Holden's story may derive at least indirectly from David's); both try to "find themselves" and thus exhibit conviction as a main source of strength (but also of weakness).[3] Even as David describes his friend Steerforth as an adolescent Victorian immoralist, Holden presents us with Stradlater, the so-called "secret slob" and "sexy bastard."[4] Whereas one steers forth, the other does his straddling. Elsewhere, in the Simonson-Hager collection *Salinger's "Catcher in the Rye*," Carl Strauch comments further on the Dickens-Salinger "literary parallel" (48).

That Salinger's popular novel has, in spite of some controversy, certain convincing literary antecedents is now a commonplace; however, so far commentary has limited itself to some general consideration of the place of his work in the history of the picturesque tradition and, in particular, in its relation to Twain's *Huckleberry Finn*.[5] Yet perhaps especially because of Twain's having been so often compared with Dickens, notably by Joseph Gardner in *PMLA*, the Dickensian element in Salinger's novel should be taken well into account too. It might be remarked that this is part of the "catch" to *The Catcher*, for Salinger had literary resonances in the back of his mind and not merely in the implicit allusion to Robert Burns in his title ("coming through the rye"). Granted, however, Alan Trudgett has commented in the London *Sunday Times* that the Salinger title relates also to a fielding position in baseball, the catcher of the ball being in rye grass and "positioned out on the boundary," thus, like Holden Caulfield, "observes rather than participates" (21 Aug. 1994).

The Romantic element in *David Copperfield* is more striking in various ways. Holden's adoration of his little sister points back to David's puppy love for Little Emily. Even the overt profanity in Salinger might have been indirectly suggested by Dickens—that is, if Salinger had in mind the expression "what the dickens" as a euphemism he wished to overcome and in doing so unconsciously linked the phrase with the earlier novelist. We might be reminded that Dickens himself, in performing in a production of Shakespeare's *The Merry Wives of Windsor*, was attracted to the expression "the dickens his name is" (3.2.16). All told, the most evident connection is that of nomenclature. Yet it would be carrying coals to Newcastle to proceed a step farther and maintain that even the forename, Holden, has a hidden resonance from the Copperfield novel (Mr. Gummidge there being the "old 'un"). More likely Holden would signify something generally in the past through the connotation of "olden," thereby not ruling out some Dickensian association either. Moreover, surely Caulfield's former teacher, *Antolini*, represents a collapsed form of yet another name in Dickens: *Mantolini*.

In any event, Dickens himself considered *David Copperfield* to be the hero of his own favorite novel, so not to be discountenanced is the fact that the protagonist's initials happen to be the same as those of his author, though in reverse.

NOTES

[1]See Bernard S. Oldsey's "The Movies in the Rye" as reprinted then in the Simonson and Hager collection on the Salinger novel,

[2]See again the Simonson-Hager collection.

[3]Janet H. Brown's "The Narrator's Role in *David Copperfield*" is helpful here.

[4]Strauch's "A Reading of *Salinger's The Catcher in the Rye*" is of special help here.

[5]Numerous articles can be informally cited, e.g. in *College English* 18 (1956):76-80; *American Quarterly* 9 (1957): 144-58; *Ohio University Review* 2 (1960): 31-42.

A RESPONSE

[Professor Jane Vogel of Ithaca College, author of *Allegory in Dickens* (1977), has sent a response to my essay on the Copperfield / Caulfield relationship, which was first published in *Notes on Contemporary Literature* [1973] and then in somewhat revised form in *Word Ways* [1994], now revised again. She indicated in her letter that she would not mind if her material was made use of and published under "both our names."]

I instantly, long ago, linked in mind p. 1 of *David Copperfield* and p. 1 of *Catcher*: "Caul," yes indeed, surely. As David ran away from the deadly Murdstone-Creakle world, Holden ran away in the wee hours from "Egypt," Pencey Prep, and, like David, wanders among monsters (the Go-roo man). Holden is among monsters like Maurice, the hotel elevator "boy" pimp. As Steerforth misleads David, so "Luce," the former dorm advisor, pulls stunts on Holden. So there's a long night's journey for both David and Holden.

Yes, as David idealizes and stores Agnes in his soul's deepest sanctuary, its Holy of Holies, so Holden stores Jane Gallagher, the pure and wounded girl who "kept her kings in the back row." When Stradlater takes Jane out—when Holden knows she is in the back seat of a car with hotshot, filthy, carnal, cold Stradlater—he goes wild, punches, carries on. When David hears Uriah Heep daring to claim Agnes, *he* thinks of running Uriah through with a hot poker! Jane is never seen, so, like Agnes, she is ethereal, a goddess. Steerforth is to Little Emily as Stradlater to Jane too.

*Holden* proves to be a Dickens sort of name: at times he's barely holdin' on; his mania to save catch-falling people, the way he *holds on* too tightly to Allie, the dead little brother, pities *even* enemies (Sunny, Maurice, dumb "Ackley"—*acne* with those pimples!); he is too quick to be *caught*; he's *too* much of a "catcher"—retains *too* much sorrow and the past. No one is holdin' *him* (except Phoebe). And, like David, Holden is literary: invents scenes, plays parts (as with Ernie Morrow's mother on the train, when Holden plays Rudolph Schmidt!). An author *manqué*. . . . Stradlater and Steerforth: the handsome boys; the roommate, schoolmate, who gets away with everything and dazzles and corrupts the girls.

Yes, the "little sister" motif: Emily lost. And Holden's little Phoebe is so vulnerable—she's ready to run away *with* him near the end. That's what saves him: he sees his wild flailings are harrying her, harming and endangering *her* life: she *must* stay in school and play Benedict Arnold in the school play. . . .

David's rising up from *his* flounderings and false directions (Steerforth, law studies) seems to me like Holden's at the end. Let's hope his long Confession readies him to go back into the fray, *claim* his Agnes, Jane, feel worthy of her at last.

Is Sallie Hayes, the empty silly show-off, a sort of *Dora Spenlow*, the wrong girl in David's life? A temporary infatuation with no *moral* base? Not quite.

Agnes Wickfield is under the shadow of her drunken, troubled father—Jane Gallagher, under the shadow of her lecherous (we assume), drinking step-father—and both are vulnerable, sad, approached by profane eyes: Uriah's, Stradlater's. And David and Holden are helpless to prevent this, deeply troubled to look on such desecration.

Tim Phoebe calls herself "Hazel Weatherfield," girl sleuth. Copperfield—Weatherfield—Caulfield.

Dickens! The *Dicksteins* live next door to the Caulfields—the only other family on the floor—one door away, symbolically speaking. It *is* a Dickensian allegory of sorts.

[There is much more.]

# CHAPTER XXVII

# HOW BIGGER'S NAME WAS BORN

Creation is an ontological phenomenon. When Richard Wright wrote his explanatory essay "How 'Bigger' Was Born," he was in essence making a distinction between intention and accomplishment: showing that the birth of Bigger Thomas in *Native Son* had various possible origins. Yet just as we can never be sure, from a religious standpoint, when the soul enters the body—or, if it be at the moment of conception, whether what is meant is the conception of the fetus or of a person—so it is difficult to pinpoint the moment when a finished literary product received the spiritual impetus which resulted in its being. The answer to be provided here is one that may or may not have been in the author's conscious intent, but the point is that it exists just as surely as creation exists, and just as surely as there is a difference between intent and creation. So the ultimate relevance of intent to accomplishment is moot. One qualification is relevant here: the answer is not, and should not be, at variance with, or contradictory to, whatever other intentions Wright may have originally had. The answer posed here is that Bigger's name owes something to Shakespeare.

In his essay "How 'Bigger' Was Born,"[1] Wright tells of five possible Biggers that influenced his own Bigger, but he does not explicitly deal with the *name* as such. At one point, in discussing "Bigger No. 3," he tells that "the white folks" called him "a 'bad nigger'" (ix); a colleague at the largely African American state university where I teach has suggested to me that the deletion of three letters (*a, d, n*) results in *Bigger*, a point which is acceptable up to a point, but may appear a bit superficial. The same can be said for the suggestion that his surname, *Thomas*, is simply derived from *Uncle Tom's Cabin* titularly. Of course there is no question that Wright had that novel partly in mind; he refers to his own earlier work *Uncle Tom's Children* in "How 'Bigger' Was Born." Yet a subtle difference exists between *Tom* and *Thom*as, and the idea that Bigger is just an Uncle Tom who has acquired racial dignity of sorts and hence has become literally bigger, acquiring also more formality and distinction even in his nominal promotion from *Tom* to *Thomas*, is a bit simplistic. Certainly it is not unfair to Wright to suggest that his creation involved a more serious genesis.

The Bigger Thomas name specifically derives from that of Othello. This statement can be proved on various levels: historically, psychologically, and linguistically. In brief, the first three letters of the surname constitute a linguistic transformation of the first three letters of Othello's, a shift in the vowel or phoneme "o." The result is metathetic. Shakespeare's own names, for example, provide numerous instances of metathesis already; the most well-known is the *Caliban / can(n)ibal* suggestion. *Holofernes* in *Love's Labour's Lost* has been considered a partial anagram for John Florio's name (especially because Florio himself used partial anagrams); in the same play the character of Moth reflects *Thom*(as) Nashe, and with that we have an exact equivalent to what Wright did with the Moor's name. I say that it is an "exact" equivalent insofar as the effect in both cases involves the Thomas name, though the way in which the shift was made constitutes a reversal. Again, few scholars debate the problem of whether or not Shakespeare was consciously or only subliminally aware of all the linguistic shifts that he created.

Bigger Thomas's first name also resulted from the Othello influence. What must have happened is that Wright's awareness of the fact that the suffix *-ello* is an Italian diminutive ending prompted him to create an Othello who was not diminutive—hence a *bigger Oth-* (thus a Bigger *Tho-*). No doubt he was bothered by the discrepancy he saw between the stature of the Noble Moor and that diminutive ending to Othello's name, and he resolved to settle the problem in his own way. This change is the psychological aspect of the name-change, and more can be said about it later.

As for the historical connection, there is no doubt that *Native Son* was strongly inspired by Shakespeare's tragedy of the Noble Moor. When the source of Bigger's name first came to my awareness, I considered the probability of the indebtedness and found that I have been preëmpted. In an important article, K. Kinnamon points out some of the striking parallels:

> (1) "Stated bluntly, Bigger Thomas is Othello to Mary Dalton's Desdemona";
> (2) "like Desdemona, Mary is misunderstood by her father, whom she deceives";
> (3) "Like Othello, Bigger kisses ere he kills"

and so on.[2] The most startling correspondence is, of course, that both Othello and Bigger Thomas kill twice; Othello kills the white woman who loves him just as Bigger assassinates the white woman who befriends him, and both do so in precisely the same manner: by smothering their victims in bed. The second killings are not comparable, but these do not really have to be, for the tragedy that ensues in both accounts in certainly comparable. Indeed, Kinnamon overlooks one of the most important associations between them, namely the psychological component: both Othello and Bigger were acting under duress to an extent that suggests that they were temporarily insane.

Othello's Iago becomes in effect the predominantly white society for Bigger Thomas. Just as Iago represents a devil figure, so the white man emerges as such in *Native Son*. Just as Iago tells the audience that Othello is epileptic and breaks out into savage madness, so an attempt is made at the trial scene in the novel to reveal Bigger's lack of mental and emotional equilibrium. One difference is that Othello says that he acted "not wisely, but too well," but Bigger Thomas does not allow himself an apologia.

Although *Native Son* has come in for comparison with Dostoievski's *Crime and Punishment* more than with *Othello*, the parallels with the drama are, on the whole, much more obvious and significant. Indeed, the only points of interest favoring the influence of the Russian are that his work is also in the genre of the novel and that Wright is known to have admired him. But Wright knew *Othello* as well, if not better. As Kinnamon shows, "J. Saunders Redding first met Wright in the summer of 1942 at a performance of the Paul Robeson *Othello*, at which time Wright demonstrated a close knowledge of the play" (358n2).[3]

What Wright probably did not know is anything about the origin of Othello's name. It is quite possible that he *was* aware that it is not to be found in Shakespeare's major source, Cinthio's *Ecatommithi*, not in the French translation by Chappuys, which the evidence suggests Shakespeare used. This was common knowledge. The only name in the Italian-French tales that is the same as a character's in the play in any way is that of *Disdemona* (called *Disdemone* in the French version), which then became *Desdemona*. Wright most likely assumed that Shakespeare wanted an Italian name for his black hero and simply invented one, adding the *-ello* ending. I doubt that he was aware that the final effect is not at all Italian-sounding (Verdi's *Otello* being named after the fact) and that *-ello* is, though a diminutive to be sure, not one for proper names (where *-ino* and *-etto* are used instead, except in dialects sometimes). Yet that is of little consequence. What is more interesting—again a point that I suspect escaped Wright's attention, largely because the scholarship on it appeared only many years later—is that Shakespeare more than likely partly derived the name *Othello* from *Othoman*. The article by F. N. Lees pointing out that Shakespeare was influenced by Othoman and his entourage as reported in Richard Knolles's *The History of the Turks* also suggests that the *-ello* ending was for a diminutive effect, that the Moor was, in a word, a "little Othoman" rather than another Othoman the Great.[4]

Since, however, this suggestion may appear to detract from the Moor's tragic stature, I have proposed (in *Names*, XXII, 183-84, but see Ch. V here) that the final *ello* was metathesis for the name of Leo, since it is known that John Leo's career and book, *The History and Description of Africa* in translation, most probably influenced Shakespeare in writing the tragedy of the Noble Moor.[5] At least there is very strong circumstantial evidence to this effect, as reported by the leading source-hunter Bullough and the African scholar Eldred Jones.[6] Just as Othello reveals some of the effects of Christianization, so Leo happened to have his name converted from that of Pope Leo X. Othello was thus an Othoman-Leo or a converted Moor in more ways than one, for he may well have initially been a Moslem, then had to accept Christianity for a marriage to Desdemona in Catholic Italy.

It is not so surprising to connect Bigger Thomas with the Noble Moor even though the reversal makes of Thomas more of an *I*gnoble Moor, even if one for which society is mainly to blame. As one critic has put it in trying to relate Bigger to another Shakespearean hero, "Like Macbeth, Bigger believes 'all the world's a stage,' and that his share in the drama of life must be *big* enough and *violent* enough and *dramatic* enough to be permanently etched in the sands of time."[7] But Bigger is more like Othello than Macbeth—even in name, as I have shown. As Kinnamon rightly says, "It is not, after all, surprising that in writing his American tragedy of race and sex, Wright turned to the greatest English work dealing with similar themes" (359). Though ironically not a "bigger Othello," Bigger Thomas begets his name from the Moor, among other sources, and the transformation process tells us something about the interplay of history and psychology as well as significant linguistic changes.[8]

## NOTES

[1]Originally in *The Saturday Review of Literature* (1 June 1940), it was reprinted in the introduction to Wright's *Native Son* in 1966.

[2]This was reported in "Richard Wright's Use of *Othello* in *Native Son*" in the journal of the African American College Language Association in 1969. It might be mentioned that analogously Romeo also kisses, then kills, in his own way.

[3]Kinnamon cites here *Anger and Beyond: The Negro Writer in the United States* 200.

[4]See his "Othello's Name" in the *Oxford Notes and Queries* as well as an opposing view published ten years later there by T. Sipahigil which does not provide any exact Italian equivalent. Lees has been indirectly corroborated by Geoffrey Bullough, whose *Narrative and Dramatic Sources of Shakespeare, Vol. III: Major Tragedies* cites Knolles's work and adds that the name *Angelus* as cited in Knolles was apparently also transformed into that of *Angelo* in *Othello*.

[5]Lois Whitney's major article "Did Shakespeare Know *Leo Africanus*?" points this out.

[6]See his *Othello's Countrymen* 21-25.

[7]Amis 240. The source for the quotation is *As You Like It* (2.7.139).

[8]Since this essay was initially printed in *Studies in Black Literature*, in an early draft form, another interpretation of Bigger's name has emerged which is also valid, if a bit minuscule. It connects the forename with the meaning of *bugger* ("and while Bigger may not be a sodomite his offense is sexual") along with other connotations, e.g.: "Bigger's first name has the appearance of an adjective in the comparative form. The bigness thus attributed to him is in part ironic, but if he is the representative black, perhaps that which he would be bigger than is the representative white, and this makes him even more fearsome to whites. Or perhaps he is a bigger doubter and bigger martyr than other Thomases, for his challenge to white society effectually expresses doubt of that society, and he is

martyred in the cause of blackness (and perhaps of all people). . . . His name thus appears in the form of modifier-plus-first name, a form favored by condescending whites in addressing blacks, as in 'Uncle Tom,' 'Aunt Jemima,' 'Little Black Sambo,' 'Ole Black Joe.' Bigger's name thus resembles those which whites have used when trying to keep blacks 'in their places'—but in the novel Bigger breaks out of 'his place'" (B. L. Clark 80).

# CHAPTER XXVIII

## *AMERIKA* AND AMERICA:
## NOMENCLATURAL PARALLELS IN KAFKA,
## LEWIS, AND DICKENS

Aside from their common ties in confronting our "brave new world," Franz Kafka and Sinclair Lewis are akin at least in one key respect: both were, in their own way, following the satiric lead of Dickens, who likewise satirized America. No attempt will be made here to posit any distinctive *thematic* debt of Lewis to Kafka (or vice versa for that matter, which may be possible), though such historical correlations are hardly entirely out of the question. To start with, in a general sense they both happened to take a very special interest in the genius of Charlie Chaplin.[1]

Before my concentrating on onomastic analogies, some background material may be imperative. To begin, if the essence of fine writing is at least partly in its individuality, a commonly accepted dictum, then it is well to recognize from the outset how such an effect was here obtainable through a broad satire of American standardization. Because Kafka is comparable enough with other satirists as diverse as Swift, to correlate him also with Lewis need not be thought ungermane if it can fill a certain comparatist gap. With regard to Lewis, true, a closer affinity is detectable, in general, between his work and the later and shorter German novels of Martin Walser,[2] yet the Dickensian tie-in at least is what makes our own subject particularly fascinating. For Kafka truly admitted to basing much in *Amerika*, notably even the opening chapter, on his reading of Dickens.[3] In turn worth examining in this connection is E. W. Tedlock's valuable analysis of Kafka's appropriation of *David Copperfield*, but that would entail a separate study.

At the outset, let us accept an obvious *donnée*: that Kafka and Lewis, like virtually any two major novelists, clearly offer many more divergencies than acute similarities—for example, Kafka symbolizing the individual as such in his "K." and Karl Rossmann, Lewis epitomizing overstandardization instead in *Main Street* and *Babbitt*. Still, the model role of *David Copperfield* evidently affected both novelists, notably in such popular works of theirs, respectively, as *Amerika* and *Babbitt*, Lewis being stimulated in a more cursory manner admittedly than was the German author. (Though Kafka's name derives from his home country, Czechoslovakia, he wrote in German and died in Germany.) Whereas George F. Babbitt and his ilk indulge in humdrum concern with the capitalistic minutiae of daily living such as advertising, Copperfield becomes sensitive to less mercenary elements in human behavior. Nonetheless, Babbitt is truly just as ego-centered and, though much older, "bounces about," as it were, like a rabbit (hence, in part, his name's connotation here) and with nearly as much vigor. Such a verbal nonce term is used advisedly in that Dickens, too, has a certain "bouncy" quality, in effect chooses to bounce the reader from one point of view to another as in telling his supreme story of *Bleak House*. In his turn, Kafka's youthful hero Karl Rossmann has a symbolic surname literally standing for "horse-man" in order to provide some exuberance of his own, especially when he finally applies to "The Nature Theatre of Oklahoma" for a position.

Now what else does the Rossmann name intone? Several studies are of some help, notably Elisabeth Rajec's Germanic monograph on Kafkaesque onomastics and later Jean Jofen's anagogical study. Rajec, for example, finds the symbolic horse-rider conception pointing to Rossmann's eventual pseudonym; insofar as such a rider can be easily recognized in *Amerika* as non-Caucasian (as, let us say, an Indian), so Karl's final acceptance of the sobriquet *Negro* reflects that somewhat. (Here we might want to recollect that Franz Kafka's own surname happened to mean *blackbird*.)

Jofen sees the horse / man combination (apropos of letters between Kafka and Max Brod) in terms of the following query: "Am I a circus rider on two horses?" She infers from this seeming contradiction that what Kafka must mean is that he "cannot be both 'the most Jewish' and 'the most German writer' at the same time" (x). Related to this anomaly, she would assert, is such a Yiddish saying as "Mit eyn tokhes" (With a single backside) one cannot sit on two tables. The basic overall inference therefore is that Kafka is more Jewish than German in his ethnicity and thinking, and that that is what colors this novel. (But at the same time he happens to be also more Germanic than Czech.)

Such an intercultural dilemma is worth tackling on its own, but somewhat outside the scope of this essay, in which onomastically the problem is with the meaning of "K." in *The Trial* and *The Castle*. Most readers accept the commonplace that this initial stands primarily for Kafka himself, but then could it not represent something else as well, even, say, *Kristus* (Czech for *Christ*) or *Krist* (German for *Christ*, in some cases)? Rajec does admit this plausibility, finding in the initial "K.," as she puts it, "Ein weiteres Kryptogram (Christus Kafka Karl)" (111). If that assumption is at all valid, could then the forename *Josef* when attached to "K." refer not only to the blessed son of Jacob, but even to Jesus born as *ben*-Joseph and at one time at least so called by Jewish historians?

Such a question is perilous to be apodeictic about, especially when Kafka's own particular background would have to come into vital play as well. For example, he is known for having substituted the name *Georg* for *Karl* in some manuscripts of *Amerika*, since he had a younger brother with that name. Likewise, even as Karl's uncle is called *Jakob*, so Kafka's grandfather happened to possess that very name too. Whether this would then relate back to Joseph as the son of Jacob more than to Joseph as the earthly father of Jesus constitutes another problem, not one for me to indulge in here.

Clearly some connection with the family name is to be discerned in both the full names *Joseph K.* and *Karl Rossmann*, the added vowel in the latter forename (K-*a*) lending itself in a dual capacity to the same concatenation in the name of *Kafka*. Kurt Fickert of Wittenberg University in his first Kafka book, *Kafka's Doubles*, posits that "linguistically Karl has a relationship to the German 'churl,' and the name might refer to Rossmann's status as an outsider" (37). Then he adds: "On the other hand, since Kafka was fond of associating his oppressed characters, by way of paradox, with the powerful, with monarchs in particular, he may have been alluding to the Emperor Charles [Karl der Gross], for whom the German university and a famous bridge in Prague [Karlsbrücke, which Kafka cites in a story] were named" (37). That could be. Kafka's low-keyed characters have seemingly unbefitting names.

But, in terms of the present essay, with its satiric focus harking back also to Dickens, the characteristic animal imagery in the surname becomes more revealing, connecting again with not only Kafka's own name as having animal meaning (i.e., *crow*) yet with one of his other heroes waking up one fine morning in *The Metamorphosis* (*Die Verwandlung*) to find himself transformed into a vermin.[4] At any rate, animal imagery thereby predominates. At this point the biographical critic might intrude and counter this by saying that all the Rossmann surname harks back to is the name of the ship Kafka's editing friend Artur Holitscher had used, but why not respond that such a prosaic genesis should easily here be dispensed with? What is rather more notable then is that Kafka's animal imagery eventually reverts back to the ebullient fantasy of Dickens, whose fertile animism is so often seen as a chief source of his imaginative vitality. Sideways, as it were, it would also call forth Lewis's poignant use of animal descriptions, such as his barnyard effects in *Elmer Gantry*, also indebted strongly to Dickens's lively fantasy.[5]

The best overall approach to the issue of social satire in both Kafka and Lewis is apropos of the attitude expressed toward not Jewish people alone, but African Americans and native Indians. Recollect here Kafka's "wünsch, Indianer zu werden" (wish to become an Indian). Truly Rossmann's assuming the pseudonym of *Negro* toward the end of *Amerika* is, in effect, an ironic commentary on overstandardization in our land of limitless possibilities. Consider especially Richard Malmsheimer's commentary:

> Although quickly discovered to be unqualified as an engineer, Karl is at least reassured by the man in charge who tells him: "There is no need to worry. We can employ everybody" (284). In his relief, Karl is unaware of the underlying irony of the man's statement. The Nature Theatre of Oklahoma, which gives him refuge, does not accept individuals as individuals, only as representations of the undiscriminated, mass "everyone." With no papers to identify him and no qualifications to recommend him, Karl becomes known to others simply as "Technical Worker." This way he achieves his own kind of miscellaneous status.[6]

But what is the association between the name *Negro* and the sort of occupation he finally accepts? If the job represents a form of black *death*, as has been suggested (for example by Jofen), then the dark effect already in his name's meaning is symbolic. Granted, it *is* somewhat misleading to identify blackness here aesthetically with both skin pigment and "obliteration of self," in that the consequence of such a correlation could be playing into the hands of racists who seek to divide and rule by stressing only the so-called mediocre or undifferentiated qualities of African Americans. One Kafka critic, Heinz Politzer, comes closer to the more essential point when he observes an association between the Rossmann nickname and the kind of work he has to perform, namely *Schwarzarbeit* ("black work") (159), but even here the irony can become elusive.

What seems most important is Karl's unconscious (or oblique) identification of his plight with that of some blacks, possibly reminding the reader that certain Africans have also been Jewish (Ethiopian and Sephardic types), thereby inherently recollecting the suffering of two ethnic groups. (Literally *Schwarzarbeit* has another meaning in Germany of course.)

This indirectly brings us now to the focus on religious satire. Here we might pause to consider one highly critical viewpoint that has been put forth, namely that the so-called "Nature Theatre" stands somehow for the Christian Church—in some ways a pantheistic thought. Yet offensive though such a bald correlation may be to some readers, it should not be totally overlooked, even as acceptance of certain stringent church dogmas can often enough be linked with a sort of death, another form of the downplaying of the self, though ideally that should hardly be the case.

Now the statues of angels at the entrance to the "Nature Theatre" evidently represent some sort of religious insignia, and certainly religious ritual has its analogies with that of the stage as well, hence duly prompting the entire "Theatre" concept. But how then would this impinge on the viewpoint that Kafka's suffering heroes also amount to sacrificial reflections, say, of the Savior, at least from an aesthetically universal point of view, if not a religious one?

In answer, revert to Kafka's "K.," who can well be thought of as something more than only a Jewish martyr (or as typifying the son Franz at the mercy of a domineering bourgeois father). For instead of being a Christ-figure as such, he might rather stand for Jesus's misunderstood, lonely, individualized existence poised against the overly standardized religion of His time. True enough, if K.'s predicament reveals that of man's inherent sinfulness, as has often been thought, he could hardly stand for Christ in any very orthodox sense. Kafka did have incidental ambiguous things to say on the subject of Original Sin and its general implications. So if K.'s name and character symbolize something spiritual, they do so more from an aesthetic rather than any formally theological point of view.

As so often with Kafka, especially in this novel, Dickens in turn bounces in once again because of this Inimitable's ambivalent attitude toward formal religion—his well-known retelling of Jesus's story for his children hardly being in any rigorous sense orthodox (though it has come to be called *The Life of Our Lord*—see Ch. XV). Likewise he made good-natured sport of well-meaning but limited ministers, notably of the Rev. Chadband in *Bleak House*, whose surname itself reflects on his oily and ultra-urbane mannerisms. And this same kind of fun is then found in Lewis's Elmer Gantry, who is at least supposedly "of the gentry," as his name's very sound may obliquely (or at least dialectally) suggest.

Finally, in summing up the satirical affinity of *Amerika* with *Babbitt*, notice a basic distinction evident from the outset: Rossmann has virtually the mentality of a child throughout, whereas the realtor, though comically naive himself about cultural values, maintains a kind of sportive manhood. Aside from their ages, the main distinction is that between introvert and extrovert, between someone at the mercy of society (hence with inferiority feelings) and a person supposedly in control of social forces (sometimes then to society's peril), thereby exhibiting a certain superiority complex. Thus Kafka's original title for Amerika, namely *Der Verschollene* (*The One Who Vanished*), points up Rossmann's eventual turning into a kind of cultural non-entity.

Still, at the end, our country begins to emerge, if somewhat ironically, as indeed the "land of unlimited possibilities," of which Kafka had dreamed. In finally becoming a part of the "Nature Theatre," then, Rossmann does achieve a certain equanimity—whereby the horse returns to nature, its pasture, as it were—even in his becoming one with "everyone." If he loses therewith some of his individuality, he nonetheless can assume the role of a modern everyman, whereby he at least finds himself free from the spying interests of an all-powerful European state. (Kafka was indeed prophetic in this respect.) As such, Karl is not really a tragic figure and even questionably a "pathetic" one; hence Max Brod's own posthumous name for the novel, *Amerika*, works. In comparison, Babbitt, too, is redeemed in spite of himself—even though his town of Zenith has been deemed ironically a hell on earth—because he has a good heart. Are we not indirectly at least reminded of Dickens once again? For the Inimitable played even with reversing his own initials in inventing

David Copperfield the same way that Lewis then acted in *The Man Who Knew Coolidge*—an anomaly that is commonly enough recognized now.

So if Kafka's vision of the United States is, as at least one reviewer had put it, "baroque," *Babbitt* can be seen as representing at least a milder, more realistic refraction of the American scene. It holds its own even when placed against the output of a genius like Kafka, just as its own authenticity provides a salutary antidote to the Kafkaesque superimposition of Old World values upon an America of the twentieth century.

## APPENDIX:
## A SAMPLE TABLE OF CORRELATIONS

1 *Bigness*

Lewis:  Babbitt respects bigness in anything: in mountains, jewels, muscles, wealth, or words.

Kafka:  "For two days and two nights they journeyed on. Only now did Karl understand how huge America was. Unweariedly he gazed out of the window" (*Amerika* 275). The descriptions of skyscrapers and large highways serve as illustrations.

2 *Technocracy*

Lewis:  Babbitt is keenly interested in cars.

Kafka:  Rossmann's admiration of a modernized desk is seen as a "strangely empirical, insight into the future of American automation" (Politzer 136).

3 *Theatricality*

Lewis:  Above all, Babbitt is theatrical. Lewis's own interest in drama led to his collaborations with Sidney Howard. Again evidence of Dickensian influence appears obvious. (Dickens was a dramatist as well as novelist.)

Kafka:  The theatricality of his characters set against a labyrinth of corridors, seemingly endless highways, and the like is surrealistic. Kafka's own interest in the Yiddish theater is germane. When *Amerika* turns to "The Nature Theatre," a Dickensian parallel seems obvious.

194

### 4 *Egotism*

Lewis: "What's the best ole town in the U. S. A.?' 'Zeeeeeen-ith!'" (*Babbitt* 161)

Kafka: Because Kafka never traveled to or in America, he did not have first-hand accounts of such egotism, but he was aware of the chauvinism ascribed to Americans by Dickens, especially in accounts of the slave trade in 1842. This is then evident in Rossmann's appropriation of *Negro*.

### 5 *Novelty*

Lewis: Babbitt's business-like attitude is seen especially in his concern with gimmickry.

Kafka: "'So you have actually old houses in America, too,' said Karl" (*Amerika* 59)—an ironic touch.

### 6 *Tobacco*

Lewis: "By the end of three days he was trained to leave his desk, walk to the file, take out and light a cigar, without knowing that he was doing it" (*Babbitt* 40).

Kafka: "a cigar of a thickness which Karl's father in Austria sometimes mentioned as an actual fact but had probably never seen with his own eyes" (*Amerika* 56-57).

(With both Lewis and Kafka, Dickens's accounts of Americans chewing and expectorating tobacco, etc., as in his *American Notes* and letters to his biographer Forster, are worth comparing. Citations to *Amerika* are from the Edwin Muir trans., 1946; to *Babbitt* from the 1922 ed.)

### NOTES

[1]Thus cf. Lewis's *It Can't Happen Here* with Chaplin's *The Great Dictator*. As for the Kafka connections, for kind assistance in commenting on early drafts of this essay I am indebted to Kurt Fickert, Raymond Jaffe, Jean Jofen, Renate Rewald, Jane Vogel, and those attending an MLA session on "Literary Onomastics" for The American Name Society in 1992 in New York City, for which an early version was first presented.

[2]For this point I am especially indebted to Kurt Fickert.

[3]Jean Bofen has expressed to me her personal feeling that the influence would have been more that of Sholem Asch.

[4]For my association of this novel with the name of "The Beatles," see my note "The Beatles as Kafkaesque," following my hearing a major lecture on "Why the Beatles are Called the Beatles" at the second Symbiosis conference in England (1999). Partly because this group of singers based themselves on another group with an insect-sounding name, "The Crickets," I raised the issue at the meeting and in the article that they were thinking not only of the "Beat" movement but of Kafka's beatle story.

[5]See my two Dickens / Lewis articles in *The Bulletin of the New York Public Library* and *The Sinclair Lewis Newsletter*.

[6]This is what Mark Spilka, in *Dickens and Kafka*, calls a new Marxist light on a Dickensian situation (153). Modern-day concern with multiculturalism could be related. As James Atlas, in *Battle of the Books: The Curriculum Debate in America*, has it: "The new all-inclusive curriculum was like the Nature Theatre of Oklahoma . . ., where 'everyone is welcome, everyone can be an artist.' In the universities of the 1980s, every culture was welcome" (30).

PART IV:

CONCLUSION

The question arises whether much of a conclusion to these many diverse approaches to literary onomastics is a must. As indicated at the end of my Foreword, I felt the best solution would be somehow to incorporate aspects of my three main sections, at least in terms of nationalities. For this reason, I was prompted to connect England and America this way—even then by way of a Continental relationship (thus bringing in my own heritage somewhat). Hence I deal with a British cohort, Dickens (who incidentally reworked some Shakespearean influences in part in his creativity) and how he then links with an "American Dickens" (my nomination being Sinclair Lewis rather than Mark Twain) by way of their influence upon a Continental Jew (with Czech and Germanic connections), namely Franz Kafka. I realize that such a seeming *potpourri* may not be everybody's cup of tea, so to speak, but it still synthesizes in many respects the affinities I have been tracing (my own surname, for that matter, being originally of Czech-Germanic origin). More-over, I can provide some factual basis for this relationship in terms of verbal and imagery parallels which I choose to document in the form of a listing at the end of the essay; so the correlation is by no means merely a speculative sort.

Originally I had felt no need to include an introduction to such concluding remarks, but the General Editor of this series, Dr. Leonard Ashley, felt that the last major part of the book should be specifically spaced apart and have the label of "Conclusion." So I present that herewith in the brief form of an *apologia* of sorts.

# SELECT WORKS CITED

Adams, Charles M. "Whitman's Use of 'Grass.'" *American Notes and Queries* 6 (1947): 167-68.

Alter, Robert. "Playing Host to the Doppelgänger." *Times Literary Supplement* 24 Oct. 1986: 1190.

Amis, Lola Jones. "Richard Wright's *Native Son*: Notes." *Negro American Literature Forum* 8 (Fall 1974): 240-43.

Anonymous. *The Lamentable and True Tragedy of M. Arden of Feversham.* 1592. Menston: Scolar Press, 1971.

Ashley, Leonard R. N. "Floreat Florio." *The Shakespeare Newsletter* 30 (1980): 49.

Asselineau, Roger. *The Evolution of Walt Whitman: The Creation of a Personality.* Cambridge, MA: The Belknap Press of Harvard UP, 1960.

Atlas, James. *Battle of the Books: The Curriculum Debate in America.* New York: Norton, 1992.

Aylmer, Felix. *The Drood Case.* New York: Barnes and Noble, 1965.

Baker, Richard M. *The Drood Murder Case.* Berkeley: U of California P, 1951.

Barfoot, C. C. Rev. of J. Vogel's *Allegory in Dickens*, in *English Studies* 59 (1978): 566.

Barton, Sir Dunbar Plunket. *Links Between Ireland and Shakespeare.* Dublin: Maunsel, 1919.

Bengis, Nathan L. "John Jasper's Devotion." *The Armchair Detective* 8 (Aug., 1975): 257-69.

Bernstein, Seymour. "Not in the I or the Ear of the Beholder." *Shakespeare Newsletter* 45 (1995): 53-54.

Bevington, David, ed. *The Complete Works of Shakespeare.* Glenview: Scott, Foresman, 1980.

Bhaerman, Robert D. Rebuttal to Oldsey. *College English* 23 (1962): 508.

Bleiler, Everett F. "The Names in *Drood*." *Dickens Quarterly* 1 (1984): 88-93, 137-42.

Bloom, Clive. "Capitalising on Poe's Detective: The Dollars and Sense of Nineteenth-Century Detective Fiction." In *Nineteenth-Century Suspense: From Poe to Conan Doyle.* Ed. Clive Bloom et al. New York: St. Martin's P, 1988, 14-24.

Bloom, Harold. *Shakespeare: The Invention of the Human.* New York: Pegasus, 1998.

Bloom, Harold, and Lionel Trilling. *Romantic Poetry and Prose.* The Oxford Anthology of English Literature. Oxford: Bxford UP, 1973.

Blythe, Hal, and Charlie Sweet. "The Reader as Poe's Ultimate Dupe in 'The Purloined Letter.'" *Studies in Short Fiction* 26 (1989): 313-15.

Boose, Lynda E. In Merrix and Ranson: 3-38.

Boyd, Aubrey. "A New Angle in the Drood Mystery." *Washington University Stud.* 9 (1922): 35-85.

Briggs, Arthur E. *Walt Whitman: Thinker and Artist.* New York: Greenwood, 1968.

Brody, Paula. "Shylock's Omophagia." *Literature and Psychology* 17 (1967): 229-33.

Brown, Janet H. "The Narrator's Role in *David Copperfield.*" *Dickens Studies Annual* 2 (1972): 197-207.

Brown, John Russell, ed. *William Shakespeare, "The Merchant of Venice."* 7th ed., rev. Cambridge: Harvard UP, 1959. (The Arden ed.)

Bullough, Geoffrey, ed. *Narrative and Dramatic Sources of Shakespeare.* 8 Vols. London Routledge, 1975.

Caprio, Betsey. *The Mystery of Nancy Drew.* Trabuco Canyon, CA: Source Books, 1992.

Carson, Rachel. *The Edge of the Sea.* New York: The New American Library, 1955.

Cervo, Nathan A. "Eliot's 'The Love Song of J. Alfred Prufrock.'" *The Explicator* 57 (1999): 227-29.

Chapman, Gerald W., ed. *Essays on Shakespeare.* Princeton: Princeton UP, 1965.

Chapman, Raymond. "*Arden of Faversham*: Its Interest Today." *English* 11 (1956): 15-17.

Charney, Maurice, ed. *"Bad" Shakespeare: Revaluations of the Shakespeare Canon.* Rutherford: Fairleigh Dickinson UP, 1988.

Clark, Beverly Lyon. "Bigger Thomas' Name." *North Dakota Quarterly* 47 (1979): 80.

Clayton, Thomas, ed. *The "Hamlet" First Published (Q1, 1603): Origins, Form, Intertextualities.* Newark: U of Delaware P, 1992.

Coard, Robert L. "Names in the fiction of Edith Wharton." *Names* 13 (1965): 1-10.

Coates, Richard. "A Provincial Bibliography of Names in the Works of Shakespeare." *Names* 35 (1987): 206-23.

Cox, Arthur J. "The *Drood* Remains." *Dickens Studies* 2 (1966): 34-35.

Cox, J. Stevens, ed. *The Library of Thomas Hardy*. Monographs on the Life, Times and Works of Thomas Hardy. No. 52. St. Peter Port, Guernsey: Collier, 1962.

Cox, Lee Sheridan. "The Riddle in *Twelfth Night*." *Shakespeare Quarterly* 13 (1962): 360.

Craig, Hardin. *The Literature of the English Renaissance, 1485-1660*. New York: Collier, 1962.

Craig, Patricia. Rev. of Owen Dudley Edwards, *The Quest for Sherlock Holmes*, in the *Times Literary Supplement* 24 Dec. 1982: 1414.

Crawford, Robert. *Devolving English Literature*. Oxford: Oxford UP, 1992.

Dachslager, E. L. "'The Stock of Barabas': Shakespeare's Unfaithful Villains." *The Upstart Crow: A Shakespeare Journal* 4 (1986): 8-21.

Däumer, Elisabeth. "Charlotte Stearns Eliot and *Ash-Wednesday's* Lady of Silences." *ELH* 65 (1998): 479-501.

Davis, Norman. "Falstaff's Name." *Shakespeare Quarterly* 28 (1977): 513-15.

Dawson, Giles E. "A Seventh Signature for Shakespeare." *Shakespeare Quarterly* 43 (1992): 72-79.

de Grazia, Margrete. *Shakespeare Verbatim: The Reproduction of Authenticity and the 1790 Apparatus*. Oxford: Clarendon, 1991.

Dessen, Alan C. "Weighing the Options in *Hamlet* Q1." In Clayton 65-78.

Dickens, Charles. *"Edwin Drood" and the "Uncommercial Traveller."* London: Nelson, 1926.

—. *"The Life of Our Lord": Written for His Children during the Years 1846 to 1849*. New York: Simon, 1934.

Dove, J. R., and P. Gamble. "'Our Darker Purpose': The Division Scene in *Lear*." *Neuphilologische Mitteilungen* 70 (1969): 306-18.

Dunn, Ian S. "T. S. Eliot, 'The Love Song of J. Alfred Prufrock.'" *The Explicator* 21 (1963): 1, 3.

Edwards, Owen Dudley. *The Quest for Sherlock Holmes: A Biographical Study of Arthur Conan Doyle*. New York: Barnes and Noble, 1983.

Egan, Joseph J. "The Relationship of Theme and Art in *The Strange Case of Dr. Jekyll and Mr. Hyde.*" *English Literature in Transition* 9 (1966): 28-32.

Eliot, T. S. *Inventions of the March Hare: Poems 1909-1917.* Ed. Christopher Ricks. New York: Harcourt, 1996.

—. Selected Essays 1917-1932. New York: Harcourt, 1932.

Ellison, Jerome. "When Howells' Pipedream Came True." *New England Quarterly* 42 (1969): 253-60.

Ellrodt, Robert. "Self-consciousness in Montaigne and Shakespeare." *Shakespeare Survey* 28 (1975): 37-50.

Elmessiri, Abdelwahab Muhammed. "The Critical Writings of Wordsworth and Whitman: A Study of the Historical and Anti-Historical Imaginations." Diss. Rutgers State Univ., 1969.

Engle, Eduard. "Zur Urgeschichte des Othello." *Shakespeare Jahrbuch* 35 (1899): 271-73.

Evans, G. Blakemore, gen. ed. *The Riverside Shakespeare.* Boston: Houghton Mifflin, 1974.

Farley-Hills, David. "Hamlet's Account of the Pirates." *Review of English Studies* NS 50 (1999): 320-31.

Farnsworth, Robert M. *Melvin B. Tolson, 1898-1966: Plain Talk and Poetic Prophecy.* Columbia: U of Missouri P, 1984.

Fickert, Kurt. *Kafka's Doubles.* Bern: Peter Lang, 1979.

Fiedler, Leslie A. "R. L. S. Revisited." In his *No! In Thunder: Essays on Myth and Literature.* Boston: Beacon, 1960. 77-91.

Fleissner, Robert F. "Addendum: Chasing a Ghost." *Names* 24 (1976): 75-76.

—. "A Drood Awakening." *Dickens Studies Newsletter* 11 (1980): 17-19.

—. "*Arden of Faversham.*" In *The Dictionary of Literary Biography: Elizabethan Dramatists.* Vol. 62. Ed. Fredson Bowers. Detroit: Gale Research Co., 1987. 361-64.

—. *A Rose by Another Name: A Survey of Literary Flora from Shakespeare to Eco.* Locust Hill Lit. Stud. No. 5. West Cornwall: Locust Hill P, 1989.

—. *Ascending the Prufrockian Stair: Studies in a Dissociated Sensibility.* Bern: Peter Lang, 1988.

—. "'Base Iúdean' in *Othello* Again: Misprint or, More Likely, Misreading?" *Notes and Queries* 233 (1988): 475-79.

—. "The Beatles as Kafkaesque." *Notes on Contemporary Literature* 30.2 (2000): 8-10.

—. "The Case of the 'Base Indian' Revisited." *The Upstart Crow: A Shakespeare Journal* 6 (1986): 44-53.

—. "Charles Dickens and Sinclair Lewis: An Exordium." *Sinclair Lewis Newsletter* 3 (1971): 10-13.

—. "Conan Doyle and the Shakespeare Authorship Mystery." *Baker Street Miscellanea* no. 63 (1990): 14-29.

—. "The Daemons of Frost and Keats in Perspective." *The South Carolina Review* 31 (1998): 155-61.

—. *Dickens and Shakespeare: A Study in Histrionic Contrasts.* New York: Haskell, 1965; rpt 1969.

—. "Frost's Response to Keats' Risibility." BSU *Forum* 11 (1970): 40-43.

—. "Dickens on Slavery: *Great Expectations* as a Novel for Black Students." *Negro History Bulletin* 38 (1975): 478-79.

—. *Frost's Road Taken.* Bern: Peter Lang, 1996.

—. "The Germination of 'Rosebud' in *Citizen Kane*." *Names* 27 (1979): 283-84.

—. "*Lear* and Polanski's *Tess*." *Shakespeare on Film Newsletter* 7 (April, 1983): 3, 7.

—. "The Likely Misascription of *Cardenio* (and Thereby *Double Falsehood*) in Part to Shakespeare." *Neuphilologische Mitteilungen* 97 (1996): 217-30.

—. "Love's Lost in *Othello*: What 'the base Indian' is Founded On." *English Studies* 76 (1995): 140-42.

—. "Name as Symbol: On Sherlock Holmes and the Nature of the Detective Story." *The Armchair Detective* 8 (1975): 280-87.

—. "The Name Jude." *The Victorian Newsletter* no. 27 (1965): 24-26.

—. "The 'Nothing' Element in *King Lear*." *Shakespeare Quarterly* 13 (1962): 62-71.

—. "On Spelling Out Sherlock Holmes's Secretive Initial." *Baker Street Miscellanea* no. 53 (1988): 8-13.

—. *The Prince and the Professor: The Wittenberg Connection in Marlowe, Shakespeare, Goethe, and Frost—A Hamlet/Faust(us) Analogy.* Heidelberg: Carl Winter UP, 1986.

—. "Prufrock as Touchstone." *American Notes and Queries* 11 (1972): 56-57.

—. Rev. of Lee Oser, *T. S. Eliot and American Poetry* (Columbia: U of Missouri P, 1998), in *American Literature* 71 (1999): 372.

—. "'The Secret'st Man of Blood': Foreshadowings of *Macbeth* in *Arden of Feversham.*" *U of Dayton Review* 14 (1979/80): 7-13.

—. "Shakespeare and Dickens: Some Characteristic Uses of the Playwright by the Novelist." Diss. New York University, 1964.

—. *Shakespeare and the Matter of the Crux: Textual, Topical, Onomastic, Authorial, and Other Puzzlements.* Lewiston: Mellen, 1991.

—. "Shakespeare's *Carte Blanche*—Appropriated by Marston." *English Studies* 56 (1975): 390-92.

—. "Sheerluck Holds . . . Out?: On a Piece of Promiscuous Parody." *Baker Street Dispatch* 5.4 (1995): 1-2.

—. "Sherlock Holmes Confronts *Edwin Drood.*" *The Baker Street Journal* NS 35 (1985): 199-205.

—. "Sherlock Holmes Intercepts the Frankenstein Monster." *The Sherlock Holmes Review* 1 (1986): 14-19.

—. "'Something Out of Dickens' in Sinclair Lewis: An Exordium." *Bulletin of the New York Public Library* 74 (1970): 607-16.

—. "The Title *The Life of Our Lord*: Does It Fit the Dickens Canon?" *American Notes and Queries* 22 (1983): 39-40.

Florio, John, trans. *The Essayes of Michael Lord of Montaigne.* 1603. 3 Vols. London: Dent, 1928.

Forsyte, Charles. "How Did Drood Die?" *The Dickensian* 84 (1988): 80-95.

Frank, Lawrence. "The Intelligibility of Madness in *Our Mutual Friend* and *The Mystery of Edwin Drood.*" *Dickens Studies Annual* 5 (1976): 150-95.

Franks, Jill. "Confessions of Sin and Love: Guido da Montefeltro's Relevance to J. Alfred Prufrock." *Yeats Eliot Review* 14.2 (1996): 20-25.

Furnas, J. C. *Voyage to Windward: The Life of Robert Louis Stevenson.* New York: Sloane, 1951.

Furness, H. H., ed. *A New Variorum Edition of Shakespeare: "Hamlet."* 2 Vols. Philadelphia: Lippincott, 1877.

—. *A New Variorum Edition of Shakespeare: "Othello."* Vol. VI. Philadelphia: Lippincott, 1886.

—. *A New Variorum Edition of Shakespeare: "The Tempest."* Vol. IX. Philadelphia: Lippincott, 1892.

Gager, Valerie L. *Shakespeare and Dickens: The Dynamics of Influence.* Cambridge: Cambridge UP: 1996.

Galbreath, Charles B. *History of Ohio.* 5 Vols. Chicago: The American Historical Society, Inc., 1925.

Gardner, Joseph. "Mark Twain and Dickens." *PMLA* 84 (1969): 90-101.

Gerber, Philip. "Namen als Symbol . . ." *Neue Rundschau* 83 (1972): 499-513. (Trans. by R. Fleissner in *The Armchair Detective* 8 [1975] 280-87.)

Gibson, J. M. "Shacklock to Sherlock." *The Sherlock Holmes Journal* 14 (1985) 86-87.

Gittings, Robert. *Thomas Hardy's Later Years*, Boston: Little Brown, 1978.

Goddard, Harold C. *The Meaning of Shakespeare.* 2 Vols. Chicago: U of Chicago P, 1951.

Gottschalk, Paul. "Time in *Edwin Drood.*" *Dickens Studies Annual* 1 (1970): 265-72.

Greenblatt, Stephen. *Renaissance Self-fashioning: From More to Shakespeare.* Chicago: U of Chicago P, 1980.

Griesbach, Ilse. "The Tragic Universal Sentiment as Structural Principle in Thomas Hardy's Novels in Relation to Shakespeare in his Lear and Macbeth Period." Diss. Marburg University, 1934.

Grimaud, Michel. "Hermeneutics, Onomastics, and Poetics in English and French Literature." *Modern Language Notes* 92 (1977): 888-915.

Gross, John. *Shylock: Four Hundred Years in the Life of a Legend.* London: Chatto, 1992.

Guttman, Selma. *The Foreign Sources of Shakespeare's Works: An Annotated Bibliography.* Morningside Heights: King's Crown P, 1947.

Hale, John K. "The Name 'Shylock.'" *The Shakespeare Newsletter* 48.4 (1998/99): 95.

Halliday, F. E. *A Shakespeare Companion 1564-1964.* Baltimore: Penguin, 1964.

Halliwell, J. O. "Name of Shylock." *Notes and Queries* 2 (1850): 221-22.

Hamilton, Charles. *In Search of Shakespeare: A Reconnaissance into the Poet's Life and Writing.* New York: Harcourt, 1985.

Hardy, Thomas. *Tess of the d'Urbervilles*. 1891. Ed. William E. Buckler. Boston: Houghton, 1960.

Harvey, P. D. A. "Charles Dickens as Playwright." *The British Museum Quarterly* 24 (1961): 22-25.

Hassel, Chris. "The Riddle in *Twelfth Night* Simplified." *Shakespeare Quarterly* 25 (1974): 356.

Hawkes, Terry. "'Love' in *King Lear*." *Review of English Studies* NS 10 (1959) 178-81.

Heller, Erich. "The Importance of Nietzsche." In his *The Importance of Nietzsche: Ten Essays*. Chicago: U of Chicago P, 1988, 1-17.

Hindus, Milton, ed. *"Leaves of Grass" One Hundred Years After: New Essays*. Stanford: Stanford UP, 1955.

Hinman, Chariton, ed. *The First Folio of Shakespeare*. The Norton Facsimile. New York: Norton, 1968.

Hitchin-Kemp, Frederick. "The Name Shylock." *Notes and Queries* 161 (1931): 467.

Hoff, Linda Kay. *Hamlet's Choice: "Hamlet"—A Reformation Allegory*. Stud. in Ren. Lit. No. 2. Lewiston: Mellen, 1990.

Hollis, Carroll C. *Language and Style in "Leaves of Grass."* Baton Rouge: Louisiana SUP, 1983.

Holloway, John. "Hardy's Major Fiction." In *From Jane Austen to Joseph Conrad*. Ed. R. C. Rathburn et al. 234-45.

Holly, Raymond L. "April 5, 1894." *Baker Street Miscellanea* no 34 (1983): 19-22.

Holmer, Joan Ozark. *"The Merchant of Venice": Choice, Hazard, and Consequence*. London: Macmillan, 1995.

Homan, Sidney. *When the Theatre Turns to Itself: The Aesthetic Metaphor in Shakespeare*. Lewisburg: Bucknell UP, 1981.

Honan, Park. *Shakespeare: A Life*. Oxford: Oxford UP, 1998.

Hornback, Bert G. Review of Jane Vogel, *Allegory in Dickens*, in *Dickens Studies Newsletter* 9 (1978): 54.

Hotson, Leslie. *The First Night of "Twelfth Night."* London: Macmillan, 1954.

Jackson, MacDonald P. "Material for an Edition of *Arden of Feversham*." Diss. Oxford University, 1963.

—. "Shakespearean Features of the Poetic Style of *Arden of Faversham.*" *Archiv für das Studium der Neueren Sprachen und Literaturen* 145 (1993) 279-303.

Jaggard, W. "The Name Shylock." *Notes and Queries* 161 (1931): 467.

Janowitz, Henry D. "*Marius the Epicurean* in T. S. Eliot's Poetry." *Journal of Modern Literature* 15 (1989): 589-92.

Johnson, Edgar. *Charles Dickens: His Tragedy and Triumph.* 2 Vols. New York: Simon, 1952.

Johnson, Roger, Letter. *Baker Street Miscellanea* no. 58 (1989): 33-34.

Jofen, Jean. *The Jewish Mystic in Kafka.* Bern: Peter Lang, 1979.

Jones, Eldred. *Othello's Countrymen: The African in English Renaissance Drama.* Oxford: Oxford UP, 1965.

Jones, William M. "William Shakespeare as William in *As You Like It.*" *Shakespeare Quarterly* 11 (1960): 228-31.

Kaplan, Fred. *Dickens and Mesmerism: The Hidden Springs of Fiction.* Princeton: Princeton UP, 1975.

Katz, Sandra. "Robert Frost, Humorist." *Robert Frost Review* 1 (1991) 24-29.

Kay, Denis. *Shakespeare: His Life, Work, and Era.* New York: Morrow, 1992.

Kay-Robinson, Denys. *Hardy's Wessex Reappraised.* New York: St. Martin's, 1971.

Kellogg, Richard L. "Holmes and Holmes in the Mind of Doyle." *Canadian Holmes* 10.3 (1987): 7-10.

Kermode, Frank, ed. *William Shakespeare, "The Tempest."* 5th ed. Cambridge, MA: Harvard UP, 1954. (The Arden ed.)

Kinnamon, K. "Richard Wright's Use of *Othello* in *Native Son.*" *CLA Journal* 12 (1969): 358-59.

Kittredge, G. L., ed. *William Shakespeare, "Othello."* Rev. Irving Ribner. Waltham: Blaisdell, 1966.

Krappe, A. H. "A Byzantine Source of Shakespeare's *Othello.*" *Modern Language Notes* 39 (1924): 156-61.

Kulshreshtha, R. B. "Shakespeare's Feeling for Words." *The Literary Criterion* 7 (Summer 1967): 6-19.

Lauria, Steve. "On the Birthday of Sherlock Holmes." *Baker Street Miscellanea* no. 28 (1981): 1-5.

Lees, F. N. "Othello's Name." *Notes and Queries* 206 (1961): 139-41.

Lehmann, R. C., ed. *Charles Dickens as Editor: Being Letters by Him to William Wills, His Sub-Editor.* New York: Sturgis, 1912.

Lellenberg, Jon L. "Sherlock Holmes in Parody and Pastiche, Part II. 1930-1981." *Baker Street Miscellanea* no. 28 (1981): 27-34.

Levin, Harry. "Shakespeare's Nomenclature." In Chapman 59-90.

Levith, Murray J. *Shakespeare's Italian Settings and Plays.* New York: St. Martin's P, 1989.

Lewis, Grace Hegger. *With Love from Gracie: Sinclair Lewis 1912-1925.* New York: Harcourt, 1955.

Lindsay, Jack. *Charles Dickens: A Biographical and Critical Study.* New York: Philosophical Library, 1950.

Loomis, Roger Sherman. *The Development of Arthurian Romance.* New York: Norton, 1963.

Lothian, J. M., and T. W. Craik, eds. *William Shakespeare, "Twelfth Night."* London: Methuen, 1975. (New Arden ed.)

Lower, Mark Antony. "The Name of Shylock." *Notes and Queries* 2 (1850): 184.

MacKenzie, Stanley. Rev. of Malcolm Watson and Edward La Serre, *Sheerluck Jones* (London: Peter Schoffer, 1982), in *Baker Street Miscellanea* no. 30 (1982): 35-36.

Malmsheimer, Richard. "Kafka's 'Nature Theatre of Oklahoma': The End of Karl Rossmann's Journey to Maturity." *Modern Fiction Studies* 13 (1967/68): 493-501.

Martin, R. W. F. "A Catholic Oldcastle." *Notes and Queries* 238 (1993) 185-86.

Martineau, Harriet. *Harriet Martineau's Autobiography.* 1872. Boston: Osgood, 1877.

Maule, Harry E., and Melville H. Cane, eds. *The Man from Main Street, A Sinclair Lewis Reader: Selected Essays and Other Writings.* New York: Random, 1953.

Maxwell, D. E. S. *The Poetry of T. S. Eliot.* London: Routledge, 1952.

Maynard, Theodore. "The Catholicism of Dickens." *Thought* 5 (1930): 81-105.

McAlindon, Thomas. *Shakespeare's Tragic Cosmos.* Cambridge: Cambridge UP, 1991.

McCarron, Robert M. "Folly and Wisdom: Three Dickensian Wise Fools." *Dickens Studies Annual* 6 (1977): 40-56.

McDavid, Ravin I. "Rosenkrantz and Guildenstern are Alive and Prospering." *Modern Philology* 79 (1982): 400-2.

Merrix, Robert P., and Nicholas Ranson, eds. *Ideological Approaches to Shakespeare: The Practice of Theory.* Lewiston: Mellen, 1992.

Mertins, Louis. *Robert Frost: Life and Talks-Walking.* Norman: U of Oklahoma P, 1965.

Meyers, Jeffrey. *Robert Frost: A Biography.* Boston: Houghton Mifflin, 1996.

Miller, James E. *A Critical Guide to "Leaves of Grass."* Chicago: U of Chicago P, 1957.

Millgate, Michael. *Thomas Hardy: A Biography.* New York: Random, 1982.

Milward, Peter. "More on 'the base Judean.'" *Notes and Queries* 234 (1989): 329-31.

Miyoshi, Masao. "Dr. Jekyll and the Emergence of Mr. Hyde." *College English* 27 (1966): 470-80.

Montaigne, Michel de. *Essais.* 1595. 2 Vols. Paris: Librairie de Paris, 1899.

Moody, A. D. *Thomas Stearns Eliot: Poet.* Cambridge: Cambridge UP, 1979.

Muir, Kenneth. *Shakespeare as Collaborator.* London: Methuen, 1960.

Murphy, C. N. "A Note on Iago's Name." In *Literature and Society*, ed. Bernice Slote 38-43.

Musgrove, S. "The Nomenclature of *King Lear.*" *Review of English Studies* 32 (1956): 294-98.

Narasimhaiah, C. D. "The Reputation of Robert Frost: A Point of View." *The Literary Criterion* 9 (1969): 1-10.

Naugrette, Jean-Pierre. "*The Strange Case of Dr. Jekyll and Mr. Hyde*: Essai d'Onomastique." *Cahiers Victoriens et Edouardiens* 40 (1994) 77-95.

Newlin, George, ed. *Everyone in Dickens.* 3 Vols. Westport: Greenwood, 1995.

Nye, Russell. *The Unembarrassed Muse: The Popular Arts in America.* New York: Dial, 1970.

Oates, Joyce Carol. "Jekyll/Hyde." *The Hudson Review* 40 (1988): 603-8.

O'Connor, Garry. *William Shakespeare: A Life.* London: Hodder, 1991.

Oldsey, Bernard S. "The Movies in the Rye." *College English* 23 (1961): 109-15.

Paquette, Robert, and S. Engerman, eds. *The Lesser Antilles in the Age of Expansion.* Gainesville: UP of Florida, 1994.

Parini, Jay. *Robert Frost: A Life*. New York: Holt, 1998.

Partridge, Eric. *Shakespeare's Bawdy*. New York: Dutton, 1948.

Percy, Allen. Letter. *Times Literary Supplement* 18 Sept. 1937: 675.

Petronella, Vincent F. "Anamorphic Naming in Shakespeare's *Twelfth Night*." *Names* 35 (1987): 224-31.

Peyrouton, Noel. "*The Life of Our Lord*: Some Notes of Explication." *The Dickensian* 59 (1963): 102-12.

Pickering, Samuel J. "*Dombey and Son* and Dickens's Unitarian Period." *The Georgia Review* 26 (1972): 438-54.

—. *The Moral Tradition in English Fiction*, 1785-1850. Hanover: UP of New England, 1976.

Poirier, Richard. *Robert Frost: The Work of Knowing*. Oxford: Oxford UP, 1977.

Politzer, Heinz. *Franz Kafka: Parable and Paradox*. Ithaca: Cornell UP, 1962.

Rajec, Elisabeth. *Namen und ihre Bedeutungen im Werke Franz Kafkas: Ein Interpretatorischer Versuch*. Bern: Peter Lang, 1977.

Ralli, Augustus, ed. *A History of Shakespearian Criticism*. 2 Vols. New York: Humanities P, 1965.

Rathburn, R. C., and Martin Steinmann, Jr., eds. *From Jane Austen to Joseph Conrad: Essays Collected in Memory of James T. Hillhouse*. Minneapolis: U of Minnesota P, 1958.

Redmond, Donald A. "On the Name of Sherlock." *Sherlock Holmes Journal* 8 (1967): 86-88.

Reed, Harry B. "The Heraclitan Obsession of Walt Whitman." *The Personalist* 15 (1934): 125.

Reichert, John. "How Universal is the Bard?" Rev. of *Shakespeare's Caliban* by Alden T. and Virginia Mason Vaughan, in *Amherst* (Fall 1992): 32-33.

Robson, W. W. "*The Mystery of Edwin Drood*: The Solution?" *Times Literary Supplement* 11 Nov. 1983: 1246, 1259.

Roden, Christopher. "What's in a Name?: The Genesis of Sherlock." *ACD: The Journal of the Arthur Conan Doyle Society* 3 (1992): 35-37.

Roe, Nicholas. "Authenticating Robert Burns." *Essays in Criticism* 46 (1996): 195-218.

Romig, Edna Davis. "More Roots for *Leaves of Grass*." *Elizabethan Studies: Univ. of Colorado Studies in the Human* 2 (1945): 322-27.

Rosenberg, Edgar. "Restoration in Cloisterham: The 'Clarendon Drood.'" *Dickens Studies Newsletter* 5 (Sept., 1974): 70-84.

Rosenberg, Samuel. *Naked is the Best Disguise: The Death and Resurrection of Sherlock Holmes*. New York: Bobbs-Merrill, 1974.

Rossky, William. "Hamlet as Jeremiah." *Hamlet Studies* 1.2 (1979): 101-8.

Roth, Cecil. "The Background of Shylock." *Review of English Studies* 9 (1933) 149.

Rowse, A. L., ed. *The Annotated Shakespeare*. 3 Vols. New York: Potter, 1978.

Sams, Eric. "Oldcastle and the Oxford Shakespeare." *Notes and Queries* 238 (1993): 180-85.

Samuels, Allen. Rev of Jane Vogel, *Allegory in Dickens*, in *The Dickensian* 74 (1978): 112.

Sanders, Andrew. *Charles Dickens: Resurrectionist*. New York: St. Martin's P, 1982.

Saposnik, Irving S. *Robert Louis Stevenson*. New York: Twayne, 1974.

Satin, Joseph. "The Symbolic Role of Cordelia in *King Lear*." *Forum* (Houston) 9 (Fall-Winter 1972): 15-17.

Schorer, Mark. *Sinclair Lewis: An American Life*. New York: Dell, 1961.

Schorer, Mark, ed. *Sinclair Lewis: A Collection of Critical Essays*. Englewood Cliffs: Prentice-Hall, 1962.

Schücking, L. L. *Character Problems in Shakespeare's Plays*. London: Harrap, 1922.

Schwartz, Murray M., and Coppelia Kahn. *Representing Shakespeare: New Psychoanalytic Essays*. Baltimore: Johns Hopkins UP, 1980.

Shaaber, M. A. "Shylock's Name." *Notes and Queries* 195 (1950): 236.

Shaheen, Naseeb. *Biblical References in Shakespeare's Plays*. Newark: U of Delaware P, 1999.

—. "'Like the Base Judean.'" *Shakespeare Quarterly* 31 (1980): 93-95.

—. "Shakespeare and *The True Tragedy of Richard the Third*." *Notes and Queries* 230 (1985): 32-33.

Shakespeare, William. *The Complete Works*. Gen. ed. Alfred Harbage. Rev. ed. New York: Viking, 1977.

—. *"Hamlet": The Text of the First Folio*, 1623. Menston: Scolar, 1969.

Siegel, Paul N. "The Damnation of Othello." *PMLA* 68 (1953): 1068-78.

Simonson, Harold P., and Philip E. Hager, eds. *Salinger's "Catcher in the Rye": Clamor vs. Criticism*. Lexington: Heath, 1963.

Sipahigil, T. "Othello's Name, Once Again." *Notes and Queries* 123 (1971): 141-48.

Slote, Bernice, ed. *Literature and Society*. Lincoln: U of Nebraska P, 1964.

Smith, J. C., ed. *Spenser's Faerie Queene*. 2 Vols. Oxford: Clarendon, 1909.

Sokoloff, B. A. "William Dean Howells and the Ohio Village: A Study in Environment and Art." *American Quarterly* 11 (1959): 58-75.

Southern, A. C. *Elizabethan Recusant Prose 1559-1582*. London: Sands, 1950.

Spilka, Mark. *Dickens and Kafka*. Bloomington: Indiana UP, 1963.

Stepanchev, Stephen. "The Origin of J. Alfred Prufrock." *Modern Language Notes* 66 (1951): 400-1.

Stevens, L. Holford. "'Most Lovely Jew.'" *Notes and Queries* 244 (1999) 212-13.

Stevenson, Robert Louis. *The Lantern Bearers and Other Essays*. Introd. Jeremy Treglown. London: Chatto, 1988.

Stokes, Francis Griffin. *A Dictionary of the Characters and Proper Names in the Works of Shakespeare*. London: Harrap, 1924.

Strauch, Carl F. "Kings in the Back Row: Meaning through Structure—A Reading of Salinger's *The Catcher in the Rye*." *Wisconsin Stud. in Contemp. Lit.* 2 (Winter 1961): 5-30.

Tannenbaum, S. A., ed. *Shakspere's "Othello": (A Concise Bibliography.)* New York: S. A. Tannenbaum, 1943.

Tatlock, J. S. P. *The Legendary History of Britain*. Berkeley: U of California P, 1950.

Tayler, Edward. "King Lear and Negation." *English Literary Renaissance* 20 (1990): 17-39.

Taylor, A. J. P., ed. *My Darling Pussy: The Letters of Lloyd George and Frances Stevenson, 1913-41*. London: Weidenfeld, 1975.

Tedlock, E. W. "Kafka's Imitation of *David Copperfield*." *Comparative Literature* 7 (1955): 52-62.

Thompson, Edward Maunde. "Two Pretended Autographs of Shakespeare." *The Library* 3rd Ser. 8 (1917): 207-17.

Thompson, Lawrance. *Robert Frost: The Early Years, 1874-1915*. New York: Holt, 1966.

—. *Robert Frost: The Years of Triumph, 1915-1938*. New York: Holt, 1970.

Thompson, Lawrance, ed. *Selected Letters of Robert Frost.* New York: Holt, 1964.

Thornbury, Walter. "Shakespeare's Rosencrantz." *Notes and Queries* 23 (1871): 105-6.

Thundy, Zacharias P. "The 'Divine' Caliban in Shakespeare's Postcolonial Discourse: A Re(De)Construction." *Michigan Academician* 30 (1998): 399-422.

Tobin, J. J. M. "Malvolio and His Capitals." *American Notes and Queries* 23 (1985): 69-71.

Torrey, E. Fuller. *The Death of Psychiatry.* Radnor: Chilton, 1974.

Trudgett, Alan. Letter. London Sunday *Times.* 21 August 1994. n.p.

Turberville, George, trans. *The Eclogues of Mantuan.* Ed. Douglas Bush. New York: Scholars' Facsimiles and Reprints, 1937.

Vaughan, Alden T., and Virginia Mason Vaughan. *Shakespeare's Caliban: A Cultural History.* Cambridge: Cambridge UP, 1991.

Verne, Jules. *The Mysterious Island.* New York: Scribner's, 1920.

Vogel, Jane. *Allegory in Dickens.* Studies in the Humanities No. 17. University: U of Alabama P, 1977.

von Schlegel, August Wilhelm, and Ludwig Tieck, eds. *Shakespeares Werke.* 19 Vols. Berlin: Temel Verlag, n.d.

Wagenknecht, Edward. *Cavalcade of the American Novel: From the Birth of the Nation to the Middle of the Twentieth Century.* New York: Holt, 1952.

Weber, Carl J. *Hardy and the Lady from Madison Square.* Port Washington: Kennikat, 1973.

White, Martin, ed. *The Tragedy of Master Arden of Faversham.* London: Ernest Benn, 1982.

Whitney, Lois. "Did Shakespeare Know *Leo Africanus?*" *PMLA* 37 (1922): 470-88.

Wilbern, David. "Shakespeare's Nothing." In *Representing Shakespeare: New Psychoanalytic Essays.* Ed. Murray M. Schwartz. 244-63.

Williams, George Walton. "Second Thoughts on Falstaff's Name." *Shakespeare Quarterly* 30 (1979): 82-84.

—. "Textual Studies." *Shakespeare Survey* 36 (1983): 181-95.

Williams, William Carlos. "An Essay on *Leaves of Grass.*" In *Leaves of Grass One Hundred Years After: New Essays.* Ed. Milton Hindus. 22-31.

Willmer, Caissa. "The Face of Evil, the Face of Hyde." *The Ithaca Times* 24-30 Aug. 1989: 24.

# INDEX

## Y

## STUDIES IN ONOMASTICS